Civil Society and
the Holocaust

Civil Society and the Holocaust: International Perspectives on Resistance and Rescue

Cecilia Felicia Stokholm Banke &
Anders Jerichow (Eds.)

Translations by Paul Larkin

HUMANITY IN ACTION

Humanity in Action Press
New York

Humanity in Action Press
New York

Copyright © 2013 by Humanity in Action, Inc.

Published in the United States by Humanity in Action, Inc., (New York) and simultaneously in Denmark by Humanity in Action Denmark (Copenhagen).

Originally published in hardcover in Danish by
Humanity in Action Denmark (Copenhagen).

Edited for the Danish version by Cecilie Felicia Stokholm Banke
and Anders Jerichow.

Edited for the English version by Judith Goldstein and Anthony Chase.

Translations by Paul Larkin.

The Library of Congress has cataloged this version as follows:
Banke, Cecilie Felicia Stokholm, and Jerichow, Anders (Eds.)
Civil Society and the Holocaust: International Perspectives on Resistance and Rescue

ISBN 978-0-615-88248-2

Cover Photo: *YIVO Archives* (New York)
Cover design: Rie Jerichow (Copenhagen)

Humanity in Action
www.humanityinaction.org

Printed by Specialtrykkeriet Viborg (Denmark)
www.stviborg.dk

Contents

Preface

In the fall of 2013 Humanity in Action Denmark organized an important conference on "Civil Society: Reactions to the Holocaust," The Copenhagen conference and essays in this book explore the different ways that European countries and the United States responded to the Holocaust. Given the commemoration of the 70th anniversary of the flight and rescue of Jews in Denmark, both the conference and book provide particular insights about Danish history during the Second World War. Both the conference and book draw lessons from the Holocaust and seek to strengthen the protection of minorities and the responsibilities of civil society today. These undertakings are the product of outstanding inquiries and activities that the Danish Humanity in Action Senior Fellows, board and staff have accomplished over 15 years under the leadership of Herbert Pundik, Uffe Stormgaard and Anders Jerichow.

Humanity in Action focuses on historic and contemporary challenges to vulnerable minorities in Western liberal democracies through its educational programs in Bosnia and Herzegovina, Denmark, France, Germany, Poland, the Netherlands, and the United States, Since we commenced our first program in 1999, the flight and rescue of Jews in Denmark in October 1943 has been a significant subject for our inquiries. We still find deeply complex challenges in this Danish history and the many ways in which it relates to other countries.

Claude Lanzmann, noted author and creator of "Shoah," wrote in his autobiography that "humans are human only because they have the capacity to transform that which oppresses them into something of value, and to sacrifice themselves for it. [This] is the very essence of humanity, but could also be called tradition, or even more, culture."[1] Humanity in Action probes the different cultures of civic engagement with international students and young professionals to promote democracy, justice and knowledge of his-

---

1   Lanzmann, Claude. *The Patagonian Hare*. New York: Farrar, Straus and Giroux, 2013. 312-313.

tory. The 2013 Danish commemorative conference and this signature publication make significant contributions to understanding the responsibilities and power of individual and collective action to promote the public good and civil society.

Judith S. Goldstein, Ph.D
Founder and Executive Director, Humanity in Action

Introduction

Today, a whole lifetime after the war, the Holocaust has been reduced into numbers and summaries: Who killed whom? Who were perpetrators, who were the victims?

Nearly six million murdered, most of them as industrial products – not by coincidence, but by political decision and after strict administrative preparations adhering to legal and political formulations of what was needed: The booking of train services and transport wagons – not first, second or third class carriages – cattle transport wagons would suffice. Equipping soldiers, recruiting assistants, some paid, some volunteering.

All arrangements regarding wagons and departure times were also in place when the Nazi occupiers in Copenhagen prepared to send Jews in Denmark away – South, East, in principle just away, completely away. The Danish State Railways had organized the connections, indicated where and when the train from Jutland needed to stop along the way. An unknown number of people must have known about the booking of this train. Others have noticed that the ship "Whateland" was docked in Copenhagen in the last days of September 1943 and people must have been wondering what kind of transportation was going to take place.

Today, the wagons and the ship are part of this story, the story known in Denmark as "October '43" – the story of the fate of Danish Jews.

In retrospect, it is, at the same time, one of the darkest chapters in Danish history as well as a stellar moment. A few days before October '43 the principal of Ordrup High School had been knocking on the door of several classes in the middle of their lessons and had asked students of Jewish origin come with him. "On that day my childhood was over," one of the students, the editor Herbert Pundik, wrote later. Before that day, he was just one of the boys. On this day, at this moment, he was the chosen one, the different one, and the one who was asked to find his parents and get away. Why? Ask the occupation authorities; ask Hitler. The train was booked and the "Whateland" at the quay in Copenhagen.

A dark chapter? Werner Best, the Nazi plenipotentiary, had decided that the night between October 1 and 2 should be the night for the Gestapo to knock at the doors of all Jews and take them away.

Or a stellar moment? More than 95 percent – statistics again – of Danish Jews managed to flee to Sweden, a unique event in the history of the Holocaust.

But between darkness and light, between the rector's knock on the door at the high school and Jews arriving at ports in South Sweden, between Best's decision on October 1, the eve of the Jewish New Year, and the end of October, there was uncertainty and fear for Jews in Denmark. Several thousand people could not sleep in their own bed, could not go to rest in their own home. A throng of people sought refuge with friends and neighbors and colleagues and strangers who opened their doors to them, terrified of trains and ships whose destination they did not know and yet could fear. This was not a stellar moment, certainly not for the 481 Jews who the occupying powers were successful in detaining – some of them in a famous raid on a church loft in Gilleleje, subsequently sending them off to the Southeast – to a concentration camp that few, if any, knew of that day. Theresienstadt.

In this gap between darkness and light, between Best's decision and the transports to Theresienstadt, and the lifeboats to Sweden – the boats that were much praised after the war – a society was called to account. This was only a small corner of Nazi-controlled Europe and only a small part of the history of the Holocaust. But the challenge was the same everywhere: What could European civil societies do against the decision of the Nazis to isolate a minority of citizens in order to kill them?

Today, we have the privilege of hindsight, of being able to see things in a historical mirror pointed backward. We know that "the final solution" did not come by itself and not without warning. To wish that Europe should have stopped Nazism in time is obvious. To live with the fact that it did not happen is unbearable. To understand that the intervention did not happen is hard. To understand why it did not happen is still a challenge. Hitler made no secret of his hatred of Jews, neither in his book, *Mein Kampf* when it was published in enormous numbers or when he subsequently took power in Berlin in 1933. The 'Kristallnacht' in November 1938 did not allow for any doubt about potential popular hatred. The Wannsee Conference in 1942 did not hide the intention to annihilate the Jews of Europe. And witnesses such as Jan Karski brought early wartime testimony from the Warsaw ghetto and of what went on in the death camps. When Karski went to London and Washington to inform the Polish government in exile and both the British and the American leaders, he got the response: We're not saying you're lying. But we have a hard time believing what you say.

For political leaders as well as ordinary people, the Nazi attacks on Jews were not a matter of statistics and not a matter of theory or principles. From start to finish, if you can identify the start and if you can get closure to the traumas that still torture the generations after the Holocaust, it is about people. Civil societies. Occupiers and occupied. But not only perpetrators and victims – there are witnesses, spectators, people who did not know or could not take in that they had or could have a role or responsibility. The story was not just what some people set in motion, but also what others were watching, let happen or could not prevent.

The figure of nearly six millions is in itself incomprehensible, but then there is the question of what Europeans did when confronted with what they knew about the Nazi regime's persecution of the Jews before, during and after this nightmare. What did they know? What knowledge could be of any use to them given the fact that you can't compare the conditions in different societies? What did they want? What did they do? And for that matter: What did they not do?

Jews in Denmark were historically – and statistically–"lucky" because they experienced a widespread willingness to help them, and because there was a place to escape to. A German official warned Danish politicians, who again warned their fellow countrymen and Sweden opened borders, which before the war were closed. Some will see this as a story of thousands of people who had to flee from home, others as a story of a civil society, showing its solidarity with a threatened minority. Escape or rescue? Now, after the events, we know that October '43 was about both, but during the events the anxiety of the minority, the will of the resistance fighters and the courage of the refugees' helpers – all of this was assessed differently – both regarding the individual and Denmark.

The activists, who at the time engaged in helping their Jewish fellow countrymen, did not know while they acted that "Danes were not deported to concentration camps solely for their help to Jews on the run, and [that] fisherman did not risk their lives for their actions," according to Sofie Lene Bak in her essay on Denmark in October '43. In hindsight, it may be argued that the occupation forces did not want to let the action against the Danish

Jews spoil the good cooperation with the Danish administration. But "the fishermen and refugee helpers, however, did not know this for certain at the beginning of October 1943," when thousands across the Danish civil society threw themselves into helping Danish Jews to find shelter. And by far "the majority of those helping the Jews did not get paid for their efforts."

At the other end of the Nazi nightmare we can see a Germany that Ulrich Herbert describes as a country with a clear absence of a civil society. On one hand, he finds it misleading and simplistic to claim that the genocide of the Jews of Europe and the spread of anti-Jewish attitudes in the German population would have grown out of a century old and rooted anti-Semitism of eliminatory kind. On the other hand, he finds it unavoidable to note that the German society was marked by a serious lack of orientation towards human rights and the protection of minorities. The reality was dominated by repression, accompanied by two important phenomena – namely that "a substantial proportion of the population was completely uninterested in fate of the Jews", and that "any public opposition, any protest against the anti-Jewish persecution measures of 1933 was initially limited and then completely excluded ".

In Poland where the main Nazi death camps were located "most people today do not," according to Konstanty Gebert, "recognize that the Jews suffered greater oppression than themselves during the German occupation." Well, this is not about competitive suffering; it would not be acceptable to "historically or morally downplay the enormous suffering that the Poles did indeed experience during World War II." But if the Holocaust or the "Shoah" is repressed today, this is, according to Gebert, no different from what happened during the war. A review of over 400 non-Jewish Polish eyewitnesses' contemporary and comprehensive records of the Nazi occupation reveals that "not a single ... contained the slightest reference to the Shoah." Not one. Even if they personally had not had any encounter with the 'Jewish fate,' a large number of them had, according to Gebert, access to a diverse underground press, which was informed of what took place during the Nazi occupation.

Also, Richard Breitman asks if this was known in the United States, a country far from the Nazi-controlled Europe and – to put it mildly – crucial for the evolution and course of the war. On the American side of the Atlantic, a liberal immigration policy, as in most communities in Europe, was replaced by restrictive asylum rules. The Jewish "Congress Weekly" reported from 1941 on the "killing, deportation and imprisonment of Jews in concentration camps in Central Europe." But the political debate had difficulty focusing on the 'Endlösung,' the Final Solution, in the middle of "the most immediately pressing problem: What could be done, if anything, in Europe, where the possibilities of military actions were very limited?" The United States stood in the middle of the perceived dilemma that – together with Britain – it had claimed responsibility for the fight against Nazism from the West, and to attempt to intervene with the Final Solution would frustrate, delay or interfere with that purpose. And in the midst of this dilemma, Washington was faced with the well-known demand that the Western allies should bomb the crematoria in Auschwitz. Whether they could have taken on bombing the death camps while pursuing the war and whether the bombing would have forced Hitler to change course – is still a contentious issue for the writing of counterfactual history. "It was ... much easier for the Nazis and their allies to kill than it was for outsiders far from the crime scenes to come to step in as rescuing angels".

Right up until the 1970s, historians chose far more frequently to deal with the Second World War's military developments and the contradiction between resistance and collaboration rather than focusing on the Holocaust, according to Bob Moore who writes about the evolution of the historiography of the war. This one-sided focus was replaced by a growing interest in the social historical aspects of communities' response to the Nazi invasion or occupation and the Nazi persecution of Jews. But to what extent, asks Moore, was Jewish history separated, concretely, psychologically and morally from other conflicts, from other groups in need of escape and from other victims of the resistance? And how are we today to view the options there were both for the Jewish community and the respective populations of their countries of residence to 'save' Jews from deportation and extermination, such as was the case in Denmark? Can 'rescue' only be perceived in the context of the annihilation itself, or should one indeed, as Moore argues, take a broader social history angle which also includes the situation before the war?

In France, where one part of the country was occupied and another was not, almost all Jews, according to Annette Wieviorka, had "confidence in the rule of protection." They allowed themselves to be registered at the same time as the Vichy government decreed that, for the time being, all foreign Jews were to be interned in special camps. When Jews in early summer 1941 received a "call-up," half of them voluntary reported to be interned. "France's non-Jewish population hardly noticed the episode," Wievorka writes, and they probably didn't notice that the other half left occupied Paris to reach the free zone. "At this stage, the French people are... neither hostile to the Jews, nor are they particularly helpful. They are simply indifferent." At the end of May 1943, the persecution became visible to all, as a German regulation forced all Jews over 6 years to wear a yellow Star of David on their clothes. And soon, Jews from France were deported to Auschwitz. Nevertheless, notes Wieviorka, it was easier for Jews in France to spread out in the country and escape prosecution than it was for the Jewish population of Poland. The French Jews constituted only a small minority of just under half a percent of the total population, and could more easily blend into French society, which still was predominantly helpful.

In Bulgaria the rescue of many Jews is – as in Denmark – part of national self-understanding. On the other hand, a fixed element of self-understanding is also ignoring the fact that Bulgaria had non-Bulgarian Jews deported to the two death camps, Treblinka and Auschwitz, from Bulgarian controlled areas in Greece and Serbia with local state railways as operators. Here the darkest hour and "stellar hour" occurred almost simultaneously, i.e. with the honorable rescue of Jews in one part of the country, and moral failure in the other. Does one honorable action cancel out the other or as Anthony Georgieff writes: "What counts most? Those who were saved or those who were destroyed?" Georgieff questions the collectivizing of both crimes as well as morally exemplary actions: "At the end of the day, will it not always be the individual who must bear the responsibility for everything that happens for good and bad?" The government of Bulgaria joined the Axis powers and also had to commit itself to contributing to the solution of the Nazi-dictated problem, "The Jewish question." Bulgaria had to introduce its own "Nuremberg Laws," which with a stroke of a pen made Jews statutorily inferior. And from the spring of 1943, Jews were mobilized for forced labor and selected for transport to Nazi death camps. But there were people from the government majority who fought against this. Even today there is discussion of who can be credited with the rescues and who bears responsibility for the deportations.

In the north of Europe, Sweden played an indispensable role for Jewish communities in neighboring countries. The Swedish government had been no more eager or willing than other European State governments to receive fleeing Jews from Germany and Central Europe. This has already been demonstrated by the historic conference in Evian in1938, where Sweden, just as other countries, was reluctant to "import a Jewish question," writes Karin Kvist Geverts. But Sweden was neutral and as such out of Nazi Germany's direct influence. And it was inevitable that Jews in the surrounding countries saw Sweden as a place to seek shelter. Swedish officials and politicians had realized this before Jewish refugees in large numbers began to knock on the door. Refugees in general had no easy access, and Jews – who in the Swedish bureaucracy were recorded with a small "m" for Mosaic or Jewish, were in particular not allowed in. There was enough to worry about for the Swedish refugee authorities – the Norwegian Quisling government's policy towards its Jews, the Finnish Government squeezed in its alliance with Germany and the war with Russia – and the Nazi occupying power's plans in Denmark.

While the rest of Europe and the United States, free nations, occupied states or countries at war, were trying to determine what they knew or wanted to know about the Holocaust. Sweden had free media, which, at least from 1942 and actually before that, could inform about the extermination of Jews. And when a group of Norwegian Jews was forced to board the ship SS Donau at the end of November 1942, bound for Poland and Auschwitz, the Swedish politicians went from being spectators to become rescuers. Jewish refugees were still registered "Mosaic" of race and faith. But where Jewish refugees before had been rejected because they were Jews, they now got access to Sweden precisely because they were Jews. At that time it was too late for Jews from Germany and Central Europe to escape to Sweden, but not too late for many Jews in the North. Later on, this led to a heated internal political debate on why Sweden bureaucratically and per definition chose to distinguish between Jews and non-Jews in its initial policy. The voice of civil society was here crucial for the change in Swedish refugee policy. For the Danish Jews, it was vital that Sweden opened its gates when they had to escape very quickly. Up until the week before the German plenipotentiary Werner Best put his action against Danish Jews in motion, Sweden had refused to accept Danish Jews. But on the crucial day, Sweden did not reject – so far as we know – one Jew.

Finland, writes Oula Silvennoinen, was never occupied by Nazi Germany, but chose an alliance that could have faced the Finnish government with demands for the deportation of its own or the country's foreign Jews. But things never got that far; part of the Finnish Jews used the opportunity to escape to Sweden anyway. But the Finnish politicians collaborated with the Germans and the mood of Finland was generally more anti-Communist than anti-Nazi. The Finnish situation is more comparable to the countries that also after the war were part of the Soviet Union and were cooperating with Nazi Germany was considered as a clever way to avoid Soviet occupation. In this way Finland represents one of the countries that, being in the periphery of the Holocaust, only recently and because of the changing demands on the management of the past have addressed the more unpleasant aspects of its history.

This is development is similar to that of Norway, although the Norwegian Jews' fate was different from that of the Finnish and Danish Jews. When 772 Norwegian Jews were deported to Auschwitz only 34 returned. About 60 percent, or the equivalent to about 1,100, managed to escape deportation in the fall of 1942. At this time, probably neither the Swedish, the Danish nor the Norwegian Jews were fully aware of the Final Solution. As Irene Levin describes with reference to concrete examples, the action against the Jews in Norway took place earlier than in Denmark. As the situation thus intensified in the late autumn in Norway, 1942, "there were mainly four types of escape, which the Jews could resort to." For each of these possibilities there were a variety of expressions of civil engagement. But "no matter how the escapes took place, whether they were *ad hoc* by networks of family and friends, or organized in advance, it was a case of individuals exhibiting a high degree of civic engagement and courage. They risked their lives," as Levin writes. Whether their actions were the manifestation of a extraordinary courage or whether they were rather a "ordinariness of goodness" is a question she raises in her conclusion. Is there such a thing as a common form of goodness?

Holland was occupied, and many Europeans know the story about the girl Anne Frank, who along with her family, received help over a long period of time, hiding in a secret attic. In statistical terms, Holland had a darker, terrifying fate during the war and the Holocaust. Three quarters – more than 103,000 of the 140,000 Jews in the country before the war – were murdered. This number constitutes the highest percentage in Western Europe. The soul searching is not yet over, writes Ronald Leopold. "What do these patterns teach us about ourselves and the society we are part of? What were the collaborators' motives in collaborating with the enemy? What ethics can you expect from a victim whose life is at risk? What spurred some people to help their fellow man? And why did the great majority prefer neither to help nor to cooperate?"

These are some of the questions addressed in this anthology that still haunt the liberal democracies of Western Europe and any civil society: Why and how could this happen? In the last essay of this anthology, Cecilie Felicia Stokholm Banke writes on the efforts to take this legacy and lesson seriously. As with the whole book, this last essay deals with the question of taking responsibility for what we do, what we conceal, what we witness and what happens while we are still pondering what we must do.

Cecilie Felicia Stokholm Banke
Anders Jerichow

Copenhagen, July 2013

Translation: Don Watts and Eva Bjerregaard

Copenhagen: Bright hope and deep gloom – A new view of the 1943 rescue operation in Denmark

"The rescue of Danish Jews during the second world war still has great significance for Denmark's reputation in the outside world. And for good reason. But perhaps the wrong reasons...."

Sofie Lene Bak

The rescue of Danish Jews during the Holocaust period is one of the most treasured examples of human empathy, public spiritedness and outstanding courage ever to emerge from Denmark. With the exception of the exploits of Danish Vikings, the rescue mission is perhaps the only other world famous episode in Danish history. In the space of just a few weeks in October 1943, the Danes managed to move over 7000 people – 95% of the country's Jewish population – to safety in neutral Sweden. Even as boats and vessels were still carrying fugitive Danish Jews across the Øresund strait to Sweden, the story of what the Danes were doing had already reached England and the United States, where expatriate Danes were in dire need for some kind of positive news that could help to change Denmark's dubious reputation as "Hitler's pantry." Denmark's rapid capitulation after the Nazi's occupied the country in 1940, and the extensive nature of cooperation with German forces thereafter, had marked the Danes out as little more than opportunist cowards. By 1945, however, the Danes had maneuvered themselves over to the winning side and then received de facto status as part of the allied war effort. But two decades were to pass before the outside world became fully aware of the remarkable events of October 1943.

Even though certain legends about the Danish rescue operation were already in circulation – legends that were absorbed into the Hollywood entertainment machine as early as 1960 with the film production of Leon Uris's novel "Exodus" – it was Israel's *Yad Vashem* (Holocaust Research and Museum Centre) and its granting to Denmark of the Title of Honor – "Righteous Among the Nations" in 1963 that focused world attention on Denmark. The general purpose of the establishment of the Title of Honor was to acknowledge Gentiles who helped Jews during the Holocaust period. It is also meant to serve as an important link in the creation of a new community of commemoration in the young state of Israel itself surrounding the human disaster that was the *Shoah*. When the *Yad Vashem* centre requested names of Danish people who might be considered for the Title of Honor, representatives of the Danish resistance movement requested in turn that no single individual be honored at the possible expense of others. Thus, at that time, the only monuments to the Danish rescue effort that were erected in *Yad Vashem's* memorial park were three trees and commemorative plaques: one for the Danish resistance movement, one for king Christian X and one to honor the Danish people as a whole. On the other hand, the first example of a Danish fishing boat being raised as a monument came as early as 1967 in the Israeli port of Haifa, and since then the interest and demand for any kind of Danish vessel, be that a fishing boat, dinghy, barge or lighter, that has the slightest connection to the October 1943 rescue operation has grown steadily.[1]

However, the paradox at that time (and still today) lies in the fact that an express prerequisite for possible inclusion in *Yad Vashem's* roll of honor is amongst other things that: *"the rescuer was aware that in extending such aid [to the Jews] he was risking his life, safety and personal freedom,"* and also that *"no material reward or substantial compensation was exacted by the rescuer from the rescued as a condition for extending aid."* [2] It is important to note that both conditions must be met. The paradox lies in the fact that these conditions were often far from being the case in Denmark in October 1943.

Amongst the Danes themselves, it has never been a secret that Jews had to pay for their illegal crossing to safety in Sweden. A small cartoon in the 1945 issue of the satirical magazine annual *Svikmøllen* illustrates not only the widespread awareness of these payment demands but also how much they were a point of discussion in this period – a gentleman is standing at the ticket counter for the Copenhagen boat to Malmö. The caption reads:

– How much is a ticket to Sweden?
– 5 kroner and 60 øre.
– That's cheap! The last time I paid 3000 kroner!

The cartoon only takes up 5 x 5 cm of space on the page and is hidden away in a corner and taking *Svikmøllen's* overall format into consideration (its use of whole page cartoons and so on) it must be said that this cartoon has no prominence or eye catching positioning. But it is there nonetheless. Moreover, small as it is, the cartoon highlights the sometimes astronomical sums that were being demanded for the sea crossing. Today's equivalent of 3000 Danish kroner (in 1943 money) is established by multiplying the amount by 20. At that time, the monthly salary for a fully trained worker was 414 kroner. Moreover, literature and memoirs covering this period cite examples of families paying up to 50,000 kroner for their crossing. They also mention fishermen who charged fees of 100.000 kroner to bring people across to Sweden.[3] As a comparison, the price of an actual fishing boat lay between 15,000 and 30,000 Danish kroner in 1943.

These payment demands are often justified by references to the fact that the fishermen involved were risking not only their lives but also their livelihoods in undertaking these crossings and that the money was a form of insurance for the vessel and its equipment, as well as possible compensation for their wives and families should things go awry. Accounts provided by the Jews themselves meanwhile stress the fact that the value of human life is not something that can be haggled over and that, of course, Jewish families were quite happy to hand over all they possessed, if necessary, in order that lives be saved. Valdemar Koppel was the Editor in Chief of Denmark's *Politiken* newspaper and his description of the situation caries a kind of humorous pathos:

"I have occasionally reflected on the amount I had to pay to get across to Malmö and the fact that, in peacetime, I could have travelled the world for the same price. Yes it could have been me on that luxury liner with its all its pampering and comforts, flirting with stunning, fairy tale dollar-millionaire princesses, with whom I would play badminton out on the sun kissed deck in the morning, and then in the evening we would dance cheek to cheek in one of the wonderful exclusive chandelier lit saloons. Oh what pleasures have I missed?! But for all that, I would not have changed one for the other. Because I experienced something that was infinitely more valuable. I encountered human goodness, a natural and selfless desire to help, which could not be automatically assumed beforehand, and which was both a source of great surprise and a deep, long lasting joy. Even today, one basks in warm feelings of gladness and human empathy when thinking about those days."[4]

For the record, the cost of Koppel's escape to Sweden was 20,000 Danish kroner, which in present day terms amounts to 400,000 kroner.

The disarming humor should not be interpreted as a kind of backhanded complaint. The fact is that Jews in Denmark actually did feel very grateful at that time. Nobody was interested in haggling about crossing fees in 1943, and those few that did were immediately condemned as tight fisted skin-flints. And then, after liberation in 1945, there was even less interest in discussing the reasonableness of the fees demanded. This was not just because the murder of 6 million coreligionists made any comparison with the travails and tribulations of Danish Jews impossible. For there was also the fact that the Danes themselves had paid a heavy price in their fight to liberate their country. Over 4000 people had been killed in accidents, sabotage and armed actions, in concentration camps, or as victims of German executions. Many more had suffered torture, hunger and brutality as captives of the Nazi regime. Those who managed to escape the above fates still had to put up with rationing, goods scarcity and the general decline of standards during the wartime occupation. Then came the day of judgment when an account was drawn up of which Danes had played their part in Denmark's freedom struggle and the returning Jews (who had spent the last years of the war in a neighboring country that overflowed with nylon stockings, chocolate) were met with no little suspicion and envy. Thus, at that historical point in time, nobody was going to raise a question mark over the apparently straightforward heroic feat accomplished by their compatriots in saving Jewish lives.

It would take a long time before research was carried out into the more dubious aspects of the "legend." Not until 1995 (50 years after the war), did we see the first systematic examination of the actual risks involved in helping Jews to escape. This concluded that those helping fugitives to flee Denmark had not, in fact, put their lives at risk by saving Jews. On the contrary. As a matter of routine, German police would hand over the helpers to the Danish police who would either release them immediately or issue a mild punishment, typically 3 months as a non high security prisoner. There are also instances where the helpers were sentenced but never served their time because they were slipped out via the back door of the court once judgment had been announced.[5] Moreover, the German forces of occupation regarded the "offence" of helping Jews to escape as an internal Danish problem and in this way were able to manage their fiction of a "peaceful occupation." This conceit was based on Nazi propaganda that they were simply protecting Denmark's military neutrality and did not otherwise violate Danish sovereignty. Thus, the helpers were sentenced and imprisoned in accordance with Danish law. Subsequent studies of the German police authorities in Denmark, have clearly demonstrated that whilst a comprehensive anti-Jewish *Aktion* (with more than sufficient manpower) was indeed initiated for the mass arrest operation on the 1st of October 1943, this operation was not planned to last more than 3 hours and was also constrained by a number of other provisos–first and foremost amongst these was that German police units were not allowed to use violence or forcible entry to access Jewish homes in order to make arrests.[6] Furthermore, this operation was a one-off. There were to be no more mass arrest initiatives. After the mass raids on the 1st of October, follow up searches were left in the hands of a small group of Gestapo officers in Copenhagen and Helsingør. Covering the whole of the Øresund strait between Denmark and Sweden effectively was an impossible task for such a small group. At the same time, Wehrmacht forces simply followed general instructions not to interfere with illegal marine traffic, whilst German navy vessels only involved themselves with military naval operations. Not one single vessel (out of 600 to 700 transport craft carrying Jewish fugitives/refugees) was detained at sea.[7]

More detailed studies have also revealed that the price for the crossing to Sweden swung substantially from the end of September 1943, when demand was greatest (and the availability of fishermen willing to sail was least), to the end of October, by which time the main body of Jewish refugees had been sailed across. In other words, the crossing price was dictated by the market. One of the great advantages in the way the rescue operation evolved was that price rates were kept fairly stable. Thus, the "helpers" assisting the refugees and fugitives effectively functioned as middle men who could agree to a fixed price with the fishermen who were to make the crossing. Furthermore, large amounts of finance were drawn in from private individuals and the business community. This helped defray at least some of the cost for individual refugees. A conservative estimate suggests that the combined cost for all Danish Jews who crossed to Sweden was somewhere near 20 million Danish kroner. Jewish families presumably paid around half of this amount, whilst the rest came from collections and donations.[8] Thus, no one was left behind because they could not afford to pay. However, they may have had to wait until the price fell further.

The combination of the already well established fact that by far the majority of Jews had to pay hard cash for their escape to Sweden and the new research findings (with regards to levels of risk etc.) had a devastating effect: if it was now clear that the rescue effort did not contain a large element of risk and that the fishermen received significant amounts of money to bring Jews to safety, then this surely was exploitation of vulnerable and persecuted human beings? The reaction to these revelations was not long in coming: The best gloss that could be put on things was that the new research had underestimated the subjective view of the risk involved – that the helpers *believed* they were risking their lives. The worst scenario was that the memory of the rescue helpers had been besmirched. The highly charged reaction of those who were centrally involved, both the victims themselves and their rescuers, as well as many who had played no part in the drama, demonstrated that the placatory interpretation of the payments issue had suppressed the memory of its scale. Now it was the Danes' own cherished image of themselves that was at stake.

But is it possible that the historians researching this period were applying a false hindsight that sought to cynically play down the fear factor for helpers? If this is the case, it was a more stringent hindsight view than was shared by the Danish authorities in 1945.

Shortly after the war's end, the transition government introduced a comprehensive reparation programmed, which was meant to compensate victims of the Nazi occupation. The civil servants tasked with implementing this programmed received very precise instructions as to how they should handle applications for compensation. Right from the start, they were told to be aware of the huge amounts of money that had been earned by fishermen during the Jews' flight to Sweden. Their guidelines gave the following instruction:

"It is common knowledge that a number of people, especially fishermen, involved themselves in these transport operations purely for their own personal gain and made massive profits by charging quite extraordinary "ticket prices" (what's particularly being referred to here is the period around 1-10-43). Any claim for compensation made by such people under the Reparations Act should be viewed as being doubtful in the extreme, given that their activities were, to put it mildly, a pure money making exercise and the risk of arrest or damage was covered by the 'prices' they charged."[9]

The authorities worked on the assumption that there had been no risk to life for the fishermen, so the main task was to clarify exactly how much profit an applicant for compensation had made whilst transporting fugitives/refugees. Those applicants who had received a payment for their transport services were advised to retract their application.[10]

The Reparations Act also contained a provision for the awarding of an "honor grant" for active involvement in Denmark's liberation struggle. This honor grant was an acknowledgment of the sacrifices made by the resistance movement, with many people having been deported to prisons and camps because of their nationality and/or political convictions. The award was a parallel honor to the acknowledgment and elevated status given to *political prisoners*, which was a prerequisite for compensation in other European countries after the war. [11] The Danish authorities refused to pay honor grants to fishermen who had earned money from the transportation of Jews – even when the person in question had died as a result of making an illegal crossing.

In fact, as early as 1945, the Danish authorities knew exactly how many helpers had lost their lives whilst helping Jews to escape. There were two. One of those drowned whilst attempting to row a boat carrying fugitives/refugees to Sweden. The other committed suicide in his cell after being arrested by the Gestapo on suspicion of helping fugitives/refugees.[12] The reason for incidents like this, despite the above evidence of a formerly relaxed attitude on the part of the German authorities, is that people who had taken part in the rescue operation in October 1943, but who then continued in their illegal people smuggling, ran a greater risk of being arrested, imprisoned and deported. In other words, the Nazi occupiers in Denmark were to subsequently regard people trafficking routes in the Øresund strait as a major problem and combatting these illegal activities was prioritized, not least because this sea channel was now providing a way in for saboteurs and weaponry and also facilitated the obtaining and exchange of secret intelligence between Denmark and Sweden. Overall the sharpened military situation produced a rising death toll due to things like drowning incidents, explosions and resistance/allied engagements with the occupying power, as well as accidental discharges of weaponry. This meant a continued need to keep the smuggling routes open because there were still people trying to get across to Sweden. But Danish transgressors were not deported to concentration camps if there only "crime" was helping Jews to escape, so the fishermen involved could not be said to have risked their lives in such activities.

On the other hand, Danish fishermen and those who assisted Jewish fugitives/refugees in the beginning of October 1943, could not know this for certain. However, an awareness soon developed amongst them that they were not engaging in a life or death resistance exploit. They would have also noted the fact that Wehrmacht military units showed no interest in their activities and were far more concerned with rooting out Danish spies and naval coast guard staff who were working against them. Its also true to say that many helpers would have perceived themselves as being untouchable given the huge support their activities enjoyed and the high numbers of people who became involved. The helper felt the same kind of aura of protection as the soldier in H.C. Andersen's fairy-tale *The Tinder Box* where the clever dog was able to conceal the place where the Princess had been that night by drawing a chalk cross on every door in the town, whereby it became impossible to discover which was the cross that the Princess's chamber maid had drawn on the door when she had followed the magic dog which carried the sleeping princess to the waiting soldier. This fairy-tale metaphor of crosses being drawn on all doors may explain why so many people, who otherwise might not have chosen to take part and were not experienced in illegal resistance work, found the courage to get involved in the rescue mission to help Jews get across to Sweden. The protests against the Nazi regimes *Aktion* against the Jews came from all walks of life and included many opinion makers and august institutions in the country. This had the effect of galvanizing huge support for the rescue operation. It also helped to blur the boundaries between what was seen as being legal and illegal. Because effectively there was a cross on every door in the town. Were the German forces of occupation going to arrest everybody?

In Denmark's case, and at least until the autumn of 1943, the Germans valued harmonious cooperation with the Danes higher than the need to remove 8000 Jews from the country. And even when the established policy of collaboration broke down in August 1943, and the government stepped down, Danish society was not thrown into either military or social turmoil. The police and courts still functioned and leadership of the country was taken over by civil servants. For their part, the German occupiers wished to continue with their cooperation policy in order to ensure the continued supply of vital foodstuffs and materials to Germany. Thus, from a German point of view, nothing should be done to inflame Danish sensibilities. In other words, even though an order was in place to round up all Jews in Denmark because of an ideological war, any overly harsh consequences of such a policy had to be softened. It was for these pragmatic reasons that the chief executive officer of the occupying power, Werner Best, ensured that Danish Jews received advance warning of the *Aktion* planned for the 1st of October. It was for these same reasons that police units were not activated to hunt down fleeing Jews. Thus, it is not the case that Best had suddenly become a "big softy." It was rather that a manhunt for Jews did not serve the Nazi regimes strategic interests. Best was simply keen to avoid widespread unrest amongst the wider population. Nor had he become any less anti-Semitic. The aim was still to make Denmark "judenrein" (cleansed of Jews). But whether this happened via deportation to German prison camps or via illegal flight to Sweden was irrelevant to him.

Finally, it should be pointed out that a small number of people in fact sailed to Sweden free of charge. The average price for a crossing was 1000 Danish kroner per person, a substantial sum in 1943, which for many families meant that they would have to sell everything they owned, or lend an amount they would never, in reality, be able to back. These debts remained in place when they returned to Denmark in 1945. Another distorting factor affecting the relationship between risk – subjective or not – and payment for a crossing was the price level in October 1943, after the vast majority of Danish Jews had sailed to safety in Sweden. From then on, the average price for saboteurs and members of the resistance fell to 100 kroner per. person, in a situation where the risk factor was clearly present.

Does the fruit of all this research mean that no ethical and socially valuable standards can be found in the story of the Danish rescue operation for the country's Jews? Far from it.

The vast majority of those who helped their Jewish compatriots did not receive any payment for their actions. Whilst the rescue operation was running, there was a very large group of people willing to put their own safety and livelihoods at risk in order to help Jews to escape. Thousand of people became either directly or indirectly involved in the various escape operations. They came from every social class and represented a broad range of political convictions. Some had experience of illegal work and some didn't. What was common to all of them, however, was a spontaneous urge to do something. One of the most moving aspects of the rescue operation was the goodwill that Danish Jews encountered in all situations.

During a holiday in Sweden in 1935, Grete Michel met a German-Jewish refugee called Werner. They were married that same year. In the early evening of the 29th of September 1943, the now married couple set off to visit

Grete's mother in law to celebrate *Rosh Hashanah*, the Jewish New Year. They were unaware that details of a forthcoming *Aktion* against Danish Jewish had been leaked to Danish politicians at just that point in time. From here, warnings spread like wildfire across the country. Thus, as this small family unit sat and prepared its commemorative evening meal, a knock came at the door. It was one of the neighbors who had rushed to warn them not to stay at home as anti Jewish raids were expected as soon as that very night: "We took the news fairly calmly – at any event we decided we should eat before doing anything else." As soon as the meal was over, Werner went home to pack "the bare essentials."[13] In the meantime, Grete helped her mother in law to pack her own things, but before they had finished they had received no less than three completely spontaneous visits from people offering to put the family up, look after their home and property and arrange transport out of the country. Contemporary diaries and memoirs provide a huge amount of evidence of similar spontaneous offers of assistance from not just the extended family network, friends and acquaintances, but also total strangers. Completely normal Danish people threw an arm of protection around their Jewish fellow citizens without demanding anything in return. In the 1930s, the political struggle to assert democratic values was not just about protecting the rights of minorities but also to promote the active combatting of anti-Semitism, which became characterized as an un-Danish thing to be. Questioning whether Danish Jews could actually be classed as fellow citizens was viewed as a form of approval for Nazi and thereby German ideology.[14] Now, in 1943, the deep rootedness of these humane values showed itself in widespread practice.

What was decisive for the fate of the Jewish community in Denmark was that the warnings of an impending *Aktion* against it were taken seriously. Without hesitation, Jewish families fled from their homes and apartments, leaving most of their possessions behind them, and sought refuge in the homes of neighbors and friends, in hotels and summerhouses. In the meantime, they began organizing sea crossings to neutral Sweden, which had already offered to take fugitives/refugees. However, families with young children were left with a terrible dilemma. Terrifying rumors had begun to spread about children being strangled or smothered, or even thrown overboard, because they could not keep quiet during the illegal crossing. It is true that some people-smuggling routes had doctors in attendance who were able to anaesthetize the children during the sea crossing, but full anesthesia of small children can be risky and did not always have the desired effect. A crying child would expose and endanger everybody else – fugitives/refugees and fishermen alike. Another problem was that this was October in Scandinavia. The weather was harsh – wet, very windy and cold. At the start of the rescue operations, in particular, many crossings were made using rowing boats, which had to traverse the choppy waters in pitch darkness. Jewish families were also concerned about what would happen to them once they got to Sweden. Would they end up in refugee camps? Would the family in fact be able to stay together as a unit – or would men and women be separated? A drastic decision had to be made by many parents: Was it too dangerous to bring the youngest kids with them?

At least 150 children – over 10% of all children who were victims of anti Jewish persecution – were therefore placed in hiding in Denmark when their parents fled to Sweden. The age of the children that were left behind gives its own clear indication as to the way parents felt about bringing small children with them: Almost 2/3 of the children were under 5 years of age. 25% were under or around one year old. The youngest infant was no more than 6 days old. The separation from their parents was to last for almost 2 years until the war finally ended in May 1945, but for many the emotional bond had been severed forever. The children were hidden away in children's homes and boarding schools, and also in private homes amongst families who were often complete strangers to these tiny "outcasts." Only in a very small number of cases was a payment transaction made between the relevant parties, and even then this related to specific expenditure for child clothing, toys and equipment. As far as can be ascertained, no foster parents received a payment for their undertaking. As is only natural, these small children formed a bond with their foster parents. In the vast majority of cases, these substitute parents gave much love and care to their foster children and treated them as if they were their own children.[15]

A common factor for all these "hidden" children is that they lived a completely open existence in Denmark. In contrast to Jewish children in continental Europe who had been reduced to hiding in cellars and sewage systems, lofts and attics, as well as outbuildings and henhouses (in some cases without any help from adults) all the Danish children were looked after by adults. In other words, the children did not lead lives that were cut off from the outside world, but took part in the daily life of the host family, or at a children's home, by way of a cover story or a false identity. However, the cover stories were not always that reliable, just as the foster parents or guardians were suddenly faced with a range of practical problems to do with goods shortages and rationing where any change in regular patterns risked attracting the attention of others. But not one single child was betrayed to the German police authorities. This fact alone reflects both the level of solidarity at the local level (which gave support to the actions of individual foster parents or guardians), and also the particular nature of the Nazi occupation in Denmark, where anti Jewish persecution ebbed away as early as the turn of the year – 1943/44. The spontaneous decision on the part of foster families to take in and care for Jewish children (without knowing how long this would last or the amount of risk involved) is an hitherto unknown aspect of the Danish rescue operation of 1943. The story of what happened to these children is a strong testament to the deep opposition amongst many Danes to the discriminatory policies of the Nazi occupiers and also to the determination they had to take on what was potentially the greatest responsibility of all in caring for the life of small and completely vulnerable human beings.

Thus, the much vaunted solidarity that many individual Danes showed their Jewish fellow citizens is actually confirmed as being true by the most recent research. It must also be said that this same research shows how extensive, bold and remarkable the support of the Danish state mechanism was for its Jewish population.

As early as the 2nd of October 1943, the day after the anti Jewish raids, the Copenhagen municipal authority received an unusual communiqué from the Department of Social Affairs. The ministry requested of Copenhagen Council that it take over the care and preservation of the possessions and property left behind by fleeing Jews.[16] In all, there were no less than 1970 notes received regarding empty homes and apartments or questionable circumstances in the capital area. When the municipal authority received a request, the address was visited, conditions assessed, and an inventory made of all furniture and fittings. Where it proved possible to keep the property, the rent was paid for the duration of German occupation. Where it was found that the property had been re-let, or where it appeared that it had been sublet – if, for example, the rent had been too high – all relevant possessions and property were packed into boxes and stored in specially dedicated warehouses. Contracts of custodianship for property and businesses were drawn up with neighbors, extended family and employees and further measures were taken to prevent theft and ransacking. In all, house rent and all other costs were paid for 97 premises, whilst 350 lots of household effects were stored by the local council. Subsequently, this type of assistance scheme was applied across the whole country, just as financial support was paid to wives whose Jewish partner had been forced to leave the country.

In other words, right in the middle of a Nazi occupation, the Danish state mechanism was able to enact measures that would ensure the protection of possessions and property belonging to absent Jews. The rationale behind this process was quite simply that returning Jews would have a home to which they could return! It is no less striking that these protection procedures were put in place in agreement with the German occupier. Thus, at the same time as the Gestapo was carrying out raids and arrests along the Øresund coast, the Danish Ministry of Foreign Affairs had reached an agreement with the head of the security section of the German police that the Danish authorities could take over the care of property belonging to deported Jews. In reality, the Danish side entered a grey area that went beyond what had actually been agreed, because the agreement officially only covered Jews who had been deported from the country. However the Department of Social Affairs took the agreement to mean that the Danish authorities were obliged to *expand* this duty of care to persons who "due to present circumstances (have) decided that the correct thing to do was to take steps to ensure their safety either within the country or by going abroad."

Only in a very few cases were the homes and apartments listed as being protected by the local authority vandalized by the German police. Instances of theft and burglary that were discovered were, as far as can be established, perpetrated by other Danes. There was, however, one report covering the 3rd of October 1943 that represented an exception to the rule:

"On the 3rd October 1943 Copenhagen council officials were warned that German military units had used the Synagogue at 12 Krystalgade as a rendezvous point during the raids on Jewish homes and that the premises had not been left unscathed. The congregation's white prayer shawls had been slung across the seats and various prayer books strewn across the floor. The floor around the ceremonial chair overflowed with stamped out cigarette stumps and the high hats worn by the elders, which were normally kept in a cupboard in the entrance hall, had clearly been used as footballs as they had been kicked across the floor and beneath the rows of benches. Following this incident, council officials removed what was deemed to be of value: a number of Torah scrolls, various silver artifacts and some books. With the help of Copenhagen Museum (and along with some boxes from the Mosaic Religious Community Museum at Ny Kongensgade 6) the items from the synagogue were stored in an underground crypt below one of Copenhagen's old churches. Following the Nazi capitulation in 1945, these items were once more placed into the care of a representative of the Mosaic Religious Community."[17]

Denmark stands out as one of the most remarkable paradoxes with regard to the anti Jewish policies being prosecuted by the Nazis, because in Denmark the German regime opted for a radically different strategy to the one it was using in the rest of Europe. The report detailing the desecration of the Copenhagen synagogue provokes reminders of the Nazi regime's attacks on Jewish property and religious shrines right across Europe during the period of the Holocaust. But the isolated nature of this kind of incident actually serves to highlight the special occupation strategy being pursued by the Germans in Denmark, which forbade the destruction or theft of Jewish property. In Denmark, the Gestapo issued instructions to the effect that no Jewish homes should be broken into or destroyed and household effects were not to be removed.[18] The municipal authority's own reports confirm that this instruction from the Gestapo *was in fact* respected by German police units on the ground, as it is clear that in the majority of cases the homes that were inspected did not give the impression of having been raided or ransacked. However, the monitoring work carried out by local council officials was still highly necessary. Not to protect Jewish property from German confiscation or vandalism but to secure it against theft and deliberate neglect perpetrated by their fellow Danes.

When the war was finally at an end, about 1/3 of Jewish families were able to return to a completely intact and well kept home. In other words, a large number of private individuals had selflessly (and with great care) kept a watch on the property belonging to these families. Moreover, the various local councils (with strong backing from the Department of Social Affairs) had made great efforts to ensure that Danish Jews had something to which they could return. Be that as it may, in the summer of 1945, thousands of people had returned to find that they had neither home nor a job to go to, or they had lost their business. Likewise, many found that their property and possessions had either been sold or stolen. However there was a particularly well established, and highly organized, aid centre to which they could turn.

In the immediate aftermath of returning home, people could get help from the so called "Centralkontor for særlige Anliggender" – Central Office for Special Needs, which first and foremost existed to handle the demobilization of the resistance movement and to help facilitate a smooth return to civilian life for its members. But returning Jews were included within the remit of this office from the start. The "Central Office" issued financial aid for food, rent, clothing and debts which had been incurred during the "illegal" period or whilst escaping. Payments were issued for the storage of furniture, for convalescence and rest cures and funeral costs. Resettlement grants were also made available in the form of a one off amount, of up to 1500 Danish kroner, for the setting up of independent companies or as a subvention for the purchase of work wear and equipment.

Jews returning home, who had either been in exile or in concentration camps, made up 25% of all those who received help from the Central Office. In total, 4200 people of Jewish origin received temporary financial help. Thus Jewish fugitives/refugees proved to be the largest group and the biggest recipient of help for "special needs." These figures show that at least 65% of Danish Jewish were in need of – and received – financial help in order to re-establish themselves in Denmark.

Europe was in utter ruins after the capitulation of the Nazi regime. Millions of people had either fled across land borders, had been forcibly moved or had been deported from their own countries. Many emaciated and traumatized prisoners had been freed from concentration camps. Prisoners of war and victims of forced labor had been released in large numbers, whilst others who had literally gone underground emerged from their hideouts. At the same time, hundreds of thousands of Germans, or Baltic Germans/citizens, and East Europeans were now being held in prison camps or were fleeing from the advancing Red Army.

In all, following the defeat of Germany, over 10 million people had *Displaced Person* status (DP), as they had either been driven out or forcibly moved from their homeland. Denmark experienced only a fraction of this chaos. After liberation, there were approximately 250.000 German, Baltic and East European fugitives/refugees in Denmark who were interned in barrack camps. However the Danish authorities had not anticipated the number of Danes the war would make homeless, or how long it would take for the last of those returning home to obtain permanent accommodation. In all, 1534 erstwhile fugitives/refugees and deported citizens had to be housed in refugee camps in Denmark, before they were able to set up new homes. 90-

95 % of the "inmates" at these camps were Jewish. In other words, about one fifth of all Jews returning home found themselves in refugee camps in Denmark for shorter or longer periods. Many more simply preferred a status as "homeless." The camps were the absolute last resort. Those who were able to consider alternatives, booked into hotels, lived with family, friends or neighbors, or rented temporary rooms; even allotment sheds were used as accommodation. Only around a third of Jews had the option of moving back to their original home.[19]

The Danish authorities understood that the costs and expenditure incurred by fleeing refugees was a serious burden for returning Jewish families. As we have seen above, those who fled had often paid huge sums to get across to Sweden. Moreover, many had been forced to leave their property and possessions in haste and unsecured and came back after the war to discover that these had been sold or had simply disappeared and/or that their businesses had been badly managed or had gone bankrupt. The education of their children, meanwhile, had been severely disrupted and there was also a group of women and children who had been left without a breadwinner as they had lost a husband/father. Thus, on the 1st of October 1945, the Danish parliament passed a Reparations Act for victims of the Nazi occupation in acknowledgement of the urgent need for public assistance on the part of those whose way of life and livelihoods had been destroyed by events during the war.

This act gave access to compensation for death and disability caused by acts of war, including acts of persecution and deportation carried out by the German forces of occupation and for so called tort-compensation for imprisonment and deportations. These payments were made as fixed amounts for each week of captivity that had been endured. The act also contained a compensation clause for property damage and support for the recommencing or start up of a business, as well as re-establishing a venture after "particularly heavy losses." There was also a provision for training and retraining. A total of DKK 1.1 million was paid out as tort compensation to Jewish prisoners who had been deported to the Theresienstadt camp – the equivalent of DKK 14 million in today's money. In this way, 77% of the surviving adults prisoners from Theresienstadt received reparations for their time in the camp. However, the remarkable thing about this Danish reparations act was that it also gave access to compensation for those who had fled to Sweden because of anti-Semitic persecution. This legislation made it possible not only to seek compensation for damage and misuse of possessions and property during the victim's exile, but also costs and expenditure for the escape itself. Assistance was also provided for the repayment of loans that were taken on to pay for the escape, as well as compensation for the use of one's own means, both in terms of cash or property that had to be sold as a consequence of urgent flight. Thus, in this way alone, the Danish state contributed to retrospective financing of the escape to Sweden made by Danish Jews with over DKK 700,000 being paid out – the equivalent of DKK 9 million in today's terms. In all, 1280 people who had been persecuted because of their Jewish origins made claims for compensation. In addition to this, at least one fifth of applicants made a claim for tort compensation because of Nazi persecution. The total amount paid out came to DKK 2.2 million in compensation and reparations to Danish Jews (DKK 27 million in today's money). In no way does this amount cover the real costs relating to anti Jewish persecution: many families refrained from seeking compensation because they felt ashamed at the thought of receiving public assistance, and even those who did receive compensation rarely saw their actual losses being covered, because the Reparations Act imposed a ceiling for the level of payments. Moreover, no amount of compensation could wipe out the human and emotional costs sustained by Danish Jews during the Nazi campaign of persecution. All it could do was ensure that no family went under because of poverty or financial distress.

In present day values, the combined state expenditure in relation to the Jewish flight from Denmark and the subsequent return home was at least DKK 74 million. Given that not everybody sought assistance or compensation, *even though* they too had suffered losses, the combined financial loss caused by the Nazi persecution of Jews was undoubtedly far greater than these amounts suggest.

It was the clear intent of the Danish authorities to prevent any controversy about the financial consequences of the flight across the Øresund from entering the public domain, or that a specific group of people should effectively become outcasts because of the unjust persecution they had suffered. It is an undoubted fact that, without the Reparations Act, a specific social group would have ended up on at the bottom of the social pile, from whence it would have proved very difficult to go upwards again. However there were clear lacunae in the legislation. Stateless Jewish refugees who had come to Denmark in the 1930s received neither compensation nor reparations, even though they had residence permits, apartments, permanent homes and possessions in Denmark. This was because the Reparations Act only covered Danish citizens. The financial help also helped put a lid on any discussion or debate surrounding the huge financial questions relating to the escape operations and thereby did away with any uncomfortable reminders about those who had lined their own pockets at the expense of people who were extremely vulnerable and in urgent need.[20]

It should also be remembered that the end of the Second World War in the spring of 1945 did not mean the end of violence and discrimination against Europe's Jews. If we wish to fully understand the consequences and implications of the Holocaust, we are obliged to follow the story of the survivors as they returned to their homes in continental Europe or–as was the case for many–their exodus to the United States or Israel. Examination of this aspect of the Holocaust does not harmonies with the self image that prevails in a range of countries in Western Europe and, in particular, does not sit comfortably with the proclaimed international focus on human rights and refugee policy.

In many European countries, Jewish survivors of the Holocaust and Nazi persecution experienced further discrimination with regards to compensation and invalid pensions, because they became classed as "random" victims as opposed to active political prisoners who had been sent to concentration camps because of their political convictions, or because of their active roles in the resistance. By comparison, the state backed assistance to Danish Jewish on their return home in 1945 was unique and once again confirms Denmark's status as an exception to the rule (as explained above) during the period of the Holocaust. It should, however, be noted that at least half of the Danish Jews who returned home encountered some kind of friction or problems resulting from their long absence. For example, they found that their homes had been rented out to others, or their possessions stolen. Likewise their businesses or workshops had often been sold or damaged. Thus, even though their motives were not perhaps directly anti-Semitic, many Danes had more or less consciously failed to show the responsibility and respect that was required of them. For Jews, this situation was all too familiar in the rest of Europe. In fact in Holland, this very situation created a new concept in the Dutch language: "bewariërs," which was a play on the word to "defend" or "keep" but applied to a person who was reluctant to give back possessions and property appropriated during the war.[21] On the other hand, it is ironic that in

Denmark the suppression of uncomfortable reminders of what happened in the Holocaust period has also drawn a veil over the story of the unique care shown by the Danish state towards its Jewish citizens. They are two sides of the same historic coin.

The rescue of Danish Jews during the Second world War still has great significance for Denmark's reputation in the outside world. And for good reason. But perhaps the wrong reasons. It seems that the fishing boat as a universal symbol of altruism and heroic valor needs to be revised. However, finding a replacement image is not that straightforward. The civil servants (who stood behind the well organized system of aid and assistance after the period of persecution and the Holocaust) with their panoply of governmental devices, laws and budget systems, hardly carry the same appeal as a simple boat braving the dark waves in freedom's name, and the collaboration policies practiced by those self same civil servants complicates their role even further. The truth is that the reaction and behavior of Danes was far more nuanced than has preciously been assumed. The type of cynical behavior and avarice that during the period of goods and accommodation shortage drove Danes to commit the theft and misuse of Jewish property can be found side by side with the many reports of simple, ordinary people who spontaneously opened their homes to both neighbors, colleagues and even total strangers, at the same time as they showed great love and care towards their children. In other words, in terms of moral and social solidarity, the narrative has lost its black and white character. But then, we recognize that this is part of life's complexity as we live it in our own times.

IMPORTANT DETAILS AND FACTS
Denmark:

Approx. 7500 Jews at the start of the war, of which 1500 Jewish fugitives/refugees from Germany, Austria and Czechoslovakia.
7056 people from Jewish families brought to safety in Sweden in October 1943, that is to say 95% of the Jewish population [as well as 686 non Jewish spouses – in all 7742].
472 deported to Theresienstadt prison camp.
Deaths in concentration camps: 53.
Deaths by suicide, sickness, exhaustion and drowning: 42.

Shot dead by German police: 2.

In all, at least 104 people died as a direct result of the Nazi's anti Jewish *Aktion* of 1943.

Returned home from exile and captivity: 7.374.

98% of the Dano-Jewish population survived the Holocaust period.

References

Bak, Sofie Lene, *Jødeaktionen oktober 1943. Forestillinger i offentlig og forskning*, København: Museum Tusculanums forlag, 2001.

Bak, Sofie Lene, *Dansk Antisemitisme 1930-1945*, København: Aschehoug, 2004.

Bak, Sofie Lene, „Indtil de vender hjem. Københavns Socialtjeneste og de danske jøder 1943-45." I: Peter Henningsen og Rasmus Mariager (red.), *Strenge tider. København i krig og fred 1943-49*, København: Københavns Stadsarkiv, 2006 (*Historiske Meddelelser om København* 2006), s. 11-43.

Bak, Sofie Lene, *Ikke noget at tale om. Danske jøders krigsoplevelser 1943-45*, København: Dansk Jødisk Museum, 2010. /*Nothing to speak of. Wartime Experiences of Danish Jews 1943–1945*, Copenhagen: The Danish Jewish Museum, 2011.

Bak, Sofie Lene, *Da krigen var forbi. De danske jøders hjemkomst efter besættelsen*, København: Gyldendal, 2012.

Bertelsen, Aage, *Oktober 43*, [1952], 5. udgave, København: Gyldendal,1993.

Bankier, David (ed.), *The Jews are coming back. The Return of the Jews to their Countries of Origin after WWII*, Jerusalem: Yad Yashem & Berghahn Books, 2005.

Blüdnikow, Bent og Klaus Rothstein (red.), *Dage i oktober 43. Vidnesbyrd*, København: Forlaget Centrum & Det Mosaiske Trossamfund, 1993.

Caestecker, Frank, "The reintegration of Jewish Survivors into Belgian Society." In: David Bankier (ed.), *The Jews are coming back. The Return of the Jews to their Countries of Origin after WWII*, Jerusalem: Yad Yashem & Berghahn Books, 2005, s. 72-107.

Følner, Bjarke, "Mindesmærker og erindringskultur. Efterskrift. I: Sofie Lene Bak, *Ikke noget at tale om. Danske jøders krigsoplevelser 1943-45*, København: Dansk Jødisk Museum, 2010, s. 211-245./"Memorials and Memorial Culture." In: Sofie Lene Bak, *Nothing to speak of. Wartime Ex-*

periences of Danish Jews 1943–1945, Copenhagen: The Danish Jewish Museum, 2011, p. 215-249.

Kreth, Rasmus og Michael Mogensen, *Flugten til Sverige. Aktionen mod de danske jøder oktober 1943, København: Gyldendal*, 1995.

Lagrou, Pieter, "Return to a Vanished World. European Societies and the Remnants of their Jewish Communities, 1945-1947." In: David Bankier (ed.), *The Jews are coming back. The Return of the Jews to their Countries of Origin after WWII*, Jerusalem: Yad Yashem & Berghahn Books, 2005, s. 1-24.

Lundtofte, Henrik, *Gestapo! Tysk politi og terror i Danmark 1940-45*. København: Gads forlag, 2003.

Yahil, Leni: *Et demokrati på prøve. Jøderne i Danmark under besættelsen.* København: Gyldendal, 1967.

Notes

1 Bjarke Følner, "Mindesmærker og erindringskultur. Efterskrift." I: Sofie Lene Bak, *Ikke noget at tale om. Danske jøders krigsoplevelser 1943-45*, København: Dansk Jødisk Museum, 2010, s. 224./"Memorials and Memorial Culture." In: Sofie Lene Bak, *Nothing to speak of. Wartime Experiences of Danish Jews 1943–1945*, Copenhagen: The Danish Jewish Museum, 2011, p. 228.

2 The home page of the Israeli Department of Foreign Affairs, http://www.mfa.gov.il/MFA/MFAArchive/2000_2009/2003/6/The+Righteous+Among+the+Nations.htm (visited 5th March 2013)

3 Aage Bertelsen, *Oktober 43*, [1952], 5. udgave, København: Gyldendal,1993, s. 84ff.

4 Account in Ole Barfoed's collection, (National Archive). Published in Bent Blüdnikow and Klaus Rothstein (eds.), *Dage i oktober 43. Vidnesbyrd,* Copenhagen: Publisher – Centrum Mosaic Religious Community, 1993.

5 Rasmus Kreth og Michael Mogensen, *Flugten til Sverige. Aktionen mod de danske jøder oktober 1943, København: Gyldendal*, 1995.

6 Henrik Lundtofte, *Gestapo! Tysk politi og terror i Danmark 1940-45, København:* Gads forlag, 2003.

7 Kreth og Mogensen.1995, s. 135.

8 Sofie Lene Bak, *Jødeaktionen oktober 1943. Forestillinger i offentlig og forskning,* København: Museum Tusculanums forlag, 2001, s. 82.

9 "Guidelines for The Central Office's processing of compensation claims: Materials for compensation claims, Lot. 28, Archive of Central Office for Special Needs (National Archive for Zealand). All quotes in the article have been adjusted to suit modern spelling and punctuation.

10 Sofie Lene Bak, *Da krigen var forbi. De danske jøders hjemkomst efter besættelsen,* København: Gyldendal, 2012, s. 131.

11 See for ex Frank Caestecker, "The reintegration of Jewish Survivors into Belgian Society." In: David Bankier (ed.), *The Jews are coming back. The Return of the Jews to their Countries of Origin after WWII,* Jerusalem: Yad Yashem & Berghahn Books, 2005, s. 72-107.

12 Journalsag 15.555 og 15.951, Erstatningsrådets arkiv (Rigsarkivet). Se også Centralk-ontoret for særlige Anliggenders kartotek over "Danske statsborgere, der mistede livet i forbindelse med besættelsen" (1945-1947) (Rigsarkivet).

13 Grethe Michels diary 18th October – 20th November 1943, JDK207X71 (Danish Jewish Museum).

14 Sofie Lene Bak, *Dansk Antisemitisme 1930-1945*, København: Aschehoug, 2004.

15 The story of these hidden children is described in Sofie Lene Bak, *Ikke noget at tale om. Danske jøders krigsoplevelser 1943-45*, København: Dansk Jødisk Museum, 2010. /*Nothing to speak of. Wartime Experiences of Danish Jews 1943–1945*, Copenhagen: The Danish Jewish Museum, 2011.

16 The local authority unit – *Socialtjenesten* (Social Services) was tasked to handle this issue. Social Services was actually set up in the spring of 1943 to look after billeting and catering for people whose homes had been damaged or evacuated temporarily due to war related in-cidents, i.e in the first instance air raids. Contingencies were also planned for catastrophes relating to mass evacuations, water supply and food supply/catering – see Sofie Lene Bak, "Indtil de vender hjem. Københavns Socialtjeneste og de danske jøder 1943-45." I: Peter Henningsen og Rasmus Mariager (red.), *Strenge tider. København i krig og fred 1943-49*, København: Københavns Stadsarkiv, 2006 (*Historiske Meddelelser om København* 2006), s. 11-43 og Bak 2012.

17 Report af 25th June 1946, Socialdirektoratets oplysningskontor, Socialtjenesten: Diverse 1943-45 (Københavns Stadsarkiv).

18 See Leni Yahil, *Et demokrati på prøve. Jøderne i Danmark under besættelsen*. København: Gyldendal, 1967, s. 173 and Kreth og Mogensen 1995, s. 32.

19 Bak 2010, s. 77ff.

20 For an overall description of the return home of Danish Jews, see Bak 2012.

21 Pieter Lagrou, "Return to a Vanished World. European Societies and the Remnants of their Jewish Communities, 1945-1947." In: David Bankier (ed.), *The Jews are coming back. The Return of the Jews to their Countries of Origin after WWII*. Jerusalem: Yad Yashem & Berghahn Books, 2005, s. 1-24.

Warsaw: The guilt of indifference

Konstanty Gebert

It his World War II memoirs, written after the events, Polish artist Jeremi Przybora describes a scene he had witnessed after leaving a concert in occupied Warsaw. On the street "sat a Jewish child. A living little skeleton, covered in parchment skin, with a skull in which only the huge, silent, terrified black eyes were alive…A small crowd stood there motionless, and wordlessly watched, as if hypnotized, this small death, huddled there, in still broad daylight, in the very heart of the lively "Aryan" district, in a basement niche, as if it had just emerged from under the ground, and threatened no-one, until you take it by the hand. So no-one dared to take this child by the hand. And neither did I. But it did not forgive me, did not allow itself to be erased from memory. And I know that the death which will come for me will neither be an old lady with a scythe, nor the knight from Bergman's film."[1] During the German occupation of Poland in WWII hundreds of thousands, possibly millions of Poles had had similar experiences: the Nazis had designated Poland as the killing fields of the Shoah, and of its six million victims, half had been Polish Jews.

On the face of it, it seems impossible for Poles not to have known what was happening to the Jews, in front of their own eyes, on their own, if occupied soil. And yet this cannot be stated with full certainty. In contemporary sociological research, most Poles do not recognize that Jews suffered greater oppression under German occupation than Poles did.[2] It would be anachronistic to project this finding backwards in time, and it certainly would be historically and morally unacceptable to belittle the huge suffering ethnic Poles were subject to in WWII.[3] Yet – given the fact that basic education about the Shoah was present, even if in curtailed form, in school curricula of Communist Poland, and that in any case restrictions on what can be taught were eliminated after the transition to democracy in 1989 – one has to consider the hypothesis that the understanding of what was happening to the

Jews in WWII was flawed to begin with, and that it was then passed along in its flawed form. This hypothesis is impossible to prove, of course, but circumstantial evidence can be brought to bear. And so, the eminent contemporary Polish historian Feliks Tych, former head of the Jewish Historical Institute in Warsaw, after having studied more than 400 WWII extensive documentary records written by non-Jewish Polish eyewitnesses of the occupation[4] – both contemporary diaries and memoirs written after the fact, published as well as unpublished – has discovered that most of these records do not contain any reference to the Shoah. None.

This essay will look at possible explanations of this staggering finding. It will therefore concentrate on what ethnic Poles knew, under German occupation, of the fate of the Jews. For lack of space, it will not apply a historical perspective, even though the Poles' knowledge would have obviously been radically different in 1940 and four years later, nor a sociological one, even if the level of knowledge between different groups might have been high. It will look, rather unsystematically, at two sources – diaries and the underground press–for information which would help elucidate the question. It will not attempt to address what people belonging to other ethnic groups into which the Germans had classified their occupied Polish subjects (in particular Germans, and the Jews themselves) knew. But it will try to reconstruct the Poles' knowledge – and to account for it.

It is of course theoretically imaginable that the 400+ sample Tych studied contains some kind of structural flaw which is responsible for the absence of references to the Shoah – yet no such interpretation has been advanced in the more than dozen years since the study has been published. We have therefore to accept as tentative fact that most Poles (especially since diarists are not just a random cross-section of the public, but are the more active observers of the world around them) failed to register what was certainly the most devastating crime committed ever in history, as it occurred in front of their eyes. This blind spot of monumental proportions cannot be explained by hypothetical insensitivity alone. The wartime diaries of Władysław Tatarkiewicz, a leading philosopher who could not be accused of insensitivity, for instance, contain not even one reference to the fate of the Jews, let alone the Shoah itself – yet he had spent the war in Warsaw, site of the Warsaw Ghetto and scene of its 1943 uprising.

One cannot seriously entertain the notion that the authors of these diaries and memoirs really did not know what was happening to the Jews. To be certain, inhabitants of the big cities (Jews constituted 40% of pre-war Poland's urban population) lost direct contact with their Jewish neighbors once the occupying authorities had locked them up in ghettos: in Warsaw this occurred in November 1940. Yet telephone lines still functioned, and an "Aryans only" tramline traversed the Warsaw ghetto. "I shudder at the thought that this is where my friends, and the parents of friends, live" writer Jarosław Iwaszkiewicz wrote in his diary after taking that tram. " I do get news from them occasionally, but they are written as if from the afterlife. I cannot shake off this impression."[5]

But even assuming that the ghetto walls did effectively separate Jews from non-Jews and therefore prevent the latter from realizing the fate of the former, these walls were hardly hermetic. In Warsaw, in particular, due to the pre-war intermingling of Jewish, non-Jewish and mixed neighborhoods, completely separating the ghetto from the "Aryan side" proved technically impossible, and in order to reach St. Charles Boromeus' church one had to cut across the ghetto, traffic being regulated by a system of gates alternatively blocking Jewish and non-Jewish vehicles and pedestrians. Agnieszka Hulewicz-Feillowa remembers how, en route to her own wedding, "[w]e made a mistake in reaching the church, and entered the ghetto. German police wanted to arrest us. We experienced a lot of emotion and were late to church."[6] This is the only mention of the ghetto in her extensive memoir.

But if the ghetto walls were not hermetically sealed, it was not for lack of trying by the Germans. Furthermore, the Warsaw Ghetto uprising apart (we will return to it later), the ultimate fate of the Jews locked in the big ghettos was concealed from the eyes of those on the "Aryan side": all they knew was that cattle cars would take Jews "to the East," allegedly for resettlement. The death camps were set up in relatively secluded sites, so apart from the local residents, most people would initially not be aware of their existence, let alone purpose. But in smaller towns and villages, ghetto walls, such as were set up, usually consisted of nothing more than wooden fencing and barbered wire: whatever was happening there was visible to all. Furthermore, it often was not cost-effective to transport the inmates of the small ghettos to the death camps: they would be killed on the spot. Some 1.5 million Jews were murdered by roving execution squads–the Einsatzgruppen.

Krystyna Libiszowska-Dobrska, daughter of a well-off family of landed gentry, thus described the last day of the Jews in her home-town of Przysucha (the Yiddish Pshiskhe of Hassidic fame): "Far away on the road, in the direction of Opoczno stood a long row of peasant horse-carts. It was towards them that the SS and also Jewish police directed the [Jewish] population being expelled from their homes…It would occasionally happen that somebody, buckling under the load, could not make it fast enough and stopped, or that one of the women, probably remembering that she had left behind at home something which now seemed indispensable, would attempt to turn around. Then one of the Germans standing in front of our house would take position and shoot…This murder of a defenseless population, on the elderly, women and children, was performed in cold blood, not in the amok of battle or even with robbery in mind, for all that could be robbed had already been taken away from these people. It was a planned, systematic action, thought out by the representatives of one nation in order to eliminate another one."[7] Libiszowska-Dobrska had no doubts about what she was witnessing. And yet out the 37 peasant memoirs analyzed by Tych – and one can safely assume their authors had all seen similar things – only 14 mention the Shoah, and out of those only 3 express sympathy to its victims.

Circumstances left Libiszowska-Dobrska no way out but to see what was happening, and to understand it fully. Since Iwaszkiewicz, Hulewicz-Feillowa and countless others doubtless saw, and therefore knew, what was happening in the ghettos, could it be they somehow did not understand what they were seeing? The idea is less preposterous than it may seem. In 1942 Jan Karski, an officer in the Polish underground Home Army, was smuggled out of Poland, after having been taken to the Warsaw ghetto and to Izbica Lubelska, a sub-camp of the Bełżec death camp. He was to brief Allied leaders on what he had seen. In 1943 he met in the US with Justice Felix Frankfurter. Upon hearing his report, Frankfurter for a long moment was silent.

> "Mr. Karski," Frankfurter said after a further pause, "a man like me talking to a man like you must be totally frank. So I must say: I am unable to believe you." [Polish Ambassador Jan] Ciechanowski flew from his seat. "Felix, you don't mean it!" he cried. "How can you call him a liar to his face! The authority of my government is behind him. You know who he is!" Frankfurter replied, in a soft voice filled with resignation, "Mr. Ambassador, I did not say this young man is lying. I said I am unable to believe him. There is a difference."[8]

We, who have grown up in a world of which Auschwitz and Treblinka are a part, know that they have existed, and therefore can exist again.[9] We might envy Justice Frankfurter his capacity of disbelieving the possibility of such a world, but we no longer have the option of echoing his choice. It might well have been the case that Iwaszkiewicz, a sensitive and compassionate writer, and Hulewicz-Feillowa, also tried to avail themselves of it. Libiszowska-Dobrska, confronted with the brutal murder of people she had known and liked, as her memoirs make clear, did not have that possibility. And yet the case could be made that the denial of an unacceptable reality is an attempt to preserve for oneself the vision of a saner and more moral world, and as such is an act of legitimate self-defense, if not of outright resistance.

A feeling very often expressed by those diarists who had noticed the Shoah was that of helplessness. "I shivered when I saw such scenes," writes an eyewitness of the destruction of the Vilna ghetto. "Unfortunately, only seldom was one able to help those people. For help to Jews was punished by death."[10] In an important pamphlet published underground: "Na oczach świata" ("In Front of the Eyes of the World") in reaction to the Warsaw Ghetto uprising, the writer Maria Kann states: "In front of the eyes of the world, in front of our eyes a nation was being murdered. We looked at it powerlessly. Regardless of all the outrage, we are getting used to the thought that it is possible to murder, it is possible to build crematoria for living people." While Kann, rejecting the Frankfurter option, is fully aware of the huge danger of moral complacency that such an attitude entails (she will become an activist of "Żegota," the underground Council to Save the Jews, which will dispense aid and assistance to Jews in hiding, on a scale unrivaled in occupied Europe), the already quoted Przybora takes a different position. "Among the voices raised world-wide, condemning Poles for their indifference towards the dying Jews there are no righteous who would take the danger to us into account…Let us pay homage to the heroes, let us be disgusted by the "szmalcownicy,"[11] but may no-one demand of a nation of twenty-some million to be composed of twenty-some heroes. This reasoning is probably convincing. Probably…"[12]

Kann and Przybora had drawn radically opposed conclusions from the powerlessness they had both described. For Kann, since the moral consequences of powerlessness are utterly unacceptable, therefore powerlessness is unacceptable as well. She set about doing something, became one of the heroes Przybora mentions[13]–and in the process, of course, gained full knowledge of the immensity of the crime which was being committed, a knowledge any human being could be excused for not wanting to have. Przybora, to the contrary, seems to have decided that since doing anything is impossible, then the indifference (which he does not challenge as a characteristic) which follows is morally acceptable. Yet he is much too honest a human being to fully believe that: the scene of the encounter with the Jewish child immediately follows.

The absence of references to the Shoah can then possibly be explained by a withdrawal of cognitive investment into a reality which was too horrible to contemplate, and too overwhelming to modify. And yet powerlessness, if not challenged, leads thus to indifference, and indifference in turn leads to a cognitive rearrangement of the world. This is hardly a rare or wartime-only phenomenon. Most of us, describing our everyday activities, would not include, or indeed notice, brief encounters with others who could use our help, but whom we consider beyond our sphere of responsibility: the homeless, the poor, the infirm – the list is long. It is true, we do so because we legitimately believe that someone else will help them as part of his or her professional obligations; the Jews of occupied Poland could obviously not count on such help. On the other hand, however, all that would be involved, in our case, would be an almost painless expenditure of time or money; Maria Kann, as the Vilna diarist noted, risked death. The ease with which we exclude others from the universe of shared moral obligations should serve as a reminder to those who would all too easily condemn Przybora for his depressing frankness. And yet even though he wrote years after the events of the war, he seemed not fully aware of the not only moral, but also cognitive consequences of the exclusion he had accepted. Consequences that Feliks Tych's fine research brings out in excruciating detail.

Yet personal experience was not the only way Poles learned about the fate of the Jews under German occupation. They had at their disposal a very variegated underground press (and were exposed to an ongoing barrage of Nazi propaganda, which we will not have the space to analyze here). We will investigate, however, the impact underground media might have had on what people knew of what was happening–and on what they thought about what they knew.

The underground press was a major element of the Polish resistance movement. Though its production and distribution was punished with concentration camp or death, almost two thousand different titles were published throughout the occupation, nearly twice as much as in occupied France or the Netherlands. Their print runs would vary from several dozen to thousands, and each copy, passed from hand to hand, would reach, according to historians, at least ten persons on the average. The Polish historian Paweł Szapiro, also of the Jewish Historical Institute, is conducting an extensive study of what the Polish underground press wrote about the Jews. He has published one volume so far, collecting all known reactions to the Warsaw Ghetto uprising. The anthology, culled from 153 publications of all political orientations, contains 455 texts, from very brief news items to long features.[14] They date from February 1943, when the first rumors about the planned total liquidation of the ghetto started to circulate, to November 1944, when in a final copy the material damage to Warsaw, wrought by the crushing of the uprising, was being assessed. And though the Warsaw Ghetto uprising was a truly extraordinary event – the first act of armed resistance in German-occupied Europe, and simultaneously what then seemed to be the final act of the history of Polish Jews – one can assume that the coverage it got in the Polish underground media can help shed a light on the way the fate of the Jews in general was being portrayed therein, which in turn will help us understand what the readers of that press knew at the time.

The overwhelming majority of the texts in Szapiro's anthology are informative, and rely on outside sources: Polish eyewitnesses observing the fighting in the ghetto from the "Aryan" side, and later – Allied comments on the events, as broadcast by the BBC and "Świt" – a Polish government-in-exile station broadcasting from London, but very successfully masquerading as an underground radio based in Poland. Thus, the stories focus mainly on the observable – Jews are fighting – and on reactions to that event on the Warsaw street, and eventually in the free world. Very little, for understandable reasons, is being written about the development of actual events in the ghetto, both during the course of the uprising and in the months preceding it. Only a few of the newspaper articles refer to eyewitness testimony, usually from Jews who had managed to flee the ghetto. The general impression of the course of the fighting tends to attribute more military power to the insurgents than they actually had, and also does not sufficiently describe the concentration-camp-like conditions which prevailed in the ghetto.

Yet the basic facts are very well known to the authors of the articles, and therefore to their readers. In a fundamental text published in "Biuletyn Informacyjny," the principal publication of the underground Home Army (the military organization affiliated with the government in exile), and then reprinted in at least four other publications, the anonymous author states: "After the Germans had concluded their preparations, consisting of locking up Polish Jews in ghettos, and transporting there numerous transports of Jews from Western Europe – the first act of the tragedy began. Under the orders of the death-head-marked SS-men, all kinds of German execution-ers would empty house after house, neighborhood after neighborhood, city after city, driving the hapless victims along cadaver-strewn roads, or transfer-ring them under barbaric conditions to the sites of collective execution in Treblinka, Bełżec and Sobibór. There German science had in an exemplary way resolved the issue, so attractive for it, of how to collectively annihilate, possibly without a trace, hundreds of thousands of people. Smaller Jewish centers were liquidated on the spot. Only those Jews, whose work was use-ful to the German war machine, were left behind."[15] The author quotes no sources for his description, assuming therefore it is common knowledge. As he was writing for the principal organ of the Polish underground, it is safe to surmise that this is what informed Polish opinion knew in April 1943 about the development of the Shoah.

And the description is rather accurate. It centers on the scale and planned, systematic character of "collective annihilation" (the term "genocide," though advanced by a Polish Jewish lawyer, Rafał Lemkin, already before WWII, in reference to the massacre of the Armenians in Ottoman Turkey, was not in use until after the war), identifies its two main methods: technological murder in death camps and assassination on the spot, and names three of the six death camps. It seriously underestimates, however, the number of victims (by spring 1943 some 4 million Jews had already been murdered, not "hun-dreds of thousands), but the immensity of the destruction was not obvious to any outside observers at the time. On the other hand, however, Jewish leaders whom Jan Karski had met in the Warsaw Ghetto had a better grasp of events: they told him that what was happening was "the total annihilation of the Jewish people."

Another significant omission in the "Biuletyn Informacyjny" summary of events is that it lists only three of the six death camps in operation. While one of the remaining three – Stuthoff – was the smallest one and operated on Polish territory annexed to the Reich and might have thus escaped detection, the other two – Auschwitz and Majdanek – were well-known throughout the country, as they also served as concentration camps for non-Jewish inmates. Therefore, their omission from the "Biuletyn Informacyjny" list is difficult to explain – unless their use as concentration camps for Poles prevented them from being seen as simultaneously death camps for Jews.

This interpretation may seem far-fetched, but there is some evidence to support it. Krzysztof Radziwiłł, Polish nobleman, essayist and diplomat, was an inmate at Majdanek when, on November 3, 1943, the Germans had shot 17 thousand Jewish inmates. "On the second day after this hecatomb, camp life recovered its normal appearance again, and that was when, I remember, for the first time in my life did I slap one of my Polish companions of misfortune in the face. He had offered me to join him in a drinking party to celebrate the fact that there will be so many Jews less in the future Poland"[16]. The prince's anonymous "companion of misfortune" was doubtless extremely unrepresentative (though not entirely isolated; see below) in his expression of joy; yet his fundamental belief that the victim of the massacre were "them," Jews, and not "us," Polish citizens, was widespread. A witness of the mass executions of Jews in the Ponary fort near Vilnius noted in her memoirs, written after the war: "Throughout all the post-war years I carried the thought, like a pang of conscience, of how to repay the debt towards the [ethnic] Poles who were [also] murdered at Ponary...They found themselves in the pits with a human mass which was ethnically alien to us."[17] If even sharing the death pits with murdered Jews was something that, for a Polish survivor, was unbearable, it is understandable that Jewish fate was seen as fundamentally different from Polish fate.

This is evident from the press articles. Even though only a very small minority express an outright anti-Semitic hostility akin to that revealed by Radziwiłł's "companion of misfortune" (17 out of 455),[18] many contain qualifiers clearly expressing Polish non-identification with the Jewish fate, and critical surprise at Jewish behavior. "The hitherto passive death of the Jewish masses," opines the author of the quoted "Biuletyn Informacyjny" article– "created no new values–was useless; death arms in hand might bring new values into the life of the Jewish nation, endowing the suffering of Jews in Poland with the radiance of a fight for the right to live...The fighting citizens of the Polish State from beyond the ghetto walls had become closer, more comprehensible to the community of the capital, than the passive victims, who had allowed themselves to be dragged to their deaths without resistance." There is no doubt that the author views the ghetto fighters with sympathy, as he qualifies them as "citizens of the Polish State." Yet they are not seen as a part of "the community of the capital," and their previous way of dying is seen as incomprehensible and worthless. It is a stunning paradox that, exactly at the time the Warsaw Ghetto uprising broke out, German authorities had publicized the discovery of the mass graves at Katyń[19]–where 23,000 interned Polish officers had been executed in batches by their Soviet captors. Yet though these were young and healthy military men, unencumbered by the presence of weak and powerless dependents, and not emaciated by years spent in concentration-camp-like ghetto conditions, nobody thought of criticizing them for having allowed themselves to be "dragged to their deaths without resistance."

The qualified recognition of Jews as Poles is a constant factor even in publications sympathetic to the plight of Poland's Jews. "The invader's barbaric oppression of the Jews, Polish citizens after all, directly impacts Polish raison d'état," remarked a commentator in another Home Army publication.[20] "Whatever the feelings one might have towards Jews, one has to bow one's head in front of their tragedy," concluded writing for an independent liberal democratic paper.[21] "Polish society did not recently feel any particular sympathy towards the jews (*sic*)....The cause of these antagonisms was not on the Polish side, but had its source within jewry (*sic*) itself...Regardless of all this we recognized the jews (*sic*) as human and were never able to resolve the jewish question through crime and cruelty" – another Home Army publication.[22] In a nutshell: if Jews were Polish citizens only "after all," if one had to silence one's feelings towards them in the face of their tragedy, if one felt pride that one recognized them as human – then it is hardly surprising that one did not consider them as part of one's own community. Their fate was not ours, even if we may empathize or assist. Small wonder that most diarists fail to register that fate at all. It is not that they did not know. It is that they did not consider it relevant to their own fate.

Two qualifiers, however, need to be interjected here. First, it is not at all obvious that this exclusion from the universe of shared moral obligations did in fact mean indifference – far from it. Just as the overwhelming majority of such comments on the Shoah, as were found in the diaries express compassion and outrage, the same is true of the opinions expressed in the underground press. The majority of Poles were simply too busy surviving themselves to extend enough attention to the fate of these "ethnic aliens," who were "antagonistic to the Polish side" and "incomprehensively passive" towards their own dying. Furthermore, many thought that what is happening to the Jews today might happen to the Poles tomorrow. "We stood in the same line to the Nazi annihilation, though the Jews were ahead of us," wrote the already quoted Przybora.[23] Similar sentiments were also expressed in the underground press.

The relative rarity of unconditionally anti-Semitic views expressed in the material under consideration is of course a positive phenomenon. We do know that the increasingly virulent anti-Semitism of pre-WWII Poland did not disappear under the occupation, in view of a common enemy and the immensity of Jewish suffering. On September 25, 1941, the commander in chief of the Home Army, general Stefan "Grot" Rowecki, wrote in a periodic report to the government in exile in London: "I report that all [favorable] declarations and moves by the Government and the National Council [Poland's parliament in exile] concerning Jews in Poland create inside the Country the worst impression possible and eminently facilitate propaganda unfavorable or hostile to the Government...Please accept as a completely real fact that the overwhelming majority of the country is antisemiticaly inclined. Even socialists are no exception...[and they] accept the postulate of emigration as the solution of the Jewish problem."[24] Rowecki attributes this attitude to the alleged betrayal of Poland committed by Jews under Soviet occupation.

Given this prevalence of anti-Semitism, it is to be appreciated that only a minority of the elites (as expressed in the underground media) shared it. On the other hand, however, one also needs to bear in mind that an underground paper is heavily dependent on the trust it enjoys amongst its readers – who, after all, take risks just by reading it.[25] Therefore it stands to reason that the paper would not disseminate views that its readers would reject. This holds true both of publications expressing sympathy to Jews and those expressing their hostility towards them. From a contemporary perspective, however, only the latter attitude demands investigation. Yet, if in reaction to the Warsaw Ghetto uprising, the newspapers of the rather influential right-wing organization "Miecz i Pług" (MiP, "The Sword and the Plough") wrote that "these issues [i.e. the fate of the uprising] are completely indifferent to us,"[26] and "[w]e know what immense losses did the Polish Nation incur because of precisely these jews (sic), and this is why the fate which befalls them, terrible from a purely human viewpoint, seems nonetheless just,"[27] these statements need to be treated at face value. For a part of Polish public opinion, the crushing of the Warsaw Ghetto uprising was the defeat of one enemy by another and the fate the defeated faced was fair.

Another underground publication, connected with the National Party (SN), concurs: "Simply, the jews (*sic*) finally understood that the Germans have condemned all of them, without exception, to annihilation. And having to choose between death by firing squad or by gas, or fighting arms in hand, in which it might be even possible to save themselves, they chose the latter, sure thing. There is no heroism, or even risk involved. And this has nothing whatsoever to do with the Polish cause."[28] And the Jewish peril to Poland has not disappeared with the extermination of most of the country's Jewish population: "We stress to the utmost our condemnation of the beastliness of the Hitlerite goons, but we will not renounce our economic and political struggle against jewry (*sic*), by becoming sentimental over the crocodile tears of jewish financers and politicians, who are preparing to impose their power over us. If we are to shoot at jews (*sic*) – it will probably be on the barricades, in the fire of a red revolution imposed on us"[29] warns another SN publication. The organ of the extreme right military underground NOW agrees: "Let us remember, that several hundred thousand jews (*sic*) (and this is as many as have been preserved, in the country and abroad) is enough, were they capable again to dominate our economic life and penetrate the centers of political-cultural life, to maybe even more influence the fate of Poland, than the hitherto million-strong jewish masses."[30] In all those, and other similar articles, the alleged treason of the Jews was invoked as justification of the views expressed.

Hence the logical conclusion, supporting general Rowecki's quoted report: "Today, a tear in the eye over the burned ghetto notwithstanding, the programs of all Polish movements agree on the elimination of jewish influence. Victory has been achieved,"[31] triumphs, certainly somewhat exaggeratedly, the SN. Most Poles, even if not directly concerned with the fate of the Jews, would have in all probability disagreed. And yet the support base of SM, MiP and NOW did exist. Józef Górski, a landed gentleman from near Kosów Lacki and certainly a patriot, was torn in his reaction to the Shoah. "As a Christian I could only feel compassion towards my [Jewish] brethren…" he notes, "but as a Pole I looked at these events differently. Following the ideology of [Roman] Dmowski [the leader of Poland's pre-WWII right] I considered the Jews an internal occupier…so I could only feel satisfaction that we are getting rid of that occupier, and not through our own handiwork, but through that of the other, external occupier...I could not conceal my satisfaction when I crossed our towns which have been rid of the Jews, and when I saw that the revolting, sloppy Jewish hovels with the inseparable goat have stopped spoiling our landscape."[32]

Yet even he notices there is an inconvenience to this otherwise welcome development: the demoralization of a segment of the population: "Some peasants hid Jews in their homes, and took ample compensation for it; then, when the constant danger, to which they were exposed, started to weigh on them too much, they cut the Jews' heads with axes."[33] This aspect of the Shoah—the participation of numbers of individual Poles in the murder of Jews—was not realized by Polish public opinion until the great historical debates of the early 21st century, brought about by the books of Jan T. Gross[34]. Yet at the time they occurred, these actions were already to an extent described, discussed and condemned in the underground press. The Catholic writer (and pre-war anti-Semite), Zofia Kossak-Szczucka, who was under the occupation the single most influential individual in setting up, at great personal risk, the Council to Help the Jews "Żegota," had in May 1942 published in the organ of the Catholic "Front Odnowy Polski (FOP; "Front for the Renewal of Poland") a damning report on the collaboration and demoralization of some Poles: "The question of the demoralization, savagery that the Jewish massacres generate in us is becoming a burning one. For not only the Shaulis [Lithuanian collaborationist police], Volksdeutsche or Ukrainians who are used for monstrous executions. In many localities (Kolno, Stawiski, Jagodne, Szumów, Dęblin) the local population volunteered to participate in massacres. All available means are to be used against such outrage. It is necessary to make people realize they are becoming Herod's goons, to brand them in the secret press, to call for executioners to be boycotted, and to announce against the murderers severe verdicts of the courts of the free Republic."[35] The "Jagodno" she mentions is almost certainly Jedwabne, the site of a major massacre of Jews conducted by Polish neighbors, described in Jan T. Gross's ground-breaking book. It lies next to Kolno and Stawiski, which were also sites of such massacres, while no information has been found, however, on similar events in the remaining two localities mentioned.

In retrospect, then, the absence of references to the Shoah in the majority of the diaries studied by Tych is less stunning that it would seem. Poles, as evidenced by coverage in the underground press, were reasonably well informed about the fate which had befallen their Jewish neighbors. Most withdrew their cognitive investment in that fate in part out of powerlessness, and in–clearly lesser–part out of hostility to its victims. That withdrawal led at times to agonizing moral dilemmas, but more often to the acceptance of the belief that the fate of the Jews was not something the Poles could influence, and therefore not something they should have been involved in. This in turn led to an attitude which could be characterized as indifference, even if we know that this was often not the case.

Yet for Jews who encountered that attitude – and this involved the quasi-totality of those, who were able to survive "on the Aryan side" and therefore were in daily contact with Poles – it left an indelible mark on their perception of their Gentile neighbors. "They know but they don't care" was a feeling often expressed by survivors, both during the Shoah and after. And since it was much safer for those Poles who were genuinely indifferent to the Jews' fate, or actually approved of it, to express their attitude in public – expressions of sympathy to the Jews were penalized by the German authorities – many survivors drew the conclusion that the indifference they felt masked hostility rather than powerlessness. And so a minority opinion became attributed to the majority of Poles who often, even now, react to it with the outrage of someone who is being unfairly accused but at the same time is aware that he does have something to answer for.

Notes

B.N. Dz. Rękopisów stands for National Library, Warsaw, Manuscripts Department

1   Jeremi Przybora: Przymknięte oko Opatrzności, Memuarów część II [The Closed Eye of Providence, Memoirs Part II], Warszawa 1998, p. 47. *Cit. in* Feliks Tych: Długi cień Zagłady, Warszawa 1999, p. 31.
2   Antoni Sułek: Zwykli Polacy patrzą na Żydów [Ordinary Poles look at Jews], in Gazeta Wyborcza, Jan 15, 2010.
3   It is generally believed that 3 million non-Jewish Polish citizens (mainly Poles, but also Ukrainians and Byelorussians) died in WWII, although contemporary historical estimates tend to lower this estimate somewhat.
4   *Op. cit.*
5   Jarosław Iwaszkiewicz: Notatki 1939 – 1945 [Notes 1939 – 1945]; Andrzej Zawada (Ed.), Warszawa 1991, p. 48. *Cit. in* Tych, *op. cit.*
6   Agnieszka Hulewicz-Feillowa: Rodem z Kościanek [Born in Kościanki], Kraków 1988, p. 203. *Cit. in* Tych, *op. cit.*
7   Krystyna Libiszowska-Dobrska: Trochę wspomnień z lat okupacji [Some Reminiscences from the Years of Occupation; unpublished manuscript], B.N., Dz. Rękopisów, akc. 11666, rozdz. III, k.11-12. *Cit. in* Tych, *op. cit.*

8 E. Thomas Wood and Stanislaw M. Jankowski: Karski: How One Man Tried to Stop the Holocaust, New York (John Wiley & Sons, Inc., 1994; paperback February 1996).

9 As David Rieff had said in his book "Slaughterhouse," on the Bosnian war: "After Sarajevo, after Srebrenica, we know what "Never again!" means. ``Never again" simply means ``Never again" will Germans kill Jews in Europe in the 1940's. That is all it means."

10 Leszek Jastrzębiec: Tułacze życie; Pamiętnik [A Wanderer's Life; Memoirs; unpublished] B.N. Dz. Rękopisów, akc. 9314, t. III, k. 145. *Cit. in* Tych, *op. cit.*

11 Colloquial term to designate blackmailers, who made a living out of threatening to denounce Jews.

12 Przybora, *op. cit.*, p. 47. *Cit. in* Tych, *op. cit.*

13 Poles constitute over one third of the Righteous Gentiles recognized by Yad Vashem, the single biggest national group.

14 Paweł Szapiro: Wojna żydowsko-niemiecka [The Jewish-German War], London 1992, Aneks Publishers.

15 "Ostatni akt wielkiej tragedii" [The last act of the great tragedy]", "Biuletyn Informacyjny", 17 (172), April 29, 1943. *Cit. in* Szapiro, *op. cit.* # 63.

16 Krzysztof Radziwiłł: Mój pamiętnik. Od feudalizmu do socjalizmu. [My Memoirs. From Feudalism to Socialism; unpublished manuscript], B.N., Dz. Rękopisów, akc. 9213, k. 297-298; *Cit. in* Tych, *op. cit.*

17 Helena Pasierbska: Wileńskie wspomnienia z lat wojny [Vilna Memoirs from Wartime; unpublished manuscript], B.N., Dz. Rękopisów, akc. 127715, k. 42. *Cit. in* Tych, *op. cit.*

18 It needs to be remembered, however, that the overwhelming majority of the articles culled were information, not opinion, so the relative proportion of the antisemitic texts is much larger.

19 The massacre was immediately attributed by the Germans to "Jew Bolshevik executioners", an explanation which found large credence among the Polish population, and adversely impacted its reaction to the Warsaw Ghetto uprising. In broader terms, the alleged collusion between Polish Jews and Soviet authorities during the 1939-41 Soviet occupation of Eastern Poland generated strong anti-Semitic reactions throughout the country. This is a topic, however, that cannot be addressed properly in such a brief essay.

20 "Agencja Prasowa" nr 17 (159), April 28, 1943, *Cit. in* Szapiro, *op. cit.*, #53

21 "Nowy Dzień" nr 551, April 28, 1943, *Cit. in* Szapiro, *op. cit.* # 54.

22 "Twierdza" nr 19 (122), May 8, 1943, *Cit. in* Szapiro, *op. cit.* # 130

23 Had Hitler won the war, this might have eventually become true. During the war, however, the difference between the fate of the Jews, who were to be hunted down to the last child hiding in the woods, and the Poles, who were "only" to be reduced to slave labor, remained stark, even without factoring in the fact that the Shoah had been almost completely successful, while most Poles remained brutally oppressed, but not enslaved. The fallacious argument of commonality of fate was, and continues to be used, for two very different reasons: to shame those among the Poles who would approve of Nazi policy towards the Jews, and to oppose granting Jews the moral high ground due to their unique suffering.

24 *Cit.* in Andrzej Żbikowski: Studia z dziejów Żydów w Polsce, Warszawa 1995, v. 2, p. 63

25 The author of this paper was the editor of an underground newspaper in Poland under military dictatorship in the 80s.

26 "Polska Żyje", April 24, 1943, *Cit. in* Szapiro, *op. cit.* # 37

27 "Nurt Młodych", nr 4, April 30, 1943, *Cit. in* Szapiro, *op. cit.* # 72

28 "Wielka Polska", nr 19, May 5, 1943, *Cit. in* Szapiro, *op. cit.* # 104

29 "Walka", nr 28, August 28, 1943, *Cit. in* Szapiro, *op. cit.* # 215

30 "Kierownik", nr 30, May 16, 1943, *Cit. in* Szapiro, *op. cit.* # 173

31 "Młoda Polska", nr 18 (32), October 13, 1943, *Cit. in* Szapiro, *op. cit.* # 339

32 Józef Górski: Na przełomie dziejów [At the Turning-point of History; unpublished manuscript], B.N., Dz. Rękopisów, III 9776, k. 33, 74. *Cit. in* Tych, *op. cit.*

33 *Ibidem*, k. 57,

34 Jan T. Gross: Neighbors: The Destruction of the Jewish Community in Jedwabne, Poland. Princeton, NJ: Princeton University Press, 2001; Fear: Anti-Semitism in Poland After Auschwitz. Random House, 2006; with Irena Grudzińska-Gross: Golden Harvest. New York: Oxford University Press, 2012.

35 "Prawda", nr 2, May 1942.

Sofia: Double-faced Bulgaria

"Can virtue, the other side of crime, be collectivized? Is it not individuals who are to be held responsible for whatever good or evil happens?"

Anthony Georgieff

When asked about the sources of their national pride, most educated Bulgarians do not have to think too long: "The salvation of the Bulgarian Jews from the Holocaust" is one of the top three answers. Bulgaria, they will assert, stands unique in Europe, with the exception of Denmark, in that it did not allow its Jewish citizens to be transported to extermination in the Nazi death camps. Christians, Jews, Muslims and Gypsies lived in peace and harmony, they will add, reinstating the Bulgarians' "proverbial" hospitality and tolerance. Your Bulgarian in the street will probably omit to mention the Bulgarian State Railways cattle cars that brought 11,343 Jews to Treblinka and Auschwitz from the then Bulgaria-administered territories of Aegean Thrace, Macedonia and southern Serbia. Any question likely to arise will not be about the fact of the rescue, but about who should be credited for it.

As leaders and political systems changed in Eastern Europe's post-Communist years, so did the answers to this question. Initially, the Communist school textbooks claimed that it had been the Communist Party and its leading functionaries who were to be lauded personally for the heroic deed. With the fall of Communism in 1989, perceptions and attitudes changed. The regal figure of Bulgaria's King Boris III, a war-time ally of Hitler, emerged. It was because of his cunning policies of delays and real as well as simulated reluctance to comply that the Germans were outmaneuvered and no single Jew was sent to certain death, the story went.

But it would soon transpire that things in Bulgaria's recent history were not so black-and-white. The name of Dimitar Peshev, the 1940s deputy speaker of parliament, came to the fore. Ignored and largely forgotten under Communism, Peshev now shone as a valiant citizen who not only stood against the government's intention to make Bulgaria Judenfrei, but was the organizer of a popular movement to prevent what had seemed like an accomplished deed.

These theories, of course, conflicted with each other, and Bulgaria's post-Communist leaders settled for the least controversial option. It was the Bulgarian people as a whole, they claimed, it was the Bulgarian nation as such that rose up and saved its Jews. It was a nation of selfless Raoul Wallenbergs and not a single Vidkun Quisling.

But can virtue, the other side of crime, be collectivized? Is it not individuals who are to be held responsible for whatever good or evil happens?

Any reflection on these questions will prompt other questions.

If the Kingdom of Bulgaria of The Axis is to be credited with saving about 48,000 Jews from the gas chambers, why were there so few Jews left in the People's Republic of Bulgaria when it was a member of the Warsaw Pact?

If Bulgaria did not "occupy" but just "administered" (the term being officially used by the Bulgarian establishment in 2013) what is now the former Yugoslav republic of Macedonia, northern Greece and parts of southern Serbia around Pirot, is Bulgaria to be held responsible for the 11,343 Jews the Bulgarian troops and police did deport – using Bulgarian State Railways and through Bulgarian territory – to Nazi concentration camps?

Is the one fact, the non-deportation in "Old Bulgaria," enough to make up for the other, the brutal rounding-up and the shipment of 11,343 people in the "New Lands" to death?

Would any admittance of the latter somehow tarnish, denigrate or belittle the former?

What matters more? The rescues or the deaths?

Of course, these questions are impossible to answer as they come down to a very basic thing that can have no answer: the price of human life. Are a dozen Jews from Plovdiv more expensive than a single Jew from Bitola? Or was it vice versa?

As in 2013 Bulgaria celebrates with great pomp and at a significant cost the 70th anniversary of the non-deportation of Bulgarian Jews during the Holocaust, the question of the responsibility for the 11,343 remains open. The massive Communist propaganda in 1944-1989 and the reluctance of Bulgaria's current politicians to address the issue in its complexity have led to a bizarre situation where many Bulgarians still tend to see the world in stock terms. It is either-or: you are either with us, or you are against us; you are either a victim, or a victimizer, and you can't be both at the same time – this kind of thinking goes.

Yet, the case of Bulgaria – as life itself – defies clear-cut categorizations. Bulgaria was partly a rescuer, but also a perpetrator; it was both an ally to and a bystander of Nazi Germany; it was part savior, part murderer.

In fact, the refusal of the Bulgarian establishment to admit any responsibility for what the Kingdom of Bulgaria did in Macedonia, Aegean Thrace and southern Serbia while focusing exclusively on the positive event of the rescue has little to do with Jews, Jewish affairs, the Second World War or the Holocaust. Its explanation must be sought in current political sentiments, psychological attitudes, patriotism as well as real or contrived definitions of "national pride." To understand in its entirety the complexity of this slightly schizophrenic situation one needs to consider the historical circumstances long before and long after the Second World War years. These must be seen in context because the non-deportation of the Jews in Bulgaria and the rounding-up of Jews from Macedonia, Greece and southern Serbia (in modern Bulgaria referred to as The Western Outlands) are but details in the larger picture of life in the Balkans.

To begin with, there is the history. What is now Aegean Thrace (Greece), the area around Pirot in southern Serbia and first and foremost the former Yugoslav republic of Macedonia is a Bulgarian legitimate heartland, the Bulgarians believe. Those were stripped away from Bulgaria owing to vicious neighbors, hypocritical Great Powers and an unlucky turn of events. These territories were at the core of the "Bulgarian Question" in the period 1878-1944. Bulgaria entered various alliances and counter alliances, and fought three wars, to make them its own. To Bulgarians, Macedonia is what the modern German province of Schleswig-Holstein is to Danes – ethnically, historically and culturally one's own ilk. But unlike the Danish and German governments, both the Bulgarian and the Macedonian governments feel very uneasy about it.

Then there is the interpretation of history. In the worst Balkan tradition, modern Bulgaria, as well as other Balkan countries, continue to use history in order to "prove" preconceived beliefs and notions, rather than to dispel myths and establish historical truth. This is why in the preceding paragraphs the emphasis is put on politicians speaking out about history rather than balanced historians doing this themselves.

The picture becomes even more obfuscated with the timing of events and occurrences, the justification and explanation of political, social and military actions and first and foremost with the singular Bulgarian way of defining human concepts such as honor, suffering and mercy.

Owing to the self-imposed isolation under Communism, these events, occurrences and dates are not very well-known internationally.

Bulgaria is an ancient land, first founded in 681 AD, but the modern state dates back to just 1877-1878, when Bulgaria gained independence as a result of a Russo-Ottoman imperial war.

On March 3, 1878 the Treaty of San Stefano was signed. In effect it was an armistice between Russia and the Ottoman Empire. It granted Bulgaria large territories populated mainly by ethnic Bulgarians, including Aegean Thrace, what is now the former Yugoslav republic of Macedonia, and parts of southern Serbia. The Treaty of San Stefano is perceived as the apex of the Bulgarian struggle for national independence. March 3 is celebrated as the Republic of Bulgaria's national day.

On July 13, 1878, the Treaty of Berlin, masterminded by the Great Powers, allocated much smaller territories to the new country. In fact, it split Bulgaria in two, the independent Principality of Bulgaria (now northern Bulgaria and the Sofia region), and the Ottoman province of Eastern Rumelia (now Bulgaria south of the Balkan range). Macedonia, Aegean Thrace, and southern Serbia were not included. The Treaty of Berlin is still seen by the Bulgarians as a dismemberment of their new country, a "diktat" by the Great Powers fearing a powerful, Russia-friendly Slavonic state in the Balkans.

Significantly, at the insistence of the Great Powers, the Treaty of Berlin included clauses to protect minority, including Jewish rights.

Balkan Jews went to bed in the Ottoman Empire but woke up in completely new and increasingly nationalist countries that were sometimes fiercely opposed to one another over territories, religion and minorities. However, the overwhelming majority of Jews adapted quickly to their new homelands and become loyal citizens. In 1880, a chief rabbi was elected to represent the Jewish community to Bulgarian authorities.

The Principality of Bulgaria and Eastern Rumelia united in 1885, and in 1908 Prince Ferdinand of Bulgaria unilaterally declared full independence from the Ottoman Empire, becoming king. At that time antisemitism was already present, mainly in the form of propaganda as exemplified by a number of openly antisemitic newspapers. But there was no anti-Jewish violence and Bulgaria never experienced anything nearing the Russian or Romanian pogroms.

On September 9, 1909 King Ferdinand attended the dedication of the Sofia Central Synagogue.

In 1912-1913 Bulgaria fought in the Balkan Wars. In the First Balkan War Bulgaria, Greece, Serbia and Montenegro were opposed to the Ottomans. Bulgaria made significant territorial conquests, but failed to gain Macedonia. In the second, Greece, Serbia, Romania and the Ottoman Empire fought against Bulgaria. As a result, Bulgaria lost most of the land it had conquered, including southern Dobrudzha, but did keep parts of Aegean Thrace. This was Bulgaria's "First National Catastrophe."

In 1915-1918, Bulgaria entered the First World War on the side of Germany, mainly in the hope of "regaining" Macedonia. The First World War was a complete disaster for Bulgaria and ended in the "Second National Catastrophe." King Ferdinand abdicated and left the country.

In total, 7,000-8,000 Jewish men were conscripted in the Bulgarian Army in the war with Serbia of 1885, the Balkan wars and the First World War. Of those 952 died.

At the end of the Great War in 1919, the Treaty of Neuilly-sur-Seine humiliated Bulgaria. Dobrudzha, Aegean Thrace and the Western Outlands were lost; demilitarization was ordered; and Bulgaria got to pay heavy reparations. The treaty guaranteed the rights of national minorities, Jews included.

Modeled on the famous Fridtjof Nansen plan, in 1922 ethnic Turks were relocated from Greece and Bulgaria to the Republic of Turkey; ethnic Greeks moved from Turkey and Bulgaria into Greece; and ethnic Bulgarians moved from Greece and Turkey into Bulgaria. Poverty was rampant, thousands died in transit. In Bulgaria, the government divided Jewish representation between a religious entity, represented by the chief rabbi, and a secular one, the Central Consistory and its branches in cities with Jewish communities.

In 1924, an increasing number of Jews started emigrating to British Palestine, establishing the Bet Hanan colony and a Bulgarian kibbutz in Haifa. Until 1948, about 7,000 Bulgarian Jews emigrated to Palestine.

In 1934, an outspokenly nationalist government was installed in Sofia. The first serious repercussions against Jews started. Schooling in Ladino in Jewish school was toned down, and anti-Jewish discrimination at the workplace began.

Bulgaria was becoming increasingly dependent economically on Germany. Many Bulgarians were enthusiastic about Hitler's rise to power. The government prepared for an alliance with Nazi Germany, mainly because of its hopes to regain Macedonia, Aegean Thrace, Dobrudzha and the Western Outlands.

In the following year, King Boris III assumed authoritarian powers. The country was still a parliamentary democracy with competing political parties and elections, but the king had the final say in many affairs. This political setup remained in effect until Boris's death in 1943.

From 1937 to 1944, the international Zionist movement organized the escape of 18,000 central and east European Jews to British Palestine. Many Jewish refugees left via Black Sea ports in Bulgaria and Romania.

On 9 September 1940, Jews gathered inside the Central Sofia Synagogue applauded what at the time seemed the best news of the year. Two days previously, Romania, under the Hitler-imposed Treaty of Craiova, had returned southern Dobrudzha to the Kingdom of Bulgaria.

But just a month later the Bulgarian Jews started to get cold feet. The National Assembly in Sofia began debating the draft of the Protection of the Nation Act.

At that time, Bulgaria wasn't even a part of The Axis. It was still undecided which side to back in the Second World War. The memories of the territories and populations it had lost were still fresh and painful. King Boris III, applying his notorious ability to procrastinate, was trying to play for time.

However, the countries already involved in the war needed Bulgaria as it straddled the roads to Greece and Turkey and could provide a strategic passage through the Balkans to anyone who persuaded it to join on their side.

Popular sentiment inside Bulgaria was at best contentious. Some segments of the opposition insisted on neutrality, while others backed an alliance with Britain.

The links with Germany proved too strong. During the interwar period, Bulgaria's economy had entangled itself in an intricate relationship with Germany. Revanchist feelings were high in both Bulgaria and Germany. King Boris feared any deviation from Germany would bring on Bolshevism – even though at that time Nazi Germany and the USSR were allies. The government was also pro-German. Bogdan Filov, an archaeologist who had been appointed prime minister in February 1940, was German-educated and subscribed to a number of German academic societies.

Germany succeeded in convincing Bulgaria that if it joined The Axis, it would be rewarded with most of the territories lost in 1913-1919, which now belonged to Romania, Yugoslavia and Greece.

The return of southern Dobrudzha in 1940 finally did the trick. To put it figuratively, it was the carrot that persuaded Bulgaria's politicians to back the Reich.

On 1 March 1941 Bulgaria joined The Axis. The Germans were quick to respond. With German blessing, Bulgarian troops marched unopposed into Yugoslavia and northern Greece on April 19 and 20, 1941. Bulgaria was granted the right to administer the territories it considered its own. The changing of the borders was celebrated as a national triumph, and King Boris III was lauded as "the unifying king."

Bulgarian Jews living in Palestine had declared their loyalty to Bulgaria by promising to return and enroll in the Bulgarian Army if they were summoned.

However, Bulgaria's politicians would soon discover that the carrot had a stick attached to it, and that friendship with Nazi Germany would bear a heavy price. The national economy became almost totally dependent on that of Germany and, significantly, Bulgaria would also have to tackle the "Jewish Question."

The Protection of the Nation Act was one of a number of steps in this direction. Adopted on December 24, 1940, in spite of protests by intellectuals, and enforced on January 24, 1941, it took away almost all civil rights from the 48,000 Jews living in Bulgaria proper.

Closely modeled on the infamous Nuremberg laws, it barred Jews from being able to vote, stand for office and join the armed forces. Jews were forced to list their real estate and sell to the state, at "special" prices, any agricultural land they owned. Jewish property was levied with a special, one-off tax amounting to up to 25 percent of its value. Jews were banned from owning private companies in some sectors, for example publishing and the media, while Jews with "free" professions were given local quotas.

Things took a turn for the worse for the Jews in 1942.

On June 10, 1942, a new Citizenship Act was passed. It applied to all Bulgarian lands, including the occupied territories. Significantly, Jews there were deprived of the opportunity to become Bulgarian nationals, which paved the way for their subsequent deportation as "stateless."

On August 29, Aleksandar Belev, the chief of the newly-formed Commissariat for Jewish Affairs under the Interior Ministry, was given a mandate to enforce the new restrictions against the Jews. These included, but were not limited to, Jews having to wear yellow Star of David badges; Jewish homes being signposted; and Jewish products being marked as such. To add insult to injury, Jews were banned from adding "-ov" or "-ev" (the standard Bulgarian family name-forming suffix) to their last names, and they were not allowed to take on any name except those on a list approved by the Commissariat for Jewish Affairs.

The August 19, 1942 decree ordered Jews to terminate, within three days, any kind of economic activity they conducted. Factories were told to fire Jewish workers first. The Jewish communities in the Old Lands were instructed to prepare for the deportation of all Jews within their jurisdiction. The property of any deported Jew would be nationalized. As they were not Bulgarian citizens, the Jews in the New Lands were ordered to cease all economic activity and liquidate their assets. Jewish men in Bulgaria-proper were rounded up, mobilized into "labor groups" and made to work on state projects at a pittance.

In May 1943 all the Jews in Sofia, approximately 23,000 people, were interned in the provinces. "Offenders" of the anti-Jewish legislation were sent to two labor camps, one in Pleven in northern Bulgaria and another near the village of Somovit, on the Danube. Forced Jewish labor was used mainly in road construction.

On February 22, 1943, Aleksandar Belev and SS Hauptschturmführer Theodor Dannecker, Adolf Eichmann's representative to Bulgaria, signed a confidential agreement for the deportation of 20,000 Jews from the New Lands. As there were only about 12,000 Jews there, the remaining 8,000 were to be collected from Old Bulgaria, with the communities in Kyustendil and Plovdiv targeted first. Bulgaria was preparing itself for the Final Solution.

In the meantime, the country had become one of the gateways through which Jews fleeing persecution in Europe departed for Palestine. From 1939 onwards, using Turkey's neutrality, ships with Bulgarian crew or using Bulgarian ports sent to Palestine thousands of Jews from Europe. This, however, was a dangerous affair – there were sudden storms; the danger of Soviet or German submarines; and the British ban on vessels entering Haifa without a permit. On December 12, 1941, The Salvador sank with 352 Bulgarian Jews, Jews from other countries who had been living in Bulgaria and Jews bearing non-Bulgarian passports. On 24 February 1942, with 760 Jews and all-Bulgarian crew, The Struma was torpedoed by a Soviet submarine and capsized in the Black Sea. All aboard perished.

There is no precise data, but it is believed that in 1942-1943 about 2,000 Jewish children made it to Palestine from Bulgaria. Many of them were given shelter in Bulgaria.

On March 26, 1943, shortly after the first thwarted attempt to deport the Bulgarian Jews, Berlin ordered its Sofia Embassy to immediately halt Jewish emigration from Bulgaria. The army and the heads of the Interior Ministry obeyed and demanded that each transit visa be coordinated with them. Some Foreign Ministry officials looked the other way. They continued to issue visas for Jews and at least 400 Jews from Romania, Italy, France and elsewhere left Europe in this way.

March 1943 was a terrifying month for the Jewish communities in Aegean Thrace, Macedonia and southern Serbia. Bulgarian troops and police rounded up and shipped 11,343 Jews from the New Lands to death in Treblinka and Auschwitz. The majority of those were shipped in Bulgarian State Railways cattle cars from Greece, Macedonia and Serbia to the Bulgarian port of Lom on the Danube. From there they were loaded onto barges upriver and alighted in Vienna. Northbound German trains were waiting for them there.

The Bulgarians made no pretense that they had no intention of formally incorporating the New Lands into Bulgaria-proper once the war was over. They installed a fully-functioning Bulgarian administration there, with Bulgarian police, civil service and schools. Bulgarian became the official language. The Bulgarian soldiers and police in the occupied territories were no angels, and at times resorted to unnecessary cruelty in dealing with Greeks, Albanians, Macedonians and Jews.

Against the background of this dramatic story, how could Bulgaria spare 48,000 Jews in Bulgaria-proper from the Nazi gas chambers? What were the main driving forces behind this indisputable act of courage and valour, in the case of Bulgaria, and of terror and viciousness in the case of the territories it occupied?

First, the historical facts. A few days prior to March 9, 1943, Lilyana Panitsa, the personal assistant to Aleksandar Belev, told some friends in the Central Consistory about the planned deportations. The news spread quickly and reached four MPs for Kyustendil, one of the towns whose Jews had been on the departure lists. The four consulted with Dimitar Peshev, the deputy speaker of parliament and a member of the ruling majority. Peshev was himself from Kyustendil. Collectively, they put pressure on Petar Gabrovski, the Interior Minister, to postpone the deportations.

But in those days official orders did not travel as fast as they do today. Some provincial authorities remained unaware of the change of plans. In Plovdiv, on the night of March 10, 1943, Jews were rounded up in the Jewish school. Enraged, Kiril, the Orthodox bishop of Plovdiv, marched into the school and threatened the police that if they went ahead with the deportation he would open up his churches for Jewish refugees and would hide Jews in his own home.

On March 19, Dimitar Peshev presented Prime Minster Bogdan Filov with a petition against the deportations signed by 43 MPs. On the following day two MPs withdrew their signatures.

On March 22, the Holy Synod objected to the deportations and requested a more humane implementation of the Protection of the Nation Act.

On March 26, Peshev was fired from his position in parliament.

In a April 15, meeting with the Holy Synod King Boris declared Jews were a "danger to civilization."

On May 20, Interior Minister Gabrovski presented the king with two plans for action. Plan A envisaged the deportation of all Jews from Old Bulgaria to Poland, and Plan B was resettlement of Sofia Jews to the provinces. Fearing a political backlash at home, the king settles for Plan B.

May 24, a major Bulgarian holiday, saw a massive Jewish protest against the resettlement policies. In the following melee with the police, Bishop Stefan of Sofia sheltered Rabbi Daniel Zion in his house. King Boris was nowhere to be seen as he was on holiday in his mountain retreat.

The king died in August 1943, at a time when it became increasingly clear that Germany was losing the war. Anti-Jewish measures were no longer on the agenda. In the summer of 1944, as Bulgaria became desperate to switch sides in the face of the Soviet push westwards, antisemitic legislation was relaxed.

On September 5, 1944, the Soviet Union invaded Bulgaria, and on September 9 the leftist Fatherland Front stormed Sofia, toppled the government and installed its own regime. This was the beginning of Communism in Bulgaria.

Regardless of the many theories about who did what to save Bulgaria's Jews, the fact remains that only two powers intervened directly, with real actions: the Peshev-led MPs and the Orthodox Church. These theories differ depending on the political inclinations of whoever does the talking.

Under Communism, the mainstream theory was that the Communist Party and the clandestine Communist media played the decisive role. The Communist ideologues argued that their active support for the Jews prepared the general public for the protests against the Jews' disenfranchisement and planned deportation.

After the collapse of Communism in 1989, King Boris III and his wife, Queen Giovanna, were extolled as "saviors." The king, reportedly, had agreed to the Protection of the Nation Act to appease Germany, but then dawdled in order to save the Jews.

Yet another "savior" was Petar Danov, according to a more esoteric hypothesis. A mystic and the founder of a religious sect, Danov allegedly held sway over the superstitious king. When he learned of the planned deportations in 1943, Danov is said to have told the king that if a single Jew left, the royal dynasty would be rendered heirless. The king was scared, and stopped the deportations.

Another theory proposes a more practical reason for the non-deportation of the Jews. According to it, the king did intend to turn them in, but only the "undesirable" Bolshevik element. The other Jews would be kept in Bulgaria as "essential labor" to work on roads and infrastructure: 20,000-30,000 Bulgarian workers were already employed in Germany, leading to a shortage of manpower.

One refreshing point of view is offered by Tzvetan Todorov, the French philosopher of Bulgarian origin. According to him, Bulgaria was not very different from the other European countries that did not save their Jews. What did save the Jews in Bulgaria was a fragile chain of events that could have been broken at any time: one blunder by a politician here or there, one public figure that did not stand up at the right time, a different sentiment in the Orthodox church leadership, a less crafty king – and the whole "salvation" would have turned into a journey of death.

Tzvetanov's thinking, indicating that the Bulgarians were less than noble during the Second World War, can be corroborated by the number of Righteous Among the Nations as promulgated by the Yad Vashem Remembrance Authority. According to its current lists, Bulgaria has 20 righteous. In comparison, Serbia has 131, and Greece has 313. Italy, a main German ally, has 524. Even Albania has 69.

At the present time, most Bulgarian politicians and statesmen try to avoid the controversies by claiming that the Bulgarian Jews were saved as a result of the efforts of the "whole nation."

The usual explanation for the deaths of the 11,343 from Macedonia, Aegean Thrace and Pirot who were sent to Poland when the Bulgarian Jews were rescued comes down to a verbal sleight-of-hand: Aegean Thrace, Macedonia and southern Serbia were just "administered," not occupied.

When the Communists took over on September 9, 1944, they organized mass show trials of real and supposed war criminals. The death sentences handed down on government, parliamentary, military and civil service officials outnumbered those in Nuremberg. Aleksandar Belev tried to flee the country, but was caught and was either shot or committed suicide. Petar Gabrovski was sentenced to death and executed. Dimitar Peshev received 15 years in jail on charges of "fascism and antisemitism." Prominent Communist Jewish lawyers refused to defend him. Peshev was released after 13 months and died in poverty in Sofia in 1973. Twenty of the 43 MPs who signed the Peshev petition were sentenced to death. Lilyana Panitsa was also tried, but acquitted. She died at the age of 31, probably as a result of torture by the People's Militia.

Following the 1946 referendum that abolished the monarchy, King Simeon II and his family were exiled to Spain. Simeon Saxe-Coburg-Gotha returned to Bulgaria in the 1990s as a private citizen and became prime minister in 2001-2005.

His bodyguard, Boyko Borisov, whom the former king had promoted to a top police job, has been prime minister of Bulgaria since 2009.

Having survived the war and being faced with the prospect of life in a hardline Communist country, about 38,000 of Bulgaria's Jews decided to emigrate to the newly-founded state of Israel. In the next four decades those who stayed would become a "model minority," causing no political trouble.

Jewish life rapidly declined in the 1950s-1980s. The Central Consistory was disbanded, to be replaced by a cultural organization. Jews were gradually stripped of minority rights. Dozens of synagogues were either abandoned or turned into sports or storage facilities. Some still lie in ruins. Jewish cemeteries were either destroyed, "moved" to new locations or abandoned.

Internationally, Bulgaria was toeing the Soviet line with great fervor. It broke diplomatic relations with Israel after the Six-Day War in 1967, and relations exacerbated further following the 1973 Yom Kipur War.

In 1973, Bulgaria's Communist rulers voiced their desire to put forward the name of Todor Zhivkov, the general secretary of the Communist Party and a low-ranking partisan in the war years, for the Nobel Peace Prize over his imaginary role in rescuing the Bulgarian Jews. In 1986 the government commissioned a feature film to credit Zhivkov with "saving" the Bulgarian Jews.

The Communists had managed to rid Bulgaria of its civil society. In 1984-1985 the government went ahead with a plan to forcibly Bulgarianize the country's largest minority, the Turks. The general public was at best indifferent to the repercussions that included the forcible name-changing of 800,000 Turks, the destruction of mosques and cemeteries, and the banning of the Turkish language.

Nothing like the massive response of the Bulgarian civil society to the antisemitic actions of the previous generation followed.

Todor Zhivkov was dethroned in an intra-party coup on 10 November 1989. Bulgaria started its painful attempt to democratize itself. Some Jews, especially younger ones, started a new wave of Jewish emigration, mainly to seek better lives in the West.

In 1990, the Shalom Jewish Organization was set up as the heir of the Central Consistory. It got most of the former Jewish communal properties back. Diplomatic relations with Israel were reestablished.

In 2000, to honor the war-time king and his alleged role in the rescue of the Bulgarian Jews, Bulgaria placed a monument to him and Queen Giovanna in a forest near Jerusalem. Following protests, the monument was removed. It was shipped back to Bulgaria and can now be seen in front of the Sofia City Council, next to a church.

The 1990s and 2000s saw a rebirth of antisemitism. There have been a number of attacks on Jewish properties, including the vandalizing of cemeteries. The Jewish cemetery in Kyustendil, for example, was vandalized on seven different occasions, and the home of Shalom in Burgas was unsuccessfully set on fire. The Sofia Central Synagogue was burgled. In the 2000s, extremist political leaders have taken up antisemitism as their cause célèbre. Bulgarian publishers freely publish antisemitic literature by Hitler, Goebbels, Jürgen Graf and Henry Ford, and these books can be found in most Bulgarian bookshops and street stalls. The authorities have done little if anything to curtail their distribution, nor have they properly investigated the spraying of Jewish graves with swastikas in Shumen and elsewhere.

The use of the Nazi swastika is widespread – from street gangs spraying it onto Gypsy homes and Turkish mosques, to football fans asserting their membership of a team, to anti-Communists pitching it against still widespread Red Army symbolism. The authorities usually consider it vandalism with no particular political meaning. Swastikas have been sprayed onto Jewish graves and can be seen in Central Sofia accompanied by the words "Juden Raus."

Then comes the issue of the former Yugoslav republic of Macedonia. Relations between Sofia and Skopje are at best uneasy. Macedonia declared independence in 1991 and Bulgaria became the first country to recognize it. But recognition was conditional. Macedonia's name and its political independence were fine, but Bulgaria refused to recognize its language, history and the existence of a Macedonian nation. (Greece recognizes the sovereignty of the state, its language and its nation, but refuses to recognize the name, which coincides with the name of a northern Greek province. Both Bulgaria and Greece make often completely justified claims that the current Republic of Macedonia usurps Greek and Bulgarian history as its own.)

In 2008, Macedonia opened a Holocaust Museum in Skopje. Most Bulgarian mainstream politicians and historians dismissed it as propaganda and distorted history.

In 2012, a Macedonian feature film, *The Third Half*, about the Bulgarian occupation in the 1940s and the treatment of the Macedonian Jews by the Bulgarians, infuriated Bulgaria. It was officially protested. Speaking at a joint news conference with Israeli Prime Minister Benjamin Netanyahu, Bulgarian Prime Minister Boyko Borisov asserted: "There are certain circles in the world who want to distort, to interpret and to comment on history. Yet I think that Bulgaria is a country that saved all of its Jews under Hitler, thanks to the whole Bulgarian nation."

Several months later Bulgarian producers began a TV soap about the 1943 rescue of Bulgarian Jews. The series is somewhat clumsily entitled *The Ungiven*.

A former foreign minister, who is Jewish himself, told the media Bulgaria as a nation ought to be given the Nobel Peace Prize for its rescue of the Jews in 1943.

The central issue of this article, why Bulgaria was double-faced in its treatment of the Jews during the Second World War and why its politicians, 70 years after the dramatic events of the 1940s, are so reluctant to come to terms with the country's past, becomes easier to decipher against the backdrop of the personalities, events and circumstances described above. The reasons for both the chest-thumping and the refusal to admit guilt are mainly psychological.

For one, the Bulgarian national mentality rests on several tenets. Some are readily propagated: Bulgaria's "traditional" tolerance and "proverbial" hospitality. Others are taboos. One of them is suffering, a defining concept in the Balkans, where nations still quarrel with each other over who suffered more under the Turks, under the Communists, under its neighbors, under the Great Powers, under the European Union, under the International Monetary Fund, under Angela Merkel or under an unremittingly unfavorable fate. Another is the absolute predilection to vilify anyone or anything else but oneself and one's own actions for everything that's gone wrong.

Similar attitudes seem to exist west of the border, in the former Yugoslav republic of Macedonia. There is little doubt that the striking theme park of statues being funded by the Macedonian government in Central Skopje is supposed to boost the modern Macedonians' national identity. Similarly, the Bulgarian war-time occupation of Macedonia and especially the fate of the Macedonian Jews is used as a building block in the history and mentality of the former Yugoslav republic.

Forty-five years of hardline Communism have taught at least several generations of Bulgarians and Macedonians to see the world in black-and-white rather than to explore the nuances and draw their own conclusions. Thinking, rather then memorizing dates and names, has not been on the Bulgarian school agenda for a long time.

What is more important is that unlike other former Warsaw Pact countries in Central and Eastern Europe, Bulgaria never managed to properly "de-Communize" itself. Former Communists and Secret Police functionaries have been (and in some instances still are) in charge of politics, social life and the economy. Decommunization is a complicated and painful process that will not produce black-and-white results and conclusions. Official Bulgaria so far prefers to forget, rather than to analyze so that it avoids repetitions. Like East Germany in the early 1950s, which infamously declared it had nothing to do with either Nazism or the Holocaust as those had been the deeds of West Germany's "vile capitalists," Bulgaria now finds it very uncomfortable to admit that what it did in Macedonia, Aegean Thrace and southern Serbia was morally wrong if historically inevitable.

One possible explanation is that many Bulgarians, having being brought up with the theory that the non-deportation of about 48,000 Bulgarian Jews was unique in Europe and one of the noblest events in Europe's history, fear that any admission of guilt over the 11,343 deportees will tarnish the much grander event of the rescue.

The sentiment is easy to grab by cunning politicians who would go to any length to capitalize on "national pride" as a building block for a country's national identity. The job becomes even easier in the case of Bulgaria, where the Feel-Good Factor is notoriously very low. Bulgaria remains the poorest EU state, it is currently in the grips of an economic and moral crisis, and Bulgarians can hardly find a thing to pride themselves on in their country's recent development. Why not give them something to be proud about in the past, the more distant and more spectacular, the better? Cynical, but true – Bulgarians usually vote with their feet, because they feel nothing depends on them. Yet they are ready to take up a fight if a Bulgarian Medieval king, or the Turks, are mentioned.

Furthermore, an event such as the non-deportation of Bulgarian Jews may be used to justify current ethnic tensions and strong-handed treatment of minorities, by feeding the ever-lasting "traditional tolerance" myth.

This type of attitude may suit current political ambitions and increasingly extremist public sentiments, as exemplified by a political declaration adopted unanimously by the Bulgarian parliament in March 2013. The carefully worded document reiterates the rescue of Bulgaria's Jews and does express regret over the fate of the 11,343. But it blankly refuses to even hint at any responsibility of the Bulgarians for what they did in the Kingdom of Yugoslavia and northern Greece. Analyzed carefully and in detail, the declaration indicates just one thing: that the Bulgarian establishment is set to milk the "rescue" for as long as possible while it attempts to boost the feeling of national pride and justify its disrespect for the country's civil society citing the actions of noble Bulgarians 70 years ago.

In the long run this stance is of course counterproductive.

The Bulgarians clearly need a lesson in what the Germans call Bewäl-tigung der Vergangenheit, facing and coming to terms with one's own past. What makes Bulgaria interesting is that it did not, indeed, kill about 48,000 of its Jewish citizens. This is beyond any doubt an honorable event, especially when seen against the backdrop of some of the darkest years in human history. However, it did turn in 11,343 people whom it had occupied and deprived of citizenship rights. This is the other side of the coin. The good cannot completely atone for the evil, but insisting that the evil was never committed does tarnish the image the Bulgarians are so hard trying to project both domestically and to the outside world.

Unless the Bulgarians come to terms with that, they are bound to be unable to build the Western-type of civil society that they so eagerly sought after the collapse of Communism and that saved their Jews during the Second World War.

--

Fact box
Jews in Bulgaria in 1939: estimated around 48,000.
Jews in administered territories: estimated about 12,000.
Jews in Bulgaria in 1945: 49,172.
Jews in Bulgaria now: 1,162 (2011 census results). Shalom has 6,000 members.
Jews in Greece, Serbia and Macedonia now: about 6,500. There are about 5,500 in Greece; 787 in Serbia; and 200 in the former Yugoslav republic of Macedonia.
Non-Bulgarian Jews allowed to emigrate through Bulgaria in 1939-1945: Over 10,000.
NB. A variety of sources cite different numbers for different communities. The numbers given above have gained currency, but there is an explicit disclaimer about their accurateness.

--

Further Reading

In English

Ani Avtova and Victor Melamed (Eds), Antisemitic Manifestations in Bulgaria 2009-2010, Sofia, Shalom Organization of Bulgarian Jews, 2011

Anthony Georgieff and Dimana Trankova, A Guide to Jewish Bulgaria, Sofia, Vagabond Media, 2011, ISBN 978-954-92306-3-5

Emmy Barouh (Ed), Jews in the Bulgarian Lands, Sofia, International Centre for Minority Studies and Intercultural Relations, 2001, ISBN 954-8872-35-8

Gale Stokes, The Walls Came Tumbling Down: The Collapse of Communism in Eastern Europe, USA, Oxford University Press, 1993, ISBN 0-19-506645-6

Jamila Andjela Kolomonos, Monastir Without Jews: Recollections of a Jewish Partisan in Macedonia, New York, Foundation for the Advancement of Sephardic Studies and Culture, 2008, ISBN 978-1-886857-09-4

Loise Kone and Roula Kone, Jewish-Greek Communities: Little Beloved Homes, The Ladies of the Jewish Community in Volos, Greece, 2006

Michael Bar-Zohar, Beyond Hitler's Grasp: The Heroic Rescue of Bulgaria's Jews, USA, Adams Media Corporation, 1998, ISBN 978-1580620604

Michael Berenbaum, The Jews in Macedonia During WWII, Skopje, Holocaust Fund from the Jews of Macedonia, ISBN 978-608-65129-5-8

Misha Glenny, The Balkans: Nationalism, War and the Great Powers, London, Granta Books, 2001, ISBN 978-1-862-07073-8

R. J. Crampton, A Concise History of Bulgaria, Cambridge University Press, 1997, ISBN 978-0-521-61637-9

Robert Harvey, Comrades: The Rise and Fall of World Communism, London, John Murray Publishers, 2003, ISBN 0-7195-6174-7

Robert Kaplan, Balkan Ghosts: A Journey Through History, London, Papermac, 1994, ISBN 0-333-63283-4

Shelomo Alfassa, Shameful Behavior: Bulgaria and the Holocaust, Judaic Studies Academic Paper Series, New York, 2011, ISBN 978-1-257-95257-1

Tzvetan Todorov, Voices From the Gulag: Life and Death in Communist Bulgaria, Pennsylvania State University Press, 1999, ISBN 0-271-01961-1

Tzvetan Todorov: The Fragility of Goodness: Why Bulgaria's Jews Survived the Holocaust, Princeton University Press, 2001, ISBN 0-691-11564-8

Yitzchak Mais (Ed), Macedonian Chronicle: The Story of Sephardic Jews in the Balkans, Skopje, Holocaust Fund from the Jews of Macedonia, 2011, ISBN 978-608-65129-3-4

In Italian:

Gabrielle Nissim, L'uomo che fermò Hitler. La storia di Dimitar Pesev che salvò gli ebrei di una nazione intera, Milan, Mondadori Publishers, 1999, ISBN 9788804473312

In Bulgarian

Albena Taneva (Ed), Bulgarian-Jewish Relations on the Threshold of the 21st Century, Sofia, Jewish Studies Center, Sofia University,

Albena Taneva and Vanya Gezenko (Eds), Voices in Support of Civil Society: Holy Synod Protocols on the Jewish Question (1940-1944), Sofia, Gal-Ico Jewish Studies Center, Sofia University, 2002, ISBN 954-768-004-8

David Coen, The Jews in Bulgaria 1978-1949, Sofia, Fakel-Leonidovi Publishers, 2008, ISBN 978-954-411-148-9

Isak Moskona, Language, Everyday Life and Spirituality of Balkan Jews, Sofia, Shalom Publishers, 2004, ISBN 954-8200-22-8

Samuil Arditi, The Man Who Cheated Hitler: King Boris III, Persecutor or Friend of Bulgaria's Jews?, Ruse, Avangard Print, ISBN 978-954-337-050-4

Stoyan Raychevski, Bulgarians and Jews Through the Centuries, Sofia, Bulgarian Bestseller Publishers, 2008, ISBN 978-954-463-021-8

Stoyan Raychevski, Synagogues and Jewish Cultural Heritage in Bulgaria, Sofia, Bulgarian Bestseller Publishers, 2009, ISBN 978-954-463-074-4

Ulrich Büchsenschütz and Ivo Georgiev, Bulgarian Minority Policies, Sofia, International Center for Minority Studies and Intercultural Relations, 2000

Berlin: The persecution of Jews and German society

Ulrich Herbert

How did German society react to the persecution of its Jewish citizens? And in trying to answer this question, is it possible to speak of there being an identifiable overall reaction? In fact, is it possible to speak in any sense of their being such a thing as "civil society" during Nazi rule in Germany?

At the very start of the national socialist revolution in 1933 – for there is no doubt that it was indeed a revolution – there were three population groups, of more or less equal size, confronting each other: the first group, which supported the Nazi party and helped to keep the Nazi regime in power, was primarily made up of the party's own membership and voters. The second group saw itself as a radical oppositional element to the Nazis and was comprised of the majority who supported the Social Democrats, the communists and a part of the Catholic Worker movement. The third group was made up of people who were generally indifferent to the above dividing line and whose attitude to the national socialist government depended on whether it was able to deliver advantageous political and economic results. In the following three years, group number two in this list fell victim to a campaign of political marginalization: Its leaders were imprisoned (a number of them were murdered), and in general the supporters of this second group suffered widespread intimidation. At the same time, the whole administrative apparatus of the new German state was placed under strict and targeted control from day one. All conflicting elements were shorn away and all oppositional institutions were dissolved, including other political parties, trade unions and associations. Because of the Nazi government's economic successes and foreign policy victories–the occupation of the Rhineland, the re-annexation of Saarland, etc.–the regime was soon able to win many doubters in that third group of indifferent people over to its side. Thus, in the years before the outbreak of the Second World War, the political profile of German society might be described in this way: a little over half the population were either passive or enthusiastic supporters of the regime, whilst a fifth was still indifferent and one fourth was still opposed to the Nazi dictatorship. However this latter group had been successfully cowed, was powerless and had been left isolated. Civil society, in the form of public bodies and judicial state based public and private bodies no longer existed as an independent entity in the civic sphere, or perhaps only as a neutered propaganda arm of the state–a situation that, to some extent, makes a more precise understanding of popular opinions and moods more difficult.

Nonetheless, in what follows below, I will attempt to illustrate in three phases how German society in its new manifestation interacted with the Nazi regime during its persecution of the Jews. The first phase relates to the spread of anti-Semitism; the second assesses society's reaction to the pogrom during *Reichskristallnacht* (Crystal Night) in 1938; then finally I look at the question of society's awareness of (and reaction to) the Final Solution strategy during the war itself.

I.

Let us first look at the significance of anti-Semitism. From the start of the 1920s onwards, there were several vociferous groups of radical anti-Semites which were also prepared to use violence to further their aims. However, up to the year 1933, these groups were not in a position to play any significant role. This was partly due to their violent propensities, which often led to riots and bouts of violence and which, at that time, aroused nothing more than indignation and rejection amongst most of the population, even amongst Nazi supporters.

What was of more significance though was a latent anti-Semitism, which was already quite widespread during the *Keiserreich* (Monarchical Empire), and gained further currency during the Weimar Republic, but still did not manifest itself in terms of open acts of aggression or street demonstrations. In fact, this kind of anti-Semitism was at pains to distance itself from its more "vulgar" bedfellows, or what it decried as hooligan and rabble rousing – "Radau-Antisemitismus"; be that in provocative campaigns asserting that Jews were involved, for example, in ritual murders and the people trafficking of young women. Nor did this more refined anti Jewish sentiment condone the desecration of Jewish cemeteries or street disturbances. However, many Germans did believe that Jews were an alien entity within German society and that they had enriched themselves in times of war, inflation and financial crises. If we look at anti-Semitism as a collective social phenomenon (in all its various nuances and levels of intensity), we cannot rule out the possibility that, even before 1933, a majority of Germans were hostile to the Jewish population in the country.

But even in 1933, there were still strong oppositional forces that not only objected to anti-Semitism but also directly resisted it – more than anywhere else in the labor movement and also amongst Catholic activists and liberals. In other words, regardless of how widespread anti-Semitism was before 1933–whether it reflected the views of 30, 40 or 50 per cent of the population–at that time it was still met with determined resistance.

The most important point in this debate is often overlooked: The Weimar Republic was a constitutional state based on the rule of law. So whilst it's true that a number of scandalous court rulings were handed down against Jews in this period – where anti-Semitic prejudice was clearly an overriding motive – it is also true that these rulings caused outrage throughout the state. They were still the exception and not the rule. Thus, recourse to the law following attacks, insults, annoyances or slanderous propaganda remained the preferred option for Jewish organizations in their opposition to anti-Semites. The Central Council of Jews in Germany, for example, never tired of seeking legal redress and was occasionally successful in so doing.

During the years of the Weimar Republic, anti-Semitic outrages would regularly provoke waves of public condemnation. Another important factor is that the hope amongst many German Jews was that, in historical terms, anti-Semitism was a gradually declining relic from darker, less sophisticated times and therefore would not pose a threat in the long term. To be fair, this optimistic belief and assessment of the significance of anti-Semitism on the part of German Jews was shared by the majority of Germany's left wing intellectuals. Above all, this latter group's reaction to anti-Semitism and anti-Semites was simply one of scathing sarcasm and head shaking contempt. The view held by left wing intellectuals was that the extreme right wing's militarism, and also its connections to society's most elite groups posed far more danger than anything else. Whereas the organized hatred of Jews always had, for them, something feeble minded and 'folklore-ish' about it.

From 1933 to 1938, German Jews were gradually squeezed outwards to society's edge via a plethora of laws, statutory decrees and straightforward chicanery. And now Jews were presented with a new situation – this observation may appear rather elementary, but is of huge significance: from this point onwards, opposition to anti-Semitism could no longer be expressed openly. It is true that there were still ways in which one could express one's loathing for the imposition of anti Jewish measures – for example, by going out of one's way to greet and show friendship to Jewish friends and acquaintances, maintaining social relations with old contacts or even giving direct help – though this latter gesture soon became risky. But, *Nota Bene*, these were private gestures in a period when public institutions had become a vehicle for anti-Semitism in all its various abominations.

Assertions that a significant element of those who expressed opposition to anti-Semitism prior to 1933 now began to change their opinions and gravitate towards anti-Semitism would be difficult to substantiate. However, it is clear that from 1933 onwards it was no longer seen as socially acceptable to speak out publically against the oppression of Jews in Germany. The best one could now expect on the part of those who were opposed to anti-Semitism was some form of passive avoidance of involvement in the withdrawal of rights for Jews and subsequently in their active persecution. At the same time, attacks on Jews were no longer covered by legal protection. In fact they were openly allowed by the new government; one might even say accepted. Likewise, discrimination against Jews was no longer forbidden but written into statute.

The persecution of Jews in Germany, which received very accurate coverage in broadsheet newspapers in the United States, England and France, was not brought to the center of the German public's attention until 1938. This was mainly due to the Nazi regime's mechanisms of repression and suppression, which were very quickly honed to perfection. Nobody wished to confront the Gestapo or Nazi activists by criticizing the methods being used against a group of fellow citizens, whom the majority of Germans either distanced themselves from, or were even openly hostile to. For example, in a report written in January 1936, the SPD's leadership in exile (which was far from being anti-Semitic in outlook) noted that socialist minded workers were without doubt "determined opponents of Nazi outrages." But at the same time, the exiled SPD leaders regarded it as absolutely correct and acceptable that "the Jewish financial elite should be broken once and for all and the Jews given specific areas of activity in which they could operate."

German Catholics held a similar position. Yes it is true that the Cardinal of Munich wrote to a priest, who was outraged by the persecution of the Jews, saying that the actions of the Nazis were "unchristian." But he then went on to argue that there were even greater problems: "For the spiritual hierarchy here is faced with more pressing problems...especially when we can assume that the Jews are more than capable of helping themselves, as we have already seen."

Thus, up to November 1938, anti-Jewish pogroms and persecution were not a pressing issue in the minds of most Germans. Rather, during this period, an intensive chain of large-scale events took place that generated public mobilizations and a sense of breathlessness. The Nazi regime's leadership sought to maintain this high wire atmosphere via the staging of continued high-blown and pompous public spectacles and also by constantly stressing the need for not only discrimination, but the persecution and the withdrawal of rights for all political opponents – Jews and every other group that was defined as being inimical to the "Folk Fellowship." In the light of the regime's heady successes on the economic front, given the rapid reduction in employment figures and its triumphs on the world stage, most people saw its repressive policies as an unfortunate but unavoidable corollary. Moreover, it also has to be said that many people – even those who opposed the Nazis – regarded the iron hand policy used against the Jews as a kind of 'payback' for their alleged enormous wealth and financial success in the preceding years: in other words, anti-Semitism grew to be a variant of a wider critique of capitalism.

II.

From November 8 to 10, 1938, synagogues, Jewish businesses and private homes and apartments were destroyed ransacked and/or torched by units of the SA and *Hitlerjugend*. Random passers-by and onlookers often joined in with these attacks. Around 200 Jews were murdered during these pogroms, whilst over 20,000 Jews were imprisoned in concentration camps, though only for a few weeks as this was an attempt to pressurize Jews to flee from Germany but leaving their possessions, property and assets behind them.

However, public reaction to these events was found to be either muted or downright hostile. Almost all the local branches of the Nazi party in Germany reported that the *Aktion* had been met with bewilderment and rejection amongst the wider populace. Where, two weeks previously, an attempt at the forced deportation of Polish Jews had only received limited publicity, the reports of drunken, screaming hordes of robbers and bandits was now met with outright criticism, even from the regime's own supporters. For example, in a survey that contacted local police stations, the Gestapo at Bielefeld reported exclusively negative reactions: The *Aktion* had provoked "shakes of the head and a deafening silence amongst the people." The report then went on: "The attitude of the local populace was marked by a somberness and sense of dejection. Here and there, there were clear signs of pity for the victims. By far the majority of the population have not understood the *Aktion* against the Jews and condemned it on the basis that such things should not take in place in what is supposed to be a cultured nation." Thus was the unanimous basic reaction. The public humiliation and persecution (and most of all the regular round of killings), appear to have aroused no little disapproval amongst a large majority of the population, which however does not necessarily imply a huge amount of sympathy for those being persecuted. According to reports from the domestic intelligence services, the general view amongst Germans was that the Jews should leave Germany. But public outrages of this sort would not receive the same sort of backing.

After *Kristallnacht*, the regime's anti-Jewish campaign was no longer pushed by the Nazi party apparatus and SA, but by the statutory authorities themselves; more specifically by Richard Heydrich's secret police. Drunken hordes of SA men would no longer be the spearhead of anti Jewish persecution in Germany, but rather the state's own officials in the full garb and sanction of judicial power. Thus state policy could proceed in a seamless way and without generating the kind of friction aroused by unwanted public attention. At the same time, the tempo of persecution was stepped up and the radical nature of the regime's actions dramatically sharpened.

From November 9, 1938, onwards, Germans could no longer be in any doubt as to the intentions of the national socialists: robberies, torching and arson, plunder and murder were all openly perpetrated and no one in the country could from then on claim not to understand what was happening. On the contrary, a failure to recognize with great trepidation the likely fate of the Jews after November 9 would require a willful blindness.

III.

In the first days of October 1941, the German occupation forces in Polish Galicia moved to force the whole of the Jewish population in the border town of Stanislau (today Ivano-Frankivsk) into one single residential area – thus creating a ghetto. This procedure had already been carried out in Lemberg (today Lviv) and other towns and occupied areas. In order to make this action practically feasible, the heads of the German secret police in Galicia decided to halve the number of the approximately 40,000 Jews living in Stanislau. In other words, to murder them.

On the morning of October 12, Stanislau Jews were frog-marched in columns of 250 people to the Jewish cemetery, where they were gunned down. Fifteen to 20 marksmen from the secret police and police units were positioned around two mass graves. Because of the shortage of manpower needed for the massacre, members of the railway police were also co-opted. According to investigations carried out by the Jewish Council for Jews in Germany in the wake of this mass murder, between 10,000 and 12,000 people were murdered at this site. During the executions at the cemetery, many curious onlookers gathered to observe events. They came, in particular, from the ranks of the Wehrmacht, the local police force, as well as railway staff and workers. These people witnessed the whole event and many took photographs. In the weeks that followed, the massacre in Stanislau was the prime subject of discussion, not only in the city itself but also in the district generally.

In fact, the report covering Stanislau's "Bloody Sunday" reflects what became the norm in terms of the extermination campaign against Jews. In Polish Galicia alone, there were several similar massacres, until at the start of 1942 the German authorities changed tack and proceeded to execute most Jews using gas chambers at the extermination camp at Belzec.

The report also clearly demonstrates the very public nature of these mass executions – the large number of spectators who watched the murders and the number of people who came to the scene of the crime because news of the event spread so quickly. Moreover, it shows that the scale of human involvement, either directly or indirectly, in this Nazi murder policy went far beyond the people who actually fired a weapon or switched on the gas. In contrast to the German *Reich* itself, the mass murder of Jews in the occupied areas to the east was no secret. Far too many people were involved or actually took an active part in the process of deportations, segregation, ghettoizing and forced labor (and finally in the executions themselves) for events to remain a secret. The long list included functionaries within the German forces of occupation; Nazi party and government officials; Wehrmacht units, staff working in finance and industrial sectors; state railway and works management teams and so on. From these sources, news, knowledge or awareness of the mass murder processes spread very quickly.

In Germany itself, the mass murder program against Jews was officially a secret. However, there was no shortage of reports and strong rumors, not least from soldiers returning to the *Reich* on leave, or those who simply passed conversation in their free time. This kind of talk was picked up by people like the Jewish literary figure and author Victor Klemperer who otherwise lived a completely isolated life in a "Jew House" in Dresden. He had no access to a radio or newspapers, but as early as March 1942 was able to write about a concentration camp called Auschwitz. "Death comes after a few day," he wrote in his diary. Not pursuing this multiplicity of leads and often very badly concealed indications; not wanting to know anything more specific; this was the approach taken by many Germans during these years. Here, we are talking about something other than knowledge and awareness. The technically correct term is rather – "suppression" of awareness.

IV.

If we combine all these brief outlines into a whole picture, it becomes clear that whilst in Germany at that time there was indeed a minority which was against anti-Jewish pogroms and persecution, these were effectively muzzled and in terms of numbers were dwarfed by a majority of anti-Semites. And whilst it is true that the majority of this latter group were no more than passive anti-Semites, they all agreed that Germany needed to get rid of the Jews in its midst and never bothered themselves to worry about the methods that might be used to bring this about. Furthermore, the political outlook of this group was not solely, or even primarily, characterized by anti-Semitism. However, when their Jewish neighbors were arrested and deported "to the East," this majority group did not possess sufficient political or moral convictions, which might have impelled them to refuse acceptance of, or even support of, these measures. This was even truer amongst those who after 1939 and 1941 were serving in administrative posts in the German forces of occupation outside Germany and could not fail to be aware of what was happening.

To imagine that the Jewish Holocaust and the spread of anti-Jewish sentiment amongst the German population had somehow emerged from a centuries old "underlying anti-Semitism" is both misleading and very much an oversimplification. It was rather the case that the genocide policy was able to proceed so smoothly because a substantial section of the population was completely indifferent to the fate of Germany's Jewish population. Thus, what we are actually looking at here is not a picture of a society that nurtured a burning desire to expel or murder the Jews in its midst. Rather, it bears witness to a grievous moral deficit in German society where human rights and the protection of minorities was concerned (a deficit that reached a high-water mark in the years spanning the dictatorship). This prevailing attitude must be seen in the light of the fact that, from 1933 onwards, all instances of public resistance and every protest against anti Jewish persecution policies were first subject to restrictions and then full-scale suppression.

On the other hand, it cannot be denied that a substantial element amongst the German population felt a strong antipathy to Jews, and at various levels of hatred. It is without doubt that this widely shared outlook was of central importance when it came to the implementation of the program of genocide and could also, once all public resistance was neutered as a possibly restrictive factor, be counted in itself as a driving motive that had significant impact. The number of Germans who, in this sense, were active participants in the Holocaust probably did not reach millions, but we can safely assume that it was tens of thousands of people. Moreover, the men who became the leading lights in the *Reichssicherheitshauptamt,* the SS and the large number of *Aktion* units (who have broadly come to be recognized as the actual perpetrators of the genocide) were not recruited from exterior or marginal groups in German society. Rather, they came in fact from the core of German society: that society's middle and upper echelons.

Paris: a family under German occupation

"The yellow star was imposed to separate the Jews from the others and label them. Truly, this did not stir up demonstrations against the Jews. On the contrary, the yellow star shocked, and even scandalized the mainstream opinion."

Annette Wieviorka

In September 1944, Chaskiel Perelman went back to the apartment he rented at 67 rue Rochechouart, in the 9th district of Paris. He left, with his wife and younger daughter, Rachel, the day after the *rafle* (roundup) of the Vel d'Hiv, on July 16 and 17, 1942. Under the Möbel Aktion,[1] the apartment had been emptied of all its furniture and the electric plugs had been snatched. Nothing was left from their life before. He was only with Rachel. This autumn 1944, Basia Elka, called Berthe, the elder daughter and her husband and Srulka Berneman, called Raoul, whom she married in Paris on May 20, 1941, and moved in at 7, rue Taylor with their baby girl Evelyne, born in Grenoble on July 27, 1943. This apartment was empty, too. Its tenants, the parents and the sister of Srulka, had been deported. They would never come back.

The Berneman and Perelman families are typical of those Jewish immigrant families from Poland, victims of anti-Semitic persecutions perpetrated by the Nazis and the French government of Vichy. Some of their members were murdered. Some others survived. The proportion between both for the Berneman-Perelman families is the same as for all the Jews of France. Indeed, according to the fact that 330,000 Jews lived in France in 1939, 80,000 of them (or 25%) died, most of them murdered in Auschwitz-Birkenau. Sixty-nine percent of them were foreigners, like the Berneman and the Perelman.

The first who came to France in 1923 was Chaskiel Perelman. Born in Kotsk in 1890, he first settled in Warsaw where he was a tailor.[2] A member of a communist trade union, he met Chawa Beckerkunz, born in Warsaw in 1898, whom he married. They had two children, born in Warsaw: Basia Elka (1920) and Rachmil Bochuch (1922). His wife and his two children joined him in Paris in 1924. In the beginning, they lived and worked in some unhealthy places in the slums of Paris where the immigrants lived, Jewish or not: rue des Poissonniers, in the 18th district, then 33, rue de Meaux, in the 19th where, on December 12nd 1925, at 1:20 AM Rachel was born, the first twin and Jules, the second twin. Jules lived only a few months. He died at the Herold Hospital on May 15, 1926.

At the beginning of 1930, the family moved into a middle class apartment on rue Rochechouart. It was not an immigrant neighborhood, and the Jews who lived there were French – "Israelite bourgeois," as people used to say. This new home was the proof of their social ascent. Chaskiel despised his unambitious coreligionists. At the very bottom of the scale, according to him, were the Jews living in *Pletzl*, the Saint-Paul neighborhood with the rue des Rosiers, attending the small synagogues, wearing kaftan and *payes*. Those from Belleville, even if they partly abandoned the Tradition, were no better. Not that he had given up being Jewish. Had he hoped so, it would have been impossible: he hardly spoke French and Yiddish remained his main language, his only language. Apart from his customers, his social network consisted of immigrant Jews from Poland like him. Among his customers was the very famous journalist Henri Béraud,[3] who lived in the same building. Béraud moved surreptitiously from the left to the right wing. What remained steady, with him, was his anti-communism and his anti-Semitism. What changed was his enormous weight. He received the Goncourt Prize in 1932 for *Le martyre de l'obèse* ("The Martyrdom of the Obese"). He points out his problems for dressing. He was a valuable customer for Chaskiel Perelman, who widened regularly the author's trousers. He never expressed toward him the least racial prejudice.

As many other Jewish immigrants, the Perelmans had forgotten any religious practice. They were very interested in politics, which they followed in the abundant Yiddish press, particularly the communist daily la *Naie Presse* (The New Press), published in Paris. They were not members of any political organization but belonged to the communist movement, the one of the Yiddish speaking under-section of the French Communist Party. In 1934, the parents enrolled their elder children, Berthe and Roger, at YASC, *Yiddisher Arbeyter Sport Klub*, located at the end of the Cité d'Angoulême (today rue

Jean-Pierre Timbaud), in the 11th district, in the heart of Jewish Paris. They became friends with some young communists who will become resisters and partisans of the immigrant work force.[4] Because most of them came from the YACK, they were called "the sportsmen". Neither Perelman nor Berneman became resisters.

On September 3, 1939, when France declares war on Germany, Chaskiel, now helped by his wife, now makes a good living as tailor for men. At 49, he is too old to enroll in the army as did 30,000 foreign Jewish. Roger, his son, is too young. At 17, he is a brilliant student in mathematics at the lycée Condorcet. Next year, he should pass his baccalauréat. But, because of the war, he cannot go back to lycée Condorcet, one of the oldest and boldest Parisian high schools requisitioned by the army, but to a private high school, rue du general Foy. Rachel studies accounting at rue d'Abbeville. Berthe works for a *haute couture* workshop. She is dating Srulka, called Raoul Berneman, born on April 5th 1921 in Podwialne, Poland.

For Chaskiel as for other men who have not been called by the army, the first year of war, *La drôle de guerre,* when soldiers do not fight, is a good year. His customers have grown with Polish refugees, who escaped their country split between Germany and Soviet Union. Looking at the German army entering Paris, the Perelmans act as most of the Parisians and like nearly 100,000 Jews.[5] The family leaves Paris in this great migration that is called the Exodus, as the exit of the Hebrews form Egypt. Roger is biking. The rest of the family takes the train. They arrive in Perpignan where Roger passes successfully his bacs of maths and of philosophy.

What do they know? What do they understand of the major events that occurred during their travel?

Philippe Pétain, the "winner" of Verdun, asked for an armistice with Germans. It is signed on June 22, 1940 a Rethondes. France is split in two zones. A demarcation line becomes the border between an occupied zone ruled by the German military commandment (*Miltärbefefhlshaber in Frankreich-* MBF) and a free zone. The French government, now called the French State government settles in Vichy. He runs the country by decrees that are valid in all the country, which is still administered by the French administration. Crossing the demarcation line requires a visa, called *Ausweis.* Jews cannot come back to the occupied zone when they are in the free zone.

After a short hesitation, when it is planned to flea to North Africa by Port-Bou and Spain, the family decides to come back to Paris. On a first try, they are driven back at the demarcation line. The second try works better. At the end of 1940, the family lives again on rue Rochechouart. Berthe, who was so sad, reunited with her lover, who has stayed in Paris. And life goes on normally. The war does not seem to have changed anything, or almost. Chaskiel is very busy. Roger opted for a class of *mathématiques supérieures,* a very difficult course. Because he is a foreigner, he cannot apply to Polytechnique or Normale Sup, the two best Grandes Écoles. He targets École Centrale, which admits some foreigners. He works very hard, does nothing else, does not read anymore, does not go to the movies, does not attend the YASK anymore, gets away from his old friends from the neighborhood. Rachel studies at rue d'Abbeville, as she did before the war and Berthe still works for *haute couture.*

They are worried by the first anti-Semitic measures taken by the MBF or the French state, but not enough to change anything in their daily life. The status of the Jews, enacted by Vichy on October 3, 1940, published in the *Journal officiel* on October 18th, targets primarily the foreign Jews. It provides for the internment in special camps of the foreign Jews. It is a real threat, even if no one in the family is concerned. Everyone wants to respect the law, as the huge majority of the French Jews in 1940. The family obeys the decree of September 27, 1940, that determined who is Jewish and orders everyone to register before October 20. They stand in line for hours at the police station of the rue de la Tour d'Auvergne, near their residence. The names of each member of the family are listed in the four files created and managed by the Préfecture de police by street, by nationality, by alphabetical order, by occupation. In his fitting room, Chaskiel hangs a yellow poster with black letters: *Judisches Geschaft* ("Jewish business").

On May 13, 1941, Roger walks from the lycée Condorcet by his usual itinerary: rue du Havre, rue Saint-Lazare, rue de Maubeuge, rue Pétrelle. He recounts: "It was about half past four, the air seemed light, the weather was mild, spring. It quickly appears to me that on rue Rochechouart, an abnormal number of Jews were on the sidewalks, speaking to each other, nervous and anxious; I knew them well and, to the one who asked me: 'Do you have your convocation?' I answered that I did not know. Then I came home. The convocation was there, for the morning after, at the police station of avenue de l'Opéra. My mother instinctively repeated to me not to go, but I answered: Where could I hide? We'll see well"[6]

In the memories, this convocation stayed as the "green note." "Green notes" were sent to 6694 Jews, mostly Polish, whose names where chosen in the files managed by the police headquarters. Slightly more than half of them answer, like Roger, to the convocation. All of them are interned in camps located in the Loiret: Pithiviers and Beaune-la-Rolande.

At nine in the morning, on time like the Perelman always are, Roger, accompanied by his mother and Rachel, arrives at the police station. After a short examination of his identity, he is brought into a room in the depths of the building. His mother is asked to come back with clothes and food for 24 hours. Around 2 PM, buses come to pick them up. By the window of the bus, in front of the Café de la Paix, Roger sees his sisters and Raoul who make signs with their hands in his direction. At Austerlitz station, the train does not move for a long time. And the trip, as Roger remembers it, is very long. The train stops at Pithiviers. The prisoners walk to the camp.

Berthe and Raoul marry the week after. Even if the Berneman and Perelman families have abandoned religious practice, the tradition leaves its prints: a wedding must never be cancelled, even if a relative dies. The ceremony takes place in the 10th district of Paris City Hall. The photographs show how elegant and beautiful the bride and the bridegroom were.

In fact, "the non Jewish population was not concerned. There is no record of this episode in any journal written by a non-Jew," writes Renée Poznanski[7] about those massive arrests. They were invisible.

But the difference between the number of persons that the Germans planned to arrest and the number of those who were really arrested shows that the first actors in this rescue were the Jews themselves. Some of those who went to the police station to be registered do not obey anymore and leave Paris for the free zone. The French population is neither hostile, nor helpful to the Jews, but unconcerned.

The persecution arrived in the life of the Perelmans without their anticipated it. It will never leave them in peace. The month after, just after the creation of the Commissariat aux Questions Juives, the enterprise of Chaskiel Perelman is targeted by the '*aryanisation*'–this savage word is translated from the language of the 3rd Reich to call the transfer of Jewish property to the Aryan people. On June 3rd 1941, the workshop of Chaskiel Perelman, where he works alone, gets a "trustee" whose name is M. L'Herbette, who lives 140 avenue de Paris, in Vincennes, in the near suburb of Paris. On September 25, M. L'Herbette resigns, officially because of health problems. He is replaced on November 22 by M. Lepagnot, who lives at 8, rue Eugène Besançon, in Bois-Colombes, in the western suburb of Paris. But a spelling mistake transforms Perelman into Pekelman in the files. It's under this name that the file is registered at the National Archives.[8]

Around them, in the schools, in their neighborhood, in their relationships with the trustee who, in this case, has almost nothing to direct, and seems rather friendly, no member of the family faces hostility. During this first period of persecution, the French population, as shown all the analysis,[9] is mostly unconcerned by measures taken discreetly, and quite invisible. Everybody is upset by other problems: the million and a half war prisoners, the growing difficulties to find food…

But the family is worried about Roger, who is visited by his relatives in Pithiviers, as seen from a photograph in the family's archives. The camps of Pithiviers and Beaune-la-Rolande, where 3700 Jews are interned, do not belong to the Nazi concentration universe. The men are deprived of liberty, they live in the close proximity to each other, and they do not eat their fill. But they are not victims of abuse, they can read, write letters, organize conferences and even have visitors. It is boredom that drives Roger to volunteer to work in a farm. Because of the number of war prisoners, there are not enough workers available for agriculture. Roger and seven others are sent to the farm of M. Tibout, in Guigneville, near Pithiviers. They are treated right, even if the work is hard for an urban young man. At night, they are locked in a room. A policeman, in charge of their custody, sleeps in the room beside. In the night of August 16th, the eight of them run. The lower officer Delmas, who runs the Pithiviers camp during the day, sends a report to is chief: the policeman "did not notice anything abnormal during the night."[10]

The fugitives reached the closest railway station and took the train to Paris. Then, Roger is sought after. He finds a shelter in Paris, rue Ledru Rollin, in the apartment of an unknown woman who agrees to accommodate him. But he must leave this first hiding place. Roger is badly surprised when the parents of a former school fellow refuse to shelter him. So there is no rule: some accept to help, others refuse. Those refusals can be explained by the fear, by the willingness to go on living quietly, by the fear of accepting one more person when it is more and more difficult to find food. Those behaviors can be explained by others reasons than the hatred against the Jews. Roger goes back to rue Rochechouart and obtains false papers and passes the demarcation line at Orthez. It is the beginning of a long trek to Nice then

Grenoble where he arrives at the end of October 1941. He takes back his true identity and enrolls at the faculty of science.

Of course, since the arrest of Roger and his flight from Pithiviers, disquiet has crept into the heart of the family, insomuch as the prohibitions are increasing and increasing,[11] and as the news of Jews being arrested spreads in the Jewish society of the capital. On August 20,1941, the 11th district has been locked at dawn. The *rafle* will go on the following days in all Paris. Some 4000 Jews, French or foreigners, were sent by bus to La Muette in Drancy, were they were interned in very poor conditions.[12] Once again, the results are much lower than the Nazis projections. On December 12, the Germans arrest 743 Jews who mostly belong to the French elite. They go to the camp of Compiègne-Royallieu.

Despite the multiplication of the arrest, of the departure of the first convoy to Auschwitz, on March 27, 1942, the relationships between the Jews and the French society barely change. It is with the German prescription of May 29, 1942, which imposes in the occupied zone that every Jew aged more than 6 wears the yellow star that the persecution becomes visible to everyone.

The Perelmans, as most Jews, obey this prescription. How could they act differently? Everybody knows they are Jews in their neighborhood. But they do not face any hostile reaction. When Rachel goes to her school rue d'Abbeville, she is treated by her fellows and teachers as on any other day. Chawa decides to be photographed with the star: "They will be ashamed, later," she says. Who are "they"? The Germans, probably. She and Chaskiel dress elegantly, and go to the studio of a professional photographer. They pose proudly, standing side by side. They will not have time to pick up the picture that Chaskiel will retrieve when he will be back in Paris, in the fall of 1944. The photo stays in the family archives.

The yellow star has been imposed to separate the Jews from the others and to label them in order to facilitate their arrest. In fact, it did not generate hostile reactions among the French population. On the contrary, it has shocked, and even scandalized most of the public opinion[13]. The *rafle* of the Vel d'Hiv, in July, followed in August by the arrests in the free zone, will tilt it from indifference to active help.

The Perelmans were warned of the *rafle* by a customer, a Hungarian called Leopold von Starkman. No one knows how Chaskiel met him, and the archives are generally silent about this kind of subject. Maybe by another customer. Anyway, Chaskiel is von Starckman's tailor. Does he also make suits for Germans, as Roger and Rachel's testimonies suggest? For several months, von Starckman and Chawa have acquired materials on the black market. Chawa buys fabric illegally, to supply Chaskiel who cuts and sews.

Just before the *rafle*, Leopold von Starckman informed Chaskiel that this time, the policemen would arrest women and children, too. Many Jews cannot believe this. The Perelmans do. The janitor of the building brings them into an unoccupied maids' room. Then, in a moment of panic, climbs the six floors and asks them to go back to their apartment, which they do. Chawa, who keeps a cool mind says: "We do not open. If they want to come in, they will have to break the door." Then the policemen knock at the door. Once. Twice. The policemen do not insist. They are saved. Nobody, not even the scared janitor, has denounced them. After the alert, M. Tardy, owner of the bar and tobacco shop at the corner of the street, where Chaskiel, a smoker, is a loyal customer, gives them coffee and bread and butter. When they will leave for the free zone, the Perelmans will consign the rest of their fabric to the Nannis, their neighbors, who will give it back to them after the Liberation.

All have avoided the *rafle*. Chaskiel, Chawa and Rachel rue Rochechouart, Raoul and Berthe in the apartment where they have lived since their marriage. At 7, rue Taylor, at the Berneman's parents' home, nobody believed that women and children would be arrested. Only the father, Icek, and Raoul's younger brother, Roger Berneman, born in Paris in 1930, hid. The mother, Michla, born in Kozienio (Opland) in 1901 and her daughter Edka, born in 1923 in Jedlina (Poland), an assistant accountant, are arrested, sent to the Vel d'Hiv then to the camp of Beaune-la-Rolande. They are deported by the convoy of August 5, 1942 and murdered in Auschwitz-Birkenau. Icek and Roger join Raoul in Grenoble. Icek will be arrested and deported by the convoy of January 20, 1943. He will never come back.

The story of the Perelmans and the Bernemans is not an exception. It is emblematic of what happened on July 16 and 17, 1942. The Germans, assisted by the French police, had planned to arrest 30,000 Jews: 13,157 were arrested, mostly women (5902) and children (4051). This failure – half of the number intended – is due to the information leaked form the Prefecture de Police and spread by policemen, civil servants, members of Jewish associations such as Eclaireurs Israélites. And to the ability of the Jews to hide, often thanks to their neighbors. The policemen acted in very different ways. Those in charge of the Perelmans did the minimum, and did not break the door of the apartment.[14] The behavior of the two families is not the same. The Prelmans take the rumor into account. The Berneman do not. It is hard to explain those different behaviors because those two families are very similar: same date of immigration, same profession, same number of children of almost the same age.

On September 31, 1942, F. Lepagnot, provisional trustee, sends a letter to André Lack, head of the section in charge of the clothing industry at the Commissariat aux questions Juives: "I have the honor to inform you that the Jew Perelman Chaskiel, Polish, living 67, rue Rochechouart, whom I had asked to stay on the register of artisans, has just been interned in a concentration camp." The information is not true. But it shows what this Lepagnot imagines happened to Chaskiel. He writes that a "total expulsion is in progress."

On November 21, 1942, Lack answers to Lepagnot: "As the Jew is interned, you can close this enterprise after asking the Organization committee its opinion. When you get this answer, you send it to me and I will give you all the necessary information."

It takes almost one year before the liquidation becomes official. André Lack's presentation of the enterprise is short: "Business without economic interest. No stock, small machines. Buyer's card removed. Cancelled from the register of artisans. The organization Committee agreed to the liquidation. Chaskiel Perelman is still, according to the authorities, "interned in a concentration camp". The last trustee is paid with what was still in the workshop. As Chaskiel Perelman is Polish, 83 francs and 33 centimes are sent to the Treuhand, the German financial agency that receives the money coming from the liquidation of the property of foreign Jews. At an unknown date, by a German order, the scellés will be put on the apartment of the 67 rue Rochechouart. After everything has been removed.

When Chaskiel and his younger daughter, Rachel, come back to Paris, they are lucky enough to retrieve their apartment, which has not been rented to "good faith tenants," as the people called themselves who occupied houses where the former tenants were absents. They do not find any personal papers, any photographs. The past, what existed before, is erased.

As soon as the immediate danger is gone, the family goes away, tries to find a shelter and to organize the path through the demarcation line, to reach the "free zone." As most of Jews, the Perelmans believe that only the foreigners are in danger. So the three of them walk to their friend the Zaks who are French. Their place is tiny. The Perelmans cannot stay. They walk to the house of their friend, the shoemaker Mirski, who has, on the street, a glass enclosed room and an apartment. Chawa, Chaskiel and Rachel stay there for ten days, the time to organize passing over the demarcation line, the time for Mirsky to make fake heels for Chaskiel's shoes, who hides his money in there: 150,000 francs, more than a hundred times the monthly minimum wage, as he will declare to the policeman who will question him at Sassenage on August 13, 1942. Having money is very important to survive. They plan to reach Grenoble. They decide to pass in two groups: Chaskiel, Berthe and Raoul first. Then Chawa and Rachel. They will meet in Lyon, avenue Félix Faure at their friends Blattmann, upper class people who rent a nice apartment.

"The facilitators were more than happy. The price of the pass had been multiplied by twelve to twenty," writes Renée Poznanski.[15] For the Perelman were not the only ones to try to flea the occupied zone. The *rafle* of the Vel d'Hiv generating a huge migration of Jews to the "free zone", and of a strengthening of the controls of the French and German police along the demarcation line. According to Chaskiel's testimony, the cost of the pass was 500 francs.

Chaskiel, disguised as a French worker, and Berthe and Raoul took the train at the Gare de Lyon to Chalon-sur-Saône, with a passman who took them to a nearby village, then disappeared. With other fugitive Jews, they tried to pass the line, got lost, then met a biker who helped them to pass and definitely refused the money they proposed.

Then it was Chawa and Rachel's turn. They leave Paris with a couple of young people who were not Jew but simply wanted to visit their grandmother in the free zone, and a Jewish couple. They were supposed to pass the line at Saint-Jean-des-Vignes, near Chalon-sur-Saône. The Germans saws their boat and shot. The boat returned. Rachel and the young persons swam to the free shore. Chawa and the Jewish couple sank. Her body was found. The death certificate indicates that Chawa died on July 29th at 4:30 PM. She was buried at the cemetery of Saint-Jean-des-Vignes without anybody at the burial.

The passman reimbursed Rachel. The two young persons took charge of her. She joined her father, Berthe and Raoul in Lyon.

The survivors of the family joined Roger in Grenoble. They lived in the city or in nearby neighborhoods; Sassenage, Fontaine, Domiane, Saint-Martin-d'Hère... In the beginning, they lived under their own identity: the archives of the province of Isère keeps tracks of those who were foreigners –all of them except Rachel, born in France. Roger answered to an order to join the foreign workers group of Uriage. He was locked up there. So he understood that he was in danger, even if he could not identify how. He escaped, choosing the moment when the custodians were inattentive. He jumped on the iron fence, got back to Grenoble by tramway. First, he hid at his father's, who lived in Domaine, then he reached Nice. The city, like Grenoble, was occupied by the Italians. After the armistice of "Badoglio," in September 1943, and the occupation of the whole French territory by the Germans, Chaskiel and Rachel obtained false papers. Under this false identity, they could survive unmolested.

Roger went back to Nice. Once again, he registered as Jewish in a census, as if he had learnt nothing of the two former arrests. He made a living teaching math in a private school where he was, for a short while, the director. When the Germans occupied Nice, after the armistice of Badoglio and the withdrawal of the Italian troops, hunting of Jews began. Roger took the false identity of Perrier, and went on teaching. In mid-October, after he was denounced, Gestapo policemen waited for him in the room he rented. He was arrested, brutally interrogated at Hotel Hermitage, the headquarters of the Gestapo, sent to Drancy and deported to the Auschwitz camps by the convoy of October 28, 1943. He was sent to the Janina mine, a few miles away from Auschwitz, which worked for IG Farben, For 18 months, hardly dressed, hardly fed, he went down to the bottom of the mine. He attributes his survival to the poverty of his childhood, when he had to face hunger and coldness, to his healthy body and to luck. And also to the fact that he never allowed himself to think about the past and was very eager to know all this story would end. He was one of the 2500 survivors among the 76,000 Jews deported in France.

Those destinies cannot tell everything about the story of the Jews in France. But they are emblematic. On one side, the German Nazis and the French State cooperated to persecute and to deport. One the other side, the people who, despite this persecution, show initiative to escape the trap as they understand the danger. Understanding and practical intelligence were not always enough to escape arrest and deportation. These Jewish people, in France, were, contrary to those of Poland, a very small minority: 0.5 % of the French population. They can spread and avoid persecution, as did the Perelmans. They can blend into a French society that was universally helpful.

Notes

1 The radical spoliation of Jews' homes in France, Belgium and Netherlands
2 Those informations come from private archives of the Perelman and Berneman that belong to me, from several interviews realized in 2012 and 2013 with Rachel Prelman, form Roger Perelman's autobiography, *The Life of an unimportant Jew*, Robert Laffont, 2008.
3 Henri Béraud (1885-1958) was a famous journalist who joined the extreme right newspapers in February 1934. He was sentenced to death in 1944 for collaborating and was pardoned.
4 Main d'œuvre Immigrée ou MOI. Cf Annette Wieviorka, , *Ils étaient juifs, résistants, communistes*, Denoël, 1985.
5 Poznanski, *Etre juif en France pendant la Seconde Guerre mondiale*, Hachette, p. 55.
6 Roger Perelman, *op.cit.*p. 98.
7 Renée Poznanski, *op.cit.*, p. 104.
8 AN, AJ38/18673.
9 See, among others, Pierre Laborie, *L'opinion française sous Vichy*, Seuil, 1990.
10 AD Loiret, 45/Cercil.
11 That is what Edgar Faure calls a the Nuremberg trial « the time of decrees ». Their list (more than 200) is compiled in dans *Les Juifs sous l'Occupation. Recueil des textes officiels français et allemands*, Editions du Centre, 1945.
12 See Annette Wieviorka et Michel Laffitte, À l'intérieur du camp de Drancy, Perrin, 2012.
13 See Poznanski, op.cit., p. 357-362.
14 On the preparation and realization of the rafle, see Serge Klarsfeld, *Le calendrier de persécution des Juifs de France, juillet 1940- août 1942*, Fayard, 2001.
15 Renée Poznanski, op. cit., p. 399.

Washington:
Focused on winning the war

Richard Breitman

The Holocaust was an unprecedented catastrophe. Everyone who studies it hopes to learn from it, but clear lessons are often difficult to find. This essay highlights the political contributions of some key Americans (without any claim to be comprehensive) who helped to save lives. American Jewish leaders and some non-Jews concerned about the Holocaust debated priorities and strategies for moving the government to act. Still sensitive among American Jews, this chapter of history may have some bearing on current and future humanitarian crises.

During the two years before World War II American Jewish organizations and most Jewish politicians approved of recent changes in American immigration policy tailored to the refugee crisis in Europe. President Franklin Delano Roosevelt used his executive powers to loosen immigration regulations for those seeking exit from Germany and Austria. If immigration law (quotas) set upper limits to the numbers admissible to the United States and Congress opposed any expansion, the Roosevelt administration used the full quotas and stretched them a bit. Administration officials, diplomats, and special envoys also pressed for Germany to allow Jews and other victims of persecution to leave, and they urged other countries to admit more of them. FDR put particular pressure on Britain to allow more Jews into Palestine, and on Latin American countries to accept Jewish immigrants.[1]

The war transformed American government policies and the political climate. Nazi Germany's military takeover of Norway, the Low Countries, and especially the bewilderingly rapid and thorough defeat of France convinced many that Nazi espionage, combined with propaganda, had eaten away resistance in these countries; a Nazi "Fifth Column" was at work there and had spread to the United States. American sympathy for Nazi victims diminished sharply: Nazi victories and American fears of a Fifth Column turned refugees into potential Nazi agents.[2] Anti-Semites were quite willing (and eager) to believe Jews spied for Germany out of pure greed, while others feared that Germany was forcing refugees to cooperate through threats against their relatives caught at home.[3] The popular level of fear and mistrust of aliens may be compared with that after September 11, 2001.

In this climate all the liberal American initiatives of 1937-1939 vanished. New State Department regulations and a bureaucratic labyrinth screened out most of those who were able to emerge or escape from Axis territories. Would-be immigrants had once benefited from American relatives or friends supplying affidavits of support to vouch for them financially, but now even well-connected applicants found it impossible to surmount security-related "paper walls." Among those who failed to gain entry, we learned more than five years ago, were the members of Anne Frank's family.[4]

Politics also played a role in the shift. Once President Roosevelt decided to run for an unprecedented third term, he could ill afford cases of refugee spies or Nazi agents passing for Jewish refugees. Republican critics and some Southern Democrats already regarded him and his administration as overly dependent on Jewish influence. Well after his 1940 re-election, such criticism continued. In a speech at Des Moines, Iowa, on September 11, 1941 isolationist leader Charles Lindbergh charged the British and Jewish races with trying to push America into war "for reasons which are not American." Jews allegedly endangered America, Lindbergh claimed, through their influence in Hollywood, the press, radio, and government.[5] Many Americans debated whether the United States should enter the war.

After Germany invaded the Soviet Union, the Soviet military situation was dire, and most Western observers expected a quick German victory. Nazi officials used the cover of war to veil their programs of genocide in the East. Nonetheless, some information about mass killings leaked to the West. In the fall of 1941 mainstream American newspapers covered escalating Nazi atrocities against Jews with headlines such as "Death Rate Soars in Polish Ghettoes" (*New York Times*, September 14); "New Anti-Jewish Drive Seen," (*New York Times*, October 5); "200 Jews Kill Selves Over Nazi Order to Wear a Star," (*Chicago Tribune*, October 13,); "Berlin is Swept by New Wave of Anti-Semitism" (*Chicago Tribune*, October 16); "Nazis Will Move Jews to Poland," (*Washington Post*, October 19); "German Atrocities," (*Washington Post*, October 24), and "Nazis Seek to Rid Europe of All Jews," (*New York*

Times, October 28). Whatever the American press failed to report or emphasize later, it captured clues about the first phase of what soon became a continent-wide Nazi campaign for exterminating Jews.[6]

At the end of October 1941, *Congress Weekly*, an organ of the American Jewish Congress, dramatically announced: "From Kovno in the North to Odessa in the South, a wave of outright slaughter, mass deportations and incarceration of Jews in concentration camps...." *Congress Weekly* noted that the general British and American press as well as Jewish newspapers had reported the deportation of 15,000 Hungarian and Galician Jews from Hungary to Ukraine, where they were murdered in cold blood, as well as many other killings. The unnamed author wondered how President Franklin Roosevelt and Prime Minister Winston Churchill could condemn Nazi reprisal killings of a hundred hostages in Nantes and Bordeaux and remain silent about these much larger crimes? The author then supplied his own answer, even if he rejected its validity: "Condemnation of Nazi atrocities in France are a weapon against isolationism... [but] condemnation of the atrocities against Jews would add fuel to the isolationist propaganda that the war against Hitler is a 'Jewish war.'" The general secretary of the Jewish National Workers' Alliance sent a copy of this editorial to presidential Press Secretary Stephen Early, calling for FDR to speak out on behalf of millions of suffering Jews. But until 1944 the president did not do so.[7]

After Pearl Harbor and the German declaration of war against the United States, America entered the war with overwhelming public support. The Roosevelt administration had determined that Germany represented a greater threat than Japan and decided to give the war in Europe priority over the Pacific. Still, the Allies lacked the capacity to invade or seriously threaten Axis territory in Europe. The only short-term prospect for weakening Germany was psychological warfare designed to drive a wedge between the Nazi regime and the German public. Public opinion experts hoped to avoid publicity about the fate of European Jews, since the German public was saturated with Nazi anti-Semitism. Nazi propaganda was even more strident than American isolationists in blaming the war on international Jewry. A government committee on war information policy discouraged the use of atrocity material at home as well unless it directly illuminated the nature of the enemy. In the eyes of American officials, Nazism was a threat to all humanity, not simply to the Jews. The U.S. government's most ambitious domestic propaganda initiative, the documentary film series *Why We Fight*, illustrates the official skittishness: released from 1942 to 1945, it barely touched upon Nazi killings of Jews.[8]

One advocate of loud public protest against what the Nazis called the Final Solution was a young Palestinian Jew, Hillel Kook, a Revisionist Zionist who came to the U.S. in 1940 and took the name Peter Bergson. At first, Bergson tried to use newspaper advertisements to raise American support for a Jewish army in Palestine. He wanted American pressure on Britain to mobilize Palestine's Jews in case German forces reached Palestine. David Ben-Gurion, chairman of the Jewish Agency Executive, and Chaim Weizmann, also wanted Britain to arm more Jews in Palestine, but operated without Bergson's public, anti-British clamor: they tried lobbying with key American officials, including FDR (who met with Weizmann). British authorities, worried about Arab loyalties and the attitudes of its own Moslem troops, declined to raise anything more than a Jewish brigade, and American military officials backed the British view. So did *New York Times* publisher Arthur Hays Sulzberger, who publicly denounced agitation for a Jewish army as dangerous to the Allied cause.[9]

By mid-1942, the government and a number of American Jewish organizations had moved apart. Government officials focused exclusively on the war and the general threat of Nazism. Jewish organizations were increasingly distressed about much larger incidents of mass murder of Jews in Eastern Europe and the Nazi threat to Jews in Palestine. On June 16, even the *New York Times* reported that Nazis had murdered 60,000 Jews in Vilna, Lithuania, although the story noted that accounts of the massacre from an eyewitness refugee could not be confirmed. Sources associated with the Polish-Jewish Bund, which was allied with the Jewish Labor Committee in the U.S., estimated Nazi murder and brutality had claimed the lives of 700,000 Polish Jews by the spring of 1942. The sources said that the Nazis had deployed mobile gas chambers in Poland to exterminate Jews systematically. Bund leaders called for reprisals against Germans living in Allied countries as the only way to save "millions of Jews from certain destruction." The *New York Times*, first in a brief notice on June 27 and then in a full page 6 story on July 2, carried this report with no qualifications. The mainstream press also widely covered a World Jewish Congress estimate in late June 1942 that the Nazis had killed more than a million Jews since 1939.[10]

On July 21, 1942 the American Jewish Congress, B'nai B'rith, and the Jewish Labor Committee drew 20,000 people to a rally in Madison Square

Garden to protest Nazi atrocities. Roosevelt sent a delicately worded statement for the organizers to read. He hailed the determination of the Jewish people to make every sacrifice for Allied victory. He said that Americans of all faiths shared in the sorrow of Jewish fellow citizens over Nazi savagery against helpless victims. The Nazis would not succeed, he pledged, in "exterminating their victims any more than they will succeed in enslaving mankind." This may have been the president's first public mention of Jews as Nazi victims, but he did so in a way that linked them to the general threat. He (and Prime Minister Churchill) offered only the Allied threat to punish Nazi war criminals at the end of the war as a deterrent.[11]

Critical information about the Holocaust emerged from Europe in the late summer and fall of 1942. World Jewish Congress and Agudath Israel sources in New York each received independent reports of a continuing Nazi effort to eliminate Jews in Nazi-occupied Poland. The most accurate (and most famous) report came in a telegram from Gerhart M. Riegner, representative of the World Jewish Congress in Switzerland: he had learned about Nazi use of poison gas based on prussic acid and the Nazi intention to exterminate 3.5 to 4 million Jews. A flurry of meetings within Jewish organizations and among different organizations produced ideas such as an appeal to the Nazi regime to stop the killing; an appeal to neutral countries to intercede with Germany; and a threat to take reprisals against Germans in the U.S. Even if there had been a consensus, none of these ideas had much prospect of success with the American government, let alone with the Nazi regime. Rabbi Stephen S. Wise, head of the American Jewish Congress, brought Riegner's telegram to the attention of Undersecretary of State Sumner Welles, who launched an investigation and asked Wise to avoid publicity for the time being. This investigation dragged on until late November. Once Welles told Wise that it confirmed his deepest fears, Wise immediately called a press conference and got substantial (if inadequate) coverage of the story.[12]

Clearer evidence of Nazi intentions changed the political dynamics in a number of ways. Wise and several other Jewish representatives were able to meet at the White House with FDR on December 8: that meeting, along with efforts by the Polish underground courier Jan Karski in London, led directly to an inter-Allied government statement on December 17 denouncing the Nazi plan to exterminate the Jews of Europe, which received greater publicity.[13] Equally important, the news reports and an official Allied statement mobilized a larger portion of the Jewish communities to get involved. They also gained some political support. As reports of the Final Solution circulated through Washington, 63 senators and 181 members of the House of Representatives signed a resolution drafted by Senator Robert F. Wagner of New York reaffirming their support for a Jewish homeland in Palestine.[14] In a sense, it was a significant gesture of sympathy, but it promised no action during the war. In fact, it avoided the most immediate problem – what could be done, if anything, in Europe without any military options?

While the British and American governments began to organize a confidential conference on refugee problems in Bermuda for mid-April 1943 in order to show some kind of government activity, American Jewish organizations mobilized. Jewish leaders proposed that the Allies guarantee financial support for all refugees who escaped to Turkey, Sweden, Switzerland, Spain, and Portugal. Britain could admit any who reached the British Isles. The United States could house refugees in some place such as the Virgin Islands for the duration of the war. The American Jewish Congress, in cooperation with non-Jewish organizations, organized a March 1 rally in Madison Square Garden and attracted an overflow crowd, which heard speaker after speaker plead for support to "stop Hitler now." A wide range of Jewish organizations – Zionist and non-Zionist – then formed a Joint Emergency Committee on European Jewish Affairs to strengthen their reach toward such goals. But the Joint Distribution Committee and the United Palestine Appeal sent representatives only as observers in order to avoid participating in any political goals – a sign of skittishness. Some of the mainstream organizations hoped to "educate" Allied governments; others did not mind challenging them. Even where there was agreement on goals, there were differences on means and traditional organizational rivalries.[15]

Because of its confrontational style and its advertising and fundraising techniques, the independent Bergson group aroused strong feelings – positive and negative. After reading of the evidence of the Final Solution, Bergson dropped his demand for a Jewish army in Palestine and recast his organization into the Emergency Committee to Save the Jewish People in Europe, which gained some non-Jewish backing. Bergson's organization planned its own rally for Madison Square Garden, an event cast as a memorial service or pageant called "We Will Never Die." With his knack for securing celebrity assistance, Bergson persuaded playwright Ben Hecht to write the script and composer Kurt Weill to arrange the score. The pageant filled the Garden twice in a single day and then began a tour of other cities, including Washington, D.C, where Eleanor Roosevelt, and some members of the Supreme Court and Congress attended.[16]

Bergson's committee also advertised in newspapers that the Romanian government would release Jews in return for a payment of $50 per person. Zionist leaders such as Rabbi Wise denounced as misleading and unethical appeals for donations to pay for the release of 70,000 Jews deported to Romanian-occupied Transnistria. In fact, Bergson exaggerated. Romanian intermediaries wanted more money, the Romanian government did not guarantee release of the Jews, and Germany firmly opposed Romanian plans to allow some Jewish emigration. The scheme also required the United States to repudiate its economic restrictions against financial transactions with an enemy nation and to overcome its resistance to paying ransom. Few American citizens wanted to risk violating American economic restrictions against sending funds into Axis countries when they hoped to persuade or induce the government to do more to encourage rescue or supply relief.[17]

In spite of growing awareness of the Final Solution both the American and the British governments remained focused on winning the war. Both the State Department and the Foreign Office tended to see problems with humanitarian proposals or even neutral government suggestions, rather than opportunities to save lives, which explains why only tiny proposals emerged from the April 1943 Bermuda Conference on Refugees. In a May 1943 speech in Boston Assistant Secretary of State Adolf A. Berle, by no means the least humanitarian State Department official, declared that Germany had organized a program of national murder and coerced its allies to take part, a campaign that was unique in modern Western history. But "nothing can be done to save these helpless unfortunates except through the invasion of Europe, the defeat of the German arms, and the breaking of German power. There is no other way."[18]

But there were some plausible prospects for saving lives. In April 1943 Sweden offered to try to persuade Germany to release Jews without ransom payments. The Swedish cabinet approved a proposal to take in 20,000 Jewish children if the Allies paid to maintain them and guaranteed their removal at war's end. (Some Jews had already escaped Denmark and arrived in Sweden, which had allowed them to stay.) Sweden thought these proposals might impress officials in London and Washington, but neither government offered the required guarantees.[19]

By the second half of 1943 more information about Nazi extermination camps began to filter into the general press, with some effect on media
opinion-makers. Although the *New York Times* lagged in its coverage of the
subject, other voices appeared loud and clear. Syndicated columnist Samuel
Grafton, associate editor of the *New York Post*, wrote a scathing critique of
contradictions in the Allied response to the Nazi slaughter of Jews. When
the Nazis gassed Jews in "execution caravans" in Poland, the world considered them a special problem, and Allied warnings to the Nazis against poison
gas warfare did not apply. When the Allies considered rescue, however, they
considered Jews as part of a general problem of civilian suffering, for which
the only real solution was military victory. The first step toward breaking this
mindset was to put an independent agency in charge of determining feasible
forms of rescue, Grafton wrote.[20]

Oscar Cox, a well-connected government official (then in the Foreign
Economic Administration), had recently begun to push a draft proposal to
establish an independent American board, headed by high officials, to deal
with all aspects of the war refugee problem not the direct responsibility of
the State Department. Cox's move implied that the State Department was
mishandling relief and rescue of Holocaust victims, something that he said
more or less explicitly later. It appears that Cox also had direct access to the
President or to someone who knew FDR's views. It helped politically that
Cox was a Catholic who had ties with both mainstream Jewish leaders and
with Bergson's group.[21]

One specific point of disagreement among Jewish organizations, however,
was over Palestine. Many of the mainstream Jewish organizations had committed themselves to Jewish homeland in Palestine; therefore, they wanted
Palestine available for refugees who could escape from Europe. That would
undercut the argument that there was no place for substantial numbers of
European Jews to go, and it would advance their ultimate cause. When another effort at Jewish unity called the American Jewish Conference endorsed
the establishment of a Jewish "commonwealth" in Palestine, two important
non-Zionist organizations – the American Jewish Committee and the Jewish Labor Committee – pulled out.[22]

Wise relied on a direct meeting with FDR and lobbying with high Jewish officials such as Treasury Secretary Morgenthau and White House ad-
viser and speechwriter Samuel Rosenman. Wise had to wage two separate
– if related – battles. The first was to get government approval of World Jew-

ish Congress plans to arrange for food and medicine to reach Jews in such countries as Romania and France without sending in funds violating Allied economic restrictions. The second was to ward off American endorsement of British policies in Palestine and even an Anglo-American statement that Zionist agitation had dangerous military repercussions. He had some success in both areas – calling the president's attention to the possibilities of relief and as well to the dangers of the proposed Anglo-American statement on Palestine--only to find that the State Department and the British threw up further roadblocks to relief measures.[23]

Bergson, the one-time agitator for a Jewish army in Palestine, concluded that relatively few Jews could reach Palestine and debate about Palestine might get in the way of rescue in Europe. He put his efforts elsewhere into mobilizing support in Congress for rescue. Even a determined minority there could block action on anything controversial. But Bergson at least made inroads in Congress with the introduction of a proposed (non-binding) resolution, sponsored by Senator Guy Gillette of Iowa and Representative Will Rogers, Jr. of California, urging the president to establish a rescue commission.[24]

Bergson found a way to up public pressure in October, striking an unusual alliance with the Orthodox Jewish rescue organization Vaad ha-Hatzala. Defying fears about stoking anti-Semitism, about 450 Orthodox rabbis marched to the Capitol and the White House delivering a petition calling for quick rescue action, the establishment of a rescue agency, and the opening of Palestine to Jewish immigration. Declining to meet with them, the President found a military event to attend. Bergson's allies also stepped up activities in Congress, forcing the State Department to counter with late November testimony by Assistant Secretary of State Breckinridge Long. In a confidential session of the House Foreign Affairs Committee Long read prepared testimony that inflated the numbers of refugees admitted to the U.S. since 1933 by at least 250%. When, on December 10, the committee decided to release Long's remarks in order to dampen criticism of the State Department, Long instead suffered a public relations disaster when his error became known.[25]

By that time, Morgenthau and his mostly non-Jewish subordinates had discovered worse problems. The American ambassador to Britain related that the British Foreign Office opposed World Jewish Congress proposals because of "the difficulties of disposing of any considerable number of

Jews should they be rescued from enemy-occupied territory..." The Treasury group also uncovered evidence that State Department officials had tried to stifle the flow of information about the Holocaust from Switzerland. In a showdown meeting with Secretary of State Hull and Long, Morgenthau as much as accused Long of being anti-Semitic. Hull found it necessary to break the common front with the British, but it was too late: Morgenthau now backed the establishment of a refugee agency.

Treasury official Josiah DuBois, Jr. spent much of Christmas drafting a report "on the acquiescence of this government in the murder of the Jews." He warned that Long had deliberately created a bottleneck for issuing visas to the United States. He related how other State Department officials had tried to suppress information from Switzerland about Nazi killings of Jews – and then sought to cover up what they had done. He warned that without drastic changes in American policies, the U.S. would have to share responsibility for Nazi extermination. Privately, DuBois warned Morgenthau that if the President did nothing, he would resign and take his case to the press.

Only Morgenthau had sufficient weight to persuade FDR to break cleanly with British policies toward the Jewish question in Europe. At a meeting in the White House on January 16, Morgenthau, Randolph Paul, and John Pehle summarized the report DuBois had written: Morgenthau had toned down its title to Personal Report to the President. When Roosevelt admitted that Long had soured on refugees as security risks, Morgenthau reminded the President that according to Attorney General Francis Biddle, only three Jews admitted to the U.S. during the war presented any security issues. If FDR did not act, Congress might. The President needed little persuading, quickly approving the concept of a War Refugee Board, along with an executive order that Cox had drafted establishing it.[26]

Although a comprehensive history of the War Refugee Board remains to be written, several works have devoted chapters to the Board's efforts to save lives of civilian victims of the Nazis during the last seventeen months of the war. One of David S. Wyman's chapters is entitled "Little and Late," a judgment supported in part by his next chapter detailing the Board's unsuccessful efforts to persuade the War Department to order the bombing of gas chambers and crematoria at Auschwitz. Wyman believed that such a bombing might have forced the Nazis to reconsider their policies of mass murder.[27] Although the specialists still debate the merits and feasibility of bombing

Auschwitz, few would agree that such bombing would have forced Hitler to change course.[28]

Calculations of how many people the War Refugee Board helped to save vary widely. American warnings, orchestrated by War Refugee Board officials, to the Hungarian government not to allow deportation of Hungarian Jews, were among the reasons the Horthy regime decided, in early July 1944, to suspend deportations, giving the Jews of Budapest a three-month respite. During that time, Raoul Wallenberg, Carl Lutz, and others were able to distribute protective papers and otherwise shelter tens of thousands of Jews in Budapest. More than 75,000 others there survived, simply because late 1944 killings by Nazi squads and Arrow Cross thugs were less efficient than the deportations. If those 75,000 are counted, altogether, the War Refugee Board may have helped as many as 200,000 people survive.[29]

Sweden gave Wallenberg a diplomatic appointment and sent him to Budapest with conservative instructions. The War Refugee Board encouraged him to go and to pursue humanitarian goals aggressively. It also gave him resources with which to operate and followed his reports carefully. In his last communication to Wallenberg, sent via the American Legation in Stockholm on December 8, 1944, War Refugee Board Director John Pehle struck a balance of successes and failure:

> We have followed with keen interest the reports of the steps you have taken... and the personal devotion which you have given to saving and protecting the innocent victims of Nazi persecution.... I think that no one who has participated in this great task can escape some feeling of frustration [that] our efforts have not met with complete success.... [Yet] it is our conviction that you have made a very great personal contribution to the success which has been realized in these endeavors.[30]

Arrested by the Soviets, Wallenberg undoubtedly never got this message.

Most perpetrator regimes and organizations have taken time to prepare for genocide. There were obvious advance warning signs of the Holocaust, such as *Kristallnacht*. Some people in the West saw disaster looming in Central Europe. But because the scale of Nazi killing was not yet large and there were many other forms of persecution elsewhere, relatively few people committed themselves to extracting and resettling potential Nazi victims. Getting any kind of political consensus for American governmental action was extremely difficult. Individual initiatives – inside and outside of government – mattered. It was easier to save Jews before World War II and during the early part of the war than after the Holocaust began – however one dates the start of it.

Information about the Holocaust quickly began to leak out, but the scale and magnitude of the military conflict dwarfed humanitarian concerns for most Americans. To promote humanitarian intervention in the midst of an all-out war with the survival of Western civilization at stake was an uphill battle for Jewish organizations and individuals. The time spent fighting each other could not have helped their causes.

It was also much easier for the Nazis and their allies to kill than it was for outsiders far away to save. Despite these obstacles, the United States established a War Refugee Board that managed to help save perhaps as many as 200,000 people. There was no substitute for a dedicated agency – whether public or private--intensely committed to a humanitarian effort. Despite the delay in response to news of the Holocaust, from a humanitarian perspective, what happened late in World War II was more impressive than what the United States did in late twentieth century cases of genocide, where knowledge of crimes was clearer and military options abounded.

Notes

1 Richard Breitman and Allan J. Lichtman, *FDR and the Jews* (Cambridge: Belknap Press, 2013), 98-141.
2 Francis MacDonnell, *Insidious Foes: The Axis Fifth Column and the American Home Front* (New York: Oxford University Press, 1995).
3 Breitman and Lichtman, *FDR and the Jews*, 167-170.
4 David S. Wyman, *Paper Walls: America and the Refugee Crisis, 1938-1941* (New York: Pantheon, 1985). Richard Breitman, "Blocked by National Security Fears," http://www.yivoinstitute.org/index.php?tid=154&aid=402
5 "Flyer Names War Groups," *Los Angeles Times*, 12 September 1941, p. 3.
6 Breitman and Lichtman, *FDR and the Jews*, 194.
7 Breitman and Lichtman, *FDR and the Jews*, 195-196.
8 Michaela Hoenicke Moore, *Know Your Enemy: The American Debate on Nazism, 1933-1945* (New York: Cambridge University Press, 2010), 152-153. Jeffrey Herf, *The Jewish Enemy: Nazi Propaganda During World War II and the Holocaust* (Cambridge: Belknap Press, 2008). Richard Breitman and Alan M. Kraut, *American Refugee Policy and European Jewry, 1933-1945* (Bloomington: Indiana University Press, 1987), 171-172. Michael P. Rogin and Kathleen Moran, "Mr. Capra Goes to Washington," *Representations* (fall 2003): 241.
9 Breitman and Lichtman, *FDR and the Jews*, 243-244.

10 Breitman and Lichtman, *FDR and the Jews*, 196.

11 "Nazi Punishment Seen by Roosevelt," *New York Times*, 22 July 1942, p. 1.

12 Walter Laqueur, *The Terrible Secret: Suppression of the Truth About Hitler's 'Final Solution'"* (New York: Holt Paperbacks, 1998). Walter Laqueur and Richard Breitman, *Breaking the Silence* (Hanover, N.H.: University Press of New England, 1994), esp. 143-163. Breitman and Lichtman, *FDR and the Jews*, 199-205.

13 Richard Breitman, *Official Secrets: What the Nazis Planned; What the British and Americans Knew* (New York: Hill and Wang, 1998), 144-154.

14 "Senate, House Join Palestine Plea," *New York Times*, 5 December 1942, p. 9.

15 Rabbi Stephen S. Wise to Rabbi Morton Berman, 15 February 1943, Stephen S. Wise Papers, reel 74-66, American Jewish Historical Society, New York, New York. "Save Doomed Jews, Huge Rally Pleads," *New York Times*, 2 March 1943, p. 1. Participating members of the Joint Emergency Committee were the American Jewish Committee, the American Jewish Congress, B'nai B'rith, the Jewish Labor Committee, the Synagogue Council of America, Agudath Israel, the Union of Orthodox Rabbis of the United States and Canada, and the American Emergency Committee for Zionist Affairs.

16 See the interviews with Bergson in "Not Idly By: Peter Bergson, America, and the Holocaust," 2012 film directed by Pierre Sauvage. Favorable works on Bergson's organizations include David S. Wyman and Rafael Medoff, *A Race Against Death: Peter Bergson, America, and the Holocaust* (New York: New Press, 2002); Judith Tydor Baumel, *The "Bergson Boys" and the Origins of Contemporary Zionist Militancy* (Syracuse: Syracuse University Press, 2005), espec. 116-119.

17 David S. Wyman, *The Abandonment of the Jews: America and the Holocaust, 1941-1945* (New York: Pantheon, 1984), 82-87. Wise to John Haynes Holmes, 22 March 1943, Wise Papers, reel 74-40, American Jewish Historical Society. Breitman and Kraut, *American Refugee Policy*, 185.

18 Breitman, *Official Secrets*, 186-87.

19 Breitman, *Official Secrets*, 183-185.

20 On the problems and coverage at the *New York Times*, see Laurel Leff, *Buried by the Times: The Holocaust and America's Most Important Newspaper* (New York: Cambridge University Press, 2006). On Grafton, Breitman and Lichtman, *FDR and the Jews*, 231.

21 Breitman and Lichtman, *FDR and the Jews*, 226, 228, 233-234.

22 Wyman, *Abandonment of the Jews*, 161-169. Henry L. Feingold, *Bearing Witness: How America and Its Jews Responded to the Holocaust* (Syracuse: Syracuse University Press, 1995), 220.

23 Breitman and Lichtman, *FDR and the Jews*, 227, 252-254.

24 Wyman, *Abandonment of the Jews*, 193-202.

25 For the latest version of now well-known events, Breitman and Lichtman, *FDR and the Jews*, 229-232.

26 Breitman and Lichtman, *FDR and the Jews*, 234-235.

27 Wyman, *Abandonment of the Jews*, 255-307, 335: judgment on the bombing's effect on the Nazis on 304.

28 The best collection of views regarding the bombing proposals and possibilities is *The Bombing of Auschwitz: Should the Allies Have Attempted It?*, eds. Michael J. Neufeld and Michael Berenbaum (New York: St. Martin's Press, 2000). But many articles have appeared in journals since then.

29 Breitman and Lichtman, *FDR and the Jews*, 290-294.

30 Breitman and Lichtman, *FDR and the Jews*, 288-291. Paul Levine, *Raoul Wallenberg in Budapest: Myth, History, and Holocaust* (London: Valentine Mitchell, 2010), 318.

London: The Holocaust, war and occupation in Western Europe*

Bob Moore

It comes as a great surprise to contemporary students when they discover how little attention was paid to the Holocaust in both national and international histories of the Second World War before the 1970s. Prior to this, the primary focus had been on the military aspects of the war and the civil dimension was framed by the paradigms of resistance and collaboration. The subsequent shift towards social history, in Western Europe at least, has led to a more nuanced analysis of how societies reacted to occupation and away from the simplistic resistance myths and narratives that had helped to bolster national cohesion and social reconstruction in the immediate postwar years. The comforting black and white image of a largely resistant population, with only a few clearly defined – and suitably punished and purged – collaborators was gradually replaced by approaches that gave greater weight to the shades of grey involved.[1]

Perhaps the most remarkable change in national historiographies on the Nazi occupation has been the increasing presence of the persecution of the Jews in both the narrative and also the wider analyses of societies under Nazi rule. Indeed, in recent times, it has become almost impossible to discuss the role of any state, religious or private institution during the occupation without some reference – and often quite extensive reference – to antisemitism and the fate of the Jews.[2] This has been paralleled by an increasing number of national and local studies on the persecution itself, as well as a much smaller number of overarching syntheses following in the magisterial footsteps of Raul Hilberg's *The Destruction of the European Jews*.[3] In some respects, this increasing attention should not surprise us. Hilberg listed the Jewish victims from each occupied country in 1961 but it was only when these were translated into percentages of the total Jewish populations that the huge discrepancies in mortality rates between countries became readily apparent.

This began the scholarly exploration for causation, and ultimately gave rise to the victims, perpetrators and bystanders/circumstances model that has informed so much subsequent research. This 'discovery' was particularly pertinent – and damaging – for the self-image of Netherlands in that the 75% mortality of its Jewish community was more comparable with the totals for Poland, where conditions were acknowledged to have been very much worse, and bore little relationship to those of neighboring Belgium (40%) or France (25%).[4] Given this disproportionately high Jewish mortality, it is perhaps not surprising to find that Dutch scholars have been in the forefront of continuing this comparative approach to investigate this apparent anomaly.[5] However, two other pioneers in this field, Robert Paxton and Michael Marrus, were forced to conclude that any generalizations broke apart on the 'stubborn particularities of each of [their] countries'.[6] Their comments were not intended to stifle future work, but nonetheless highlighted the problems involved – namely the vast array of changing circumstances and situations that existed within each national case study and how difficult it was to define a national picture, let alone draw parallels across national frontiers. Latterly it has been argued that even national case studies may be too diverse to provide all the answers and that regional or even local models might be more instructive.[7]

From being marginal to the history of the Second World War, the deportation of the Jews has now become center stage, at least in Western European historiography, and it is impossible for studies of the occupation period not to have a section or sections of their work dealing with this subject. It begs the question of whether this reflects the importance it held for the population at the time, or a measure of the cultural importance that the Holocaust is now perceived to have in Western society? Writing in the 1960s, the official historian of the Netherlands in the Second World War, Lou de Jong, was careful to warn against such myopia. In discussing Dutch pre-war policy on refugees, he noted that while historians might concentrate on one topic and make judgments, the reality for the actors involved was that they had perhaps hundreds of issues to consider.[8] This same maxim might equally inform the studies of the Holocaust that make assessments of how visible and how important the persecution of the Jews really was to the rest of the population? Although these observations were often made many years ago, they nonetheless suggest that it is high time that scholars re-evaluate the persecution of the Jews within the wider national and international histories of the Second World War, and specifically where it fits into the social history of Nazi occupation. What therefore follows are some observations based on a study of gentile 'rescuers' and Jewish self-help in Western Europe and how these might inform a better integration of the Holocaust into the wider history of the occupation period.

There has been a tendency in national historiographies to see the occupation period from 1940-1944/5 as a *caesura*, and thus separate from the longer run social and political history of the country concerned. This undoubtedly had advantages in allowing the occupation period to be written off as an aberration, but this exclusive concentration can mask a number of other issues that ought at least to be considered as part of the analysis and thus inform an understanding of the topic as a whole. For example, it would be difficult to understand the Jewish communities' reaction to persecution without some reference to their pre-war social, economic and organizational structures. Occupational distribution and material circumstances directly affected the ability of individuals and communities to defend themselves, and there were also major variations in their organizational structures and leadership. Much of this depended on the nature of local rabbinates and Jewish secular elites, but Zionism could also play a major mobilizing role, as could adherence to atheistic communism or social democracy. To cite just one example, the proportion of recent immigrants and refugees within Western European Jewish communities varied enormously. Of the 300-320,000 Jews in France in 1940, around 50% were non-French nationals and, of the French Jews, 37.3% had acquired their citizenship through naturalization.[9] In October 1940, the German census of all Jews in Belgium over the age of 15 showed that there were around 42,652 adult Jews in the country of whom almost 95% were foreign nationals.[10] Almost the reverse was true in the Netherlands where comparable figures enumerated approximately 118,500 indigenous Jews and only 21,750 foreign Jews or 15.5%, most of whom were recent refugees from Germany or Austria.[11] Although difficult to prove objectively, it has been suggested that these immigrants had a different response to state authority and were more aware of the threat posed by the occupying Germans.

Only a minority of Jewish survivors in Western Europe owed their salvation entirely to their own efforts and most were reliant at some point on help from others, either gentiles or fellow Jews; 'rescuers' who took risks to save others from Nazi persecution. Again, this raises the issue of how well integrated or assimilated the pre-war Jewish communities were in their respective countries and the extent to which this affected gentile responses to their subsequent persecution. Until now, academic attention has been heavily weighted towards one particular perspective, namely the 'righteousness' of gentile rescuers. This comes primarily from the recognition awarded to non-Jewish rescuers by Yad Vashem, where, by January 2013, the award of 'Righteous among the Nations' has been made to 24,811 individuals. While this has been important in bringing non-Jewish help to the forefront of discussions on Jewish survival during the Holocaust, the very criteria used by its Commissions for the Designation of the Righteous have served to create anomalies in distribution.[12] For example, there remain far more awards from the Netherlands than from neighboring Belgium, yet Jewish survival rates in the latter country were much higher.[13] There may well be international political explanations for this overrepresentation, but it is also the result of the quantity and quality of information and contemporary testimony available in the two countries. The Dutch government's decision to carry out immediate research on the occupation for a national official history undoubtedly aided the identification and honoring of rescuers in the Netherlands at an early stage. Other countries had no such in-built advantages and awards have had to rely mainly on the piecemeal and sometimes serendipitous survival of witnesses and documentation.

While this form of recognition can be seen as important in its own right, it has often led to the collection and publication of testimonies with little attention being paid to the geographical or political context in which rescues took place, or any wider analysis for the explanations behind them save for some broad categorizations.[14] This trend has been compounded by the use of sources and interviews of righteous rescuers as the basis for sociological studies on the origins of altruism and on the highlighting of Christian motivations behind acts of rescue and the behavior of particular individuals.[15] While such analyses may play a very important role within their own disciplines, their focus on individual case studies cannot encompass the wider aspects of rescue and Jewish survival and often ignore the chronological, geographical and social context to acts of rescue by non-Jews, the relationship between individual acts of rescue and the creation or existence of networks, the structure and organization of Jewish communities and the interrelationship between rescue by gentiles and Jewish self-help.

It is widely acknowledged that help for the Jews during the occupation period had to have some form of social context, but it is only in recent years that the relationships between Jews and non-Jews in the interwar period have been subjected to closer scrutiny, not only in relation to questions of rescue, but within the wider framework of non-Jews as bystanders to the Holocaust.[16] This had led to new insights into the ways Jews were perceived by their neighbors and has undoubtedly helped to shape better understanding of popular reactions when the persecutions and deportations began. There is also the vexed question of the risks run by would-be rescuers. It is often implied that rescue was invariably a matter of life and death, both for the rescuer and those rescued, but this takes no account of the fact that the laws, decrees and regulations that prohibited helping Jews varied enormously from one country to another.[17] While we should be most concerned with what the rescuers and rescued thought would happen to them if they were caught, this is difficult to ascertain at a distance, as the punishments dictated by such laws were often not rigorously or consistently implemented in practice.[18]

National studies of persecution have a tendency to underplay or ignore regional variations and often fail to identify local features such as the existence of rural traditions that had an important bearing on how Jews were perceived and treated. Likewise the concentration on interrogating and understanding the role of individuals – a tendency reinforced by the widespread collection of testimonies for the same purpose – has tended to marginalize the role played by organized networks. Yet even the most cursory examination of the subject reveals that most rescuers were ultimately linked to, or became members of, wider organizations. This in turn raises questions about how individuals became involved in rescue. Were they all motivated and drawn in by their own experiences or was their involvement prompted by others? Inevitably perhaps, the answer is complex. Many rescuers became involved through direct contact with victimized Jews or with the machinery of Nazi persecution. Some never graduated beyond being individual rescuers – albeit perhaps helped by a network later in the occupation – but there were others who expanded their commitment by drawing in family members, neighbors, professional contacts or fellow churchgoers to meet the need for hiding places for those on the run. In effect, this means that many were initially drawn in, not by individual commitment, but by prompts from others. Indeed, they often did so with some misgivings and initial reticence, as is sometimes evident in the testimonies of network organizers. Knowing how these networks developed holds the key to understanding rescue activities, and why there could be both 'havens' and 'deserts' in specific areas when it came to helping fugitive Jews.

With the exception of the Danish example, only a small number of Jews were able to flee from Nazi-occupied territory during the war, but studying the ways in which escapes were carried out shows up some other features that are too often overlooked. Switzerland and Spain were to become central to the operations of many groups helping resisters, Allied servicemen and escaping POWs as well as Jews. If nothing else, this demonstrates that the rescue of Jews was far from being an activity isolated from other forms of opposition and resistance to the Germans – even in this early stage of the occupation. Moreover, it highlights the involvement of all manner of people in these activities and a huge range of motivations from the purely philanthropic through the ideological, material and commercial to the downright exploitative. The motives of rescuers had no more than a tangential effect on the likely survival of those rescued, and even the most upright and law-abiding of rescuers could find themselves soliciting help from criminals and dubious elements within society. One telling example here is of the moral and upstanding American, Varian Fry, who soon found himself consorting with smugglers and the Marseilles underworld in order to expedite the evacuation of his charges. His experience was by no means unique and mirrored the linkages born of necessity between otherwise high-minded resisters and the criminal classes.

All too often, the rescue of the Jews is seen as a subject almost hermetically closed off from the wider history of civil opposition and resistance to Nazi rule, yet this undoubtedly misrepresents the case. From the earliest months, Jews were fugitives alongside escaping prisoners of war and political opponents of Nazism. The individuals and organizations that helped them seldom discriminated, and there were example of help for one specific group gradually being adapted to help others. That is not to say that discrimination did not exist. There are examples of help for Jews being separated off from other activities – sometimes because of the difficulties in finding help for Jews – as Jews – and sometimes because the work was thought to be inherently more dangerous and carrying more draconian penalties – and thus to be left to the 'specialists'.

There remains the danger that an approach based on the Jews as passive recipients of help from their non-Jewish neighbors ignores or downplays the steps which the Jews, both individually and communally, took to help themselves. Discussion has been heavily influenced by the assumption that the Jews were passive victims and divided among themselves, and that many community leaders were ineffective at best and collaborationist at worst. This perspective meant that steps taken by individual Jews and local organizations to avoid identification and deportation, either on their own or in collusion with non-Jewish help were often ignored. Only recently, and perhaps in a be-lated response to this perception, have scholars begun to re-evaluate self-help in Jewish resistance and Jewish survival.[19] For example, Jews could be found in the ranks of armed communist and social democratic resistance groups throughout Europe, but their presence was primarily dictated by their politi-cal allegiance rather than by their Judaism, which they had often rejected. While in most of Western Europe, Zionist Jews were not particularly nu-merous, their numbers in France allowed for the creation of the 2000-strong Organisation Juive de Combat which was ultimately incorporated into the French Forces of the Interior (FFI). Perhaps paradoxically, its history has been written separately from the wider narrative of the resistance in France.

Perhaps the best example of the integration of Jewish and non-Jewish elements can be seen in the origins and development of a (self-) help orga-nization in Belgium. The Comité de Défense des Juifs (CDJ) was formed as a national structure in the autumn of 1942 devoted exclusively to helping the Jews threatened by Nazi policies and opposed to the collaborationism of the official representative organization, the Association de Juifs de Belgique. It owed its origins to pre-war immigrant aid organizations; the communist Main d'Oeuvre Étrangère (MOE) and Solidarité Juive.[20] Its inception in response to the first threats of deportation in July 1942 owed much to ele-ments within the Independence Front (FI), a resistance movement founded in March 1941. It brought together leaders from a number of different po-litical strands and was centered in Brussels.[21] Its long-time leader was Hertz Jospa, a communist of Rumanian/Bessarabian origins whose wife, Yvonne, was also to play a major role in the organization. It also included represen-tatives from Jewish organizations from across the political spectrum, both legal and illegal, as well as non-Jews such as the left-wing-catholic Emile Hambresin,[22] Although many of the bourgeois elements involved in the cre-ation of the CDJ were wary of becoming involved with left-wing organizations and apostate Jewish communists like Jospa, they were prepared to stifle these fears in pursuit of an organization that would help the community as a whole.[23] All this was in stark contrast to the Netherlands where immigrant Jewish organizations were all-but non-existent and there was no counter-weight to the collaborationist and all-embracing Amsterdam Jewish Council. CDJ links with non-Jewish organizations allowed it better access to addresses and hiding places, and also to secure a supply of false papers through its association with the FI, and benefit from the co-operation of sympathetic local mayors and amenable civil servants who incorporated false identities into existing population records.[24] Finance came from rich Jews and later from banks and other organizations such as the JDC and Oeuvre Nationale de l'Enfance (ONE). The total expenditure for the whole of the occupation was estimated at almost BFr.48 million.[25] This integration of help from elements across the political and organizational spectrum seems to hold the key to understanding how up to 12,000 adult Jews and a further 3-4,000 children survived with the help of the CDJ, many not by hiding 'underground' but living false lives more or less in the open.

This co-operation between Jewish and non-Jewish groups also extended beyond the realms of the organized resistance. For example, after September 1939, Jewish charities in France had worked in collaboration with other Christian groups, such as the Quakers, YMCA and the Protestant Comité Inter-Mouvements Auprès d'Evacués (CIMADE), most notably in the internment camps in Southern France where Spanish Republican refugees were gradually replaced by 'enemy' German and Austrian internees. These links forged during the *drôle de guerre* facilitated further help for the Jews once the deportations began in the summer of 1942. Furthermore there is the question of individual and organized help given to the Jews through the agency of the Christian churches. In the immediate postwar era, all Christian denominations were keen to stress their opposition to Nazism during the occupation, but focused on public pronouncements and rescue activities were seldom given much prominence. In fact, the differing attitudes of leading clergymen and the very organizational structures of their churches were to have a profound effect on the incidence of rescue across the entire region, not least because of their enormous influence on the wider community.

In Belgium, the attitude of Cardinal Archbishop van Roey and prelates such as Bishop Kerkhofs in Liege have been seen as central to understanding the ways in which rescue developed in Belgium. Bishops and priests were often the first port of call for Jews who were forced to look for reliable help outside their own community. Initially this was often to obtain (false) baptismal certificates to exempt the holder from deportation, but later also encompassed requests for shelter, ration cards or help to escape the country altogether.[26] Van Roey personally intervened in some cases, but remained opposed to public appeals to the Germans, even after the deportations had begun. His reasoning was that previous appeals had achieved nothing and that any protest might bring adverse consequences for Jewish children hidden in Catholic institutions.[27] He undoubtedly knew exactly what was happening in the Catholic cloisters and orphanages across the country and he had privately sanctioned such actions. [28] He therefore trod the same tightrope as many of his colleagues elsewhere in German-occupied Europe, balancing the humanitarian and religious obligations of his office with the need to protect the secular interests of his church at a time of crisis.

The role of Marc Boegner in mobilizing Protestant communities to help Jews and other refugees in both the occupied and unoccupied zone of France is well-known, but it could be argued that some of his Catholic counterparts were just as important in harnessing their much more numerous subordinates and congregations. In spite of the Church's continually professed loyalty to Vichy, this did not prevent some leading clerics from speaking out. For example, Jules-Géraud Saliège, Archbishop of Toulouse promulgated a pastoral letter on August 23, 1942, affirming the position of the Jews as part of the human race. He was followed soon afterwards by Cardinal Archbishop Pierre-Marie Gerlier who condemned the deportations while at the same time reaffirming loyalty to the Marshal and his regime.[29] His influence was therefore largely limited to private advice to both clergy and lay-people within particular diocese to support Jews in hiding.[30] Individual prelates could also exercise influence over individual monasteries, convents, seminaries, welfare and educational institutions that were not controlled by the diocese and archdiocese but directly from Rome or by the headquarters of the order concerned. Moreover, their names could be invoked in order to encourage the laity to co-operate in sheltering Jews.[31]

In the Netherlands, Archbishop de Jong did protest when the deportations began, and his public declaration was read from every pulpit. However, this merely prompted the Germans to arrest and deport most of the Catholic converts and de Jong seems subsequently to have been less proactive than his colleagues, Cardinals Gerlier and Van Roey as the deportations continued.[32]

The actual difference may have been little more than nuances, but they were enough to have a major impact in what happened 'on the ground' in individual parishes. That said, it is also important to recognize that the Dutch Catholic Church had fewer practical resources to call upon as it had less of an 'institutional' and welfare role than its counterparts in France and Belgium. While making these comparisons at the national level, it should be remembered that local factors were still crucial and rescue often depended on the attitude of local priests. How else do we explain that some 90% of the Jews sheltered in Belgium found refuge in Wallonia and a mere 10% in Flanders? Likewise in France and the Netherlands, the degree of help for Jews from Christian communities was determined by the attitudes and mobilizing capabilities of local churchmen.

One notable feature of the literature in the last twenty years has been an outpouring of books and articles on Christians hiding Jewish children.[33] Treating them as a separate category nevertheless requires some further explanation. There is no doubt that Jewish children were a privileged group across Western Europe: widely perceived by their gentile neighbors as 'innocents' in a way that their parents were not; easier to hide as family members or evacuees; and more acceptable and less threatening as house-guests. These are all positive features that figure heavily in the narratives but it is important to show that there was also a negative side to the story that went unrecorded or was ignored in the search for the righteous. Children could be taken in to be exploited as cheap labor or worse, or in exchange for exorbitant charges for bed and board, or as targets for conversion. Such cases have been documented across Western Europe and are not peculiar to any particular social or religious milieu. Here again, the fact that the rescuers' motivations may have been far from pure was no bar to the rescue being 'successful' and the fugitive surviving the occupation. One further complication to an understanding of this topic is the acrimony caused in the postwar era by the fate of Jewish orphans. Three high profile cases in France, Belgium and the Netherlands all had similar features in that the children concerned had been successfully sheltered during the occupation but were then retained by their wartime foster parents in defiance of state authority and to the outrage of the residual Jewish communities. In each case, devout Christian rescuers claimed to see it as their duty to retain their charges within the Christian *milieu* in which they had been raised – not only as a religious obligation, but also to protect the immortal souls of the children concerned.[34]

Beyond this, there were also unlikely rescues carried out by the persecutors themselves. Even leading Nazis protected certain favored individuals in return for favors or services rendered. Lower level functionaries were likewise involved in protecting Jews and even some in particular positions who have been credited with trying to save entire groups, for example the 'racial expert' Hans-Georg Calmeyer whose executive position was used to provide temporary protection for the Sephardic Jews in the Netherlands.[35] The term 'Nazi rescuer' seems inherently contradictory, but in practice again highlights some of the problems of seeing rescue as a black and white issue. At the other end of this scale there were Jews who were formally employed by the German security services to track down and betray their co-religionists.[36] Although small in number, it could be argued that this was just another form of self-help, albeit under duress, but one that could also be portrayed as a survival strategy. Finally, not all the Jewish victims of Nazi policies were themselves law abiding citizens and there are instances of rescue through involvement with the underworld, and where discovery was often a function of criminal behavior rather than pursuit or betrayal as a Jew.

Situating self-help and rescue in a wider context has also been assisted by several recent historiographical trends. The growth of interest in other genocides has opened up new avenues for comparing rescue in Nazi occupied Europe with examples of similar behavior from other case studies.[37] Of greatest relevance here are the examples of Armenia, Bosnia and Rwanda.[38] For the most part, these studies have dealt with the rescue of civilians by other civilians, but the history of the First World War also provides us with other examples of rescue – in the help offered by civilians in German occupied Europe to allied servicemen in hiding, escaping POWs, deserters and draft-dodgers. Moreover, in the case of Belgium – overrun in 1914 and in 1940 – there are clear linkages between resistance and rescue activities in both occupations. The crucial conclusion here is that 'rescue' was not unique to the Second World War except insofar as the Jews became the primary targets of the occupation regime. Yet even this requires some qualification. Jews were by no means the only victims of Nazi persecution, albeit they were the only ones for whom capture could almost automatically be equated with death, at least after the summer of 1942. Political opponents were the first targets, as they had been in Germany in 1933, and they were followed, not just by Jews but also by many hundreds of thousands of others avoiding the imposition of German measures, most notably those related to forced labor.

Thus even when the plight of the Jews was at its height and the first mass deportations from Western Europe began in July 1942, they remained just one of the groups, albeit large in number, who were perceived as victim of the Nazis. This commonality of experience is again not often reflected in the available literature. Discussions of national resistance to Nazism often marginalize the help given to Jews and likewise, texts on the fate of Jews and the incidence of rescue often have few reflections on the wider context of resistance. There are, of course, notable and honorable exceptions but the division remains and the wider social context of rescue is often lost in the many narratives that focus purely on individuals. Without wishing to detract from the undoubted heroism of many rescuers and the bravery of the Jews who defied the Germans by refusing to allow themselves to be deported, it is important to abandon the comforting black and white assumptions about societies under occupation in order to place both self-help and rescue, as well as the persecution of the Jews itself, into a more sophisticated social history of the occupation.

Notes

* This chapter is partly adapted from Bob Moore, *Survivors: Jewish Self-Help and Rescue in Nazi-Occupied Western Europe* (Oxford: Oxford University Press, 2010) pp.1-14, and appears here with the permission of the publishers.

1 On France, see Henry Rousso, *The Vichy Syndrome. History and memory in France since 1944* (Cambridge MA: Harvard University Press, 1991). On the Netherlands, J.C.H.Blom, 'In de ban van goed en fout' In Blom, *Crisis Bezetting en Herstel,* pp..Chris van der Heijden *Grijs Verleden. Nederland en de Tweede Wereldoorlog* (Amsterdam: Contact, 2001)

2 To quote just one example, Michèle Cointet, *l'Église sous Vichy. La repentence en question* (Paris: Perrin, 1998) devotes more than a quarter of his book to the question of antisemitism and the persecution of the Jews.

3 Yehuda Bauer, *A History of the Holocaust* (New York: Franklin Watts, 2001), Doris Bergen, *The Holocaust: a new history* (Stroud: Tempus, 2008) Saul Friedländer, *The Years of Extermination. Nazi Germany and the Jews 1939-1945* (London: Weidenfeld and Nicholson, 2007) Peter Longerich, *Holocaust: the Nazi Persecution and Murder of the Jews* (Oxford: Oxford University Press, 2010)

4 Cornelis J.Lammers, 'Persecution in the Netherlands during World War Two. An Introduction' *The Netherlands' Journal of Social Sciences* XXXIV/2 (1998) pp.111-125, here p.111. This 'discovery' is often attributed to the publication of Helen Fein, *Accounting for Genocide. National Responses and Jewish Victimisation during the Holocaust* (New York: Free Press, 1979), but the raw statistics were known long before then and had been reproduced, albeit inaccurately, in Lucy Dawidowicz, *The War Against the Jews, 1933-1945* (New York: Holt, Reinhard and Winston, 1975).

5 J.C.H Blom, 'The Persecution of the Jews in the Netherlands: A Comparative Western European Perspective', *European History Quarterly,* XIX (1989).

6   M.R.Marrus and R.O.Paxton, 'The Nazis and the Jews in Occupied Western Europe 1940-1944' *Journal of Modern History* LIV (1982), pp.687-714, here p.713.

7   For the most recent Western European comparative, see Pim Griffioen and Ron Zeller, *Jodenvervolging in Nederland, Frankrijk en België* (Amsterdam: Boom, 2010) and specifical-ly on the Netherlands see Marnix Croes and Peter Tammes, *'Gif laten wij niet voortbestaan' Een onderzoek naar de overlevingskansen van joden in de Nederlandse gemeenten, 1940-1945* (Amsterdam: Aksant, 2004) J.C.H.Blom, 'Gescheidenis, sociale wetenschappen, bezetting-stijd en jodenvervolging. Een besprekingsartikel' *Bijdragen en Mededelingen betreffende de Geschiedenis der Nederlanden,* CXX (2005) pp.562-580. Marjolein J. Schenkel, *De Twentse Paradox. De lotgevallen van de joodse bevolking van Hengelo en Enschede tijdens de Tweede Wereldoorlog* (Zutphen: Walburg Pers, 2003)

8   L.de Jong, *Het Koninkrijk der Nederlanden in de Tweede Wereldoorlog*, Deel 1, ('s-Gravenha-ge: Staatsuitgeverij, 1969), p.503.

9   Jacques Adler, *The Jews of Paris and the Final Solution. Communal Responses and Internal Conflicts, 1940-1944*(New York: Oxford University Press, 1987) , pp.8-9.

10 Lieven Saerens, *Vreemdelingen in een Wereldstad. Een geschiedenis van Antwerpen en zijn joodse bevolking (1880-1940)* (Tielt: Lannoo, 2000) p.546. Lucien Steinberg, *Le Comité de Défense des Juifs en Belgique* (Bruxelles: Editions de l'Université de Bruxelles, 1973), p.15.

11 Gerhard Hirschfeld, 'Niederlande', in W.Benz, (ed.) *Dimension der Völkermords. Die Zahl der jüdischen Opfer des Nationalsozialismus* (Munich, R.Oldenbourg, 1991), p.137.

12 Paldiel, *Sheltering the Jews: Stories of Holocaust Rescuers* (Minneapolis MN: Fortress Press, 1996), p.203.

13 Paldiel, *Sheltering the Jews*, p.206. notes that mortality was much higher in Poland and the Netherlands but that rescue was also more difficult and dangerous in these countries and therefore more worthy of honour.

14 See, for example, Martin Gilbert, *The Righteous: The Unsung Heroes of the Holocaust* (Lon-don/New York: Doubleday, 2002). André Stein, *Quiet Heroes. True Stories of the Rescue of Jews by Christians in Nazi-occupied Holland* (Toronto: Lester and Orpen Dennys, 1988)

15 See especially Samuel P.Oliner and Pearl M.Oliner, *The Altruistic Personality. Rescuers of Jews in Nazi Europe* (New York: Free Press, 1988). Frederico Varese and Meir Yaish, 'Reso-lute Heroes: The Rescue of Jews During the Nazi Occupation of Europe' *Archives Euro-péenes de Sociologie*, XLVI (2005), pp.153-168. Douglas Huneke, 'A Study of Christians who saved Jews during the Nazi Era', *Humboldt Journal of Social Relations* IX/1 (1981-82) pp.144-150. Perry London, 'The Rescuers: Motivational Hypothesis about Christians Who Saved Jews from the Nazis' in: J Macaulay and L.Berkowitz (eds.) *Altruism and Hel-ping Behavior* (New York: Academic Press, 1970).

16 Vicki Caron, *Uneasy Asylum: France and the Jewish Refugee Crisis, 1933-1942* (Stanford CA: Stanford University Press, 1999). Lieven Saerens, *Vreemdelingen in een Wereldstad. Een ge-schiedenis van Antwerpen en zijn joodse bevolking (1880-1940)* (Tielt: Lannoo, 2000). Frank Caestecker, *Ongewenste Gasten. Joodse vluchtelingen en migranten in de dertiger jaren* (Brus-sel: VUB, 1993). Mark van den Wijngaert, 'The Belgian Catholics and the Jews during the German Occupation 1940-1944' in: Dan Michman (ed.) *Belgium and the Holocaust.* J.C.H.Blom and J.J.Cahen, 'Joodse Nederlanders, Nederlandse joden en joden in Neder-land (1870-1940) in: J.C.H.Blom et al (eds.) *Geschiedenis van de Joden in Nederland* (Am-sterdam: Balans, 1995)

17 Oliner, *The Altruistic Personality*, pp.1-12.

18 See for example Pierre Sauvage, 'Varian Fry in Marseille' in: John K. Roth and Elizabeth Maxwell, *Remembering for the Future. TheHolocaust in an Age of Genocide* (Basingstoke: Pal-grave, 2001), Vol.2, pp.349-350, who questions the precise levels of risk involved for neu-trals like Fry.

19 For example on France, see Lucien Lazare, *La Résistance juive en France* (Paris: Stock, 1987) and Adam Rayski, *The Choice of the Jews under Vichy* (Notre Dame IN: University of Notre

Dame Press, 2005) On Belgium, Lucien Steinberg, *Le Comité de Défense des Juifs en Belgique* (Bruxelles: Université de Bruxelles, 1973) Sylvain Brachfeld, *Ze hebben het overleefd* (Brussel: VUB, 1997). On the Netherlands, Ben Braber, *Zelfs als wij zullen verliezen. Joden in Verzet en Illegaliteit 1940-1945* (Amsterdam: Balans, 1990).

20   CEGES-SOMA R123 232.159 *8 Ans au Service du Peuple*, p.4. Maxime Steinberg, *L'Etoile et le Fusil. 1942 Les Cent Jours de la Déportation* (Bruxelles: Vie Ouvrière, 1984), pp.60-1.

21   Steinberg, *Le Comité de Défense des Juifs*, pp. 36,39. Lieven Saerens, 'Die Hilfe für Juden in Belgiën' in: Wolfgang Benz and Juliet Wetzel (eds.) *Solidarität und Hilfe für Juden während der NS-Zeit* (Berlin: Metropol, 1998), Vol.II, p.250. CEGES-SOMA AB2167 De Lathower, *Comité de Defense des Juifs*, p.2.

22   Maxime Steinberg, *L'Etoile et le Fusil: La Traque des Juifs*, I, (Bruxelles: Vie Ouvrière,1986), p.66.

23   Steinberg, *Le Comité de Défense des Juifs*, p.68.

24   CEGES-SOMA AB2167 Comité de Defense des Juifs, p.15.

25   CEGES-SOMA AB2167 Comité de Defense des Juifs, p.10, 29. CEGES-SOMA AA1915 Heiber: Dossier 13 CDJ. Ofipresse No.23, 12 October 1945. Steinberg, *Le Comité de Défense des Juifs*, p.116.

26   Saerens, 'Die Hilfe für Juden', p.258.

27   Mark van den Wijngaert, 'Les Catholiques Belges et les Juifs durant l'occupation Allemande 1940-1944' in Rudi van Doorslaer et al (eds.) *Les Juifs de Belgique. De l'Immigration au Génocide, 1925-1945* (Brussels: Centre de Recherches et d'Études Historiques de la Seconde Guerre Mondiale, 1994), p.121. Brachfeld, *Ze hebben het overleefd*, pp.72-3. Lieve Gevers, 'Catholicism in the Low Countries During the Second World War. Belgium and the Netherlands: a Comparative Approach' in: Lieve Gevers and Jan Bank (eds.) *Religion under Siege, I, The Roman Catholic Church in Occupied Europe* (1939-1950) (Leuven: Peeters, 2007), p.222.

28   Gevers, 'Catholicism in the Low Countries', p.222.

29   Francis R. Nicosia (ed.) *Archives of the Holocaust. Vol. 4 Central Zionist Archives 1939-1945* (New York: Garland, 1990) pp. 161-6 shows that these pastoral letters were widely distributed and known outside France. Rayski, *The Choice of the Jews under Vichy*, pp.118-119.

30   Jeannine Frenk, 'Righteous Among the Nations In France and Belgium: A Silent Resistance' *Search and Research* XII (2008), p.55.

31   Yad Vashem Archives M31/7529 Pierre and Henriette Ogier. Testimony of Maurice Ogier, 16 August 1996.

32   De Jong, *Het Koninkrijk*, V, p.366.

33   See in general, Deborah Dwork, *Children with a Star. Jewish Youth in Nazi Germany* (New Haven CT: Yale University Press, 1991). Anita Brostoff (ed.) *Flares of Memory. Stories of Childhood during the Holocaust* (Oxford: Oxford University Press, 1998) and on rescue, Sylvain Brachfeld, *Ils Ont Survecu:Le Sauvetage des Juifs en Belgique Occupee* (Bruxelles: Racine, 2001). Suzanne Vromen, *Hidden Children of the Holocaust. Belgian Nuns and their Daring Rescue of Young Jews from the Nazis* (New York: Oxford, 2008). Martine Lemalet, (ed.) *Au secours des enfants du siècle* (Paris: Nil, 1993). Hillel J. Kieval, 'From Social Work to Resistance. Relief and Rescue of Jewish Children in Vichy France', (BA Harvard University, 1973). Donald A Lowrie, *The Hunted Children* (New York: W.W.Norton, 1963)

34   J.S.Fishman, 'Jewish War Orphans in the Netherlands; The Guardianship Issue, 1945-1950' *Wiener Library Bulletin*, New Series 30/31 (1973-74), pp.31-6. J.S.Fishman, 'The Anneke Beekman Affair and the Dutch News Media' *Jewish Social Studies* XL/1 pp.3-24. J.S.Fishman, 'The War Orphan Controversy in the Netherlands: Majority – Minority Relations' in: J. Michman and T.Levie, *Dutch Jewish History* I (Jerusalem, 1984), Nederlands-Israëlitisch Kerkgenootschap and Portugees-Israëlitisch Kerkgenootschap, *De Verdwijning van Anneke Beekman en Rebecca Meljado: Witboek* (Amsterdam, 1954)

35 Mattias Middelberg, *Judenrecht, Judenpolitik und der jurist Hans Calmeyer in den besetzten Niederlanden 1940-1945* (Göttingen: V&R Unipress, 2005)

36 Koos Groen, *Als slachtoffers daders worden. De zaak van de joodse veraadster Ans van Dijk* (Baarn: Ambo, 1994). Steinberg *La Traque des Juifs* II, pp.32, 212-213.

37 See, for example, Jaques Semelin, Claire Andrieu and Sarah Gensberger (eds.), *La Résistance aux genocides. De la pluralité des actes de sauvetage* (Paris: Sciences Po, 2008).

38 On the Armenian genocide, see for example, Raymond Kévorkian, 'L'opposition de fonctionnaires ottomans au génocide des Arméniens' and Ugur Ümit Üngör, 'Stratégies de survie au cours du genocide des Arméniens' both in Semelin et al (eds.) *La Résistance aux genocides.*, pp.205-220 and pp.221-234. Richard G. Hovanissian, *The Armenian Genocide: History, Politics, Ethics* (New York: St.Martin's Press, 1992) Ronald Suny et al (eds.) *A Question of Genocide: Armenians and Turks at the end of the Ottoman Empire* (New York: Oxford University Press, 2013)

Amsterdam: Heroes, villains and many shades of grey

Dutch civil society under Nazi occupation: an educational perspective

Ronald Leopold

Since 2008, the Amsterdam newspaper *Het Parool*, in partnership with Amsterdam City Council, has organized the annual 'Amsterdammer of the Year' awards. Ordinary Amsterdammers who have made a positive contribution to the city can be nominated for this award, and in this way they serve as role models for their fellow citizens. In 2011, Mohamed Taha El Idrissi was voted Amsterdammer of the Year from the ten nominees, with over 18% of the votes. On a cold February evening he was walking across a bridge in his neighborhood when he heard cries for help. It soon became apparent that two people, who could not swim, had fallen in the water. El Idrissi, who suffers from reduced lung function as a result of smoking and chronic bronchitis, leapt into the ice-cold water and, with great difficulty, managed to save the pair from drowning and drag them to dry land. One of them had fallen into a coma, and the other was also in a bad way, as was El Idrissi himself. All three were taken to hospital, where they eventually recovered. El Idrissi never heard from the people he had rescued again, but he was left with a €270 hospital bill that he could not pay. Fortunately, his fellow Amsterdammers came to his aid. A fundraising drive raised more than enough to pay the bill, which had been increased by €100 due to late payment. Later El Idrissi said of his decision to jump into the water on that evening: 'Actually, that should just be a normal response. If someone's in trouble, you help them. But you often hear of people who just walk on by, or who are afraid. Then I think: well, that way things will never get better.'

Miep Gies

Would Miep Gies have been voted Amsterdammer of the Year in 1945 if the award had existed then? Probably not. Nobody had yet heard of the Diary of Anne Frank, which Miep had saved after the arrest of the people in hiding in the Secret Annexe in August 1944. So soon after the liberation, the help that she, together with her husband and three colleagues, had given to the people in hiding for a period of 25 months was just another anonymous detail among the many wartime experiences that people had endured. Many years later, when the Diary of Anne Frank had become world-renowned, Miep Gies received the honor that was due to her. In 1972 (together with her husband, whose resistance work is much less well known) she was honored as one of the Righteous Among The Nations by Yad Vashem for her help in sheltering Jews. A royal honor followed in 1995 when she was made a Knight of the Order of Orange-Nassau. She received special recognition at the Oscar ceremony in March 1996, when Jon Blair brought her on stage to join him in receiving the Oscar for his documentary *Anne Frank Remembered*. The audience gave her a standing ovation as 'a true hero'. In 2013 the city of Amsterdam added its own tribute when, on Anne Frank's birthday, a public park was named after her.

Visitors to the Anne Frank House today can see a video of Miep Gies talking about her decision to help the Frank family during their time in hiding. In fact, you can hardly call it a decision; it was more a natural, even an instinctive response to Otto Frank's plea for help. No arguments about pros and cons, no weighing up of the risks, no sleeping on it, none of that. It is as if her decision was totally self-evident; as if she was surprised she even needed to be asked. But still, in mid-1942 she must have been aware of the dangers that could result from her decision. The German occupation of the Netherlands had already lasted for two years, and the hard-hearted and highly anti-Semitic civil administration had already well and truly shown its true face. But none of that can be seen in the video. The old film images show an almost girlish young woman, and we can imagine her during that famous conversation with 'Mister Frank'. And although the circumstances are totally incomparable in so many ways, it still reminds you of the words of Mohamed Taha El Idrissi: 'Actually, that should just be a normal response. If someone's in trouble, you help them.'

Uncomfortable facts and questions

The attitude of Dutch citizens during and towards the German occupation, and especially towards the persecution of the Dutch Jews, has been a sensitive subject for research for decades. In particular, this sensitivity arises from the high percentage of Jews that were deported from the Netherlands and killed during the Second World War, both in the absolute sense and in comparison with other countries. At the outbreak of the war, in May 1940, there were an estimated 140,000 Jews living in the Netherlands. Over 103,000 – or 75% – of them were killed, by far the highest percentage in Western Europe. That painful fact looms like a dark shadow above every historical investigation into this period, and in a general sense above the constantly reinvented collective image of our nation in the period 1940 to 1945. This is particularly tangible in the commemoration and remembrance of this black page in our history. Through this commemoration and remembrance we express the values that we cherish as a society, and that were pushed aside during the German occupation.

The question of how these values relate to the extermination of the Dutch Jews, and to the attitude of the 'ordinary' non-Jewish Dutch people to this, is as relevant as it is uncomfortable. The black and white representation of occupying Germans and occupied Dutch is in any event seriously inadequate as an answer to this question. The question compels self-examination: an examination of the active and passive role of the Dutch people in implementing the persecution measures. In this context it is important to also examine the role of those who resisted the occupying forces, for example by providing help to Jews. After all, they not only represent the values we cherish, but they also give an insight into the ways in which those values are transmuted into concrete action.

That brings us to the educational relevance of our image of the persecution of the Jews. What patterns can we determine in the ways people thought and acted, and what do they teach us about ourselves and the society of which we form a part? What motivated collaborators to act in league with the enemy? What ethics can you expect from a victim whose life is at stake? What drove people to help others? Why did the vast majority neither help nor collaborate?

Research, commemoration, remembrance and education delineate our image of the past and its relevance to the present. They are dynamic in character, they influence each other, but they can also stand in uneasy relation to each other. Our self-image, both individual and collective, is fundamentally tarnished when the black and white moral perspective on the war is fragmented into countless shades of grey.

Remembrance becomes a complex issue when perpetrators are also made into kinds of victims, and vice versa. The same applies to education, as role models perish on the chopping block of academic research, or what is presented as such. Where does the Netherlands find itself today?

Growing interest

Let us begin with the good news: there is no lack of interest in the war. That can be inferred from the large number of new books with the war as their subject, from the attendance at memorial services, which is rising rather than falling, and from the amount of research that is being carried out into various aspects connected with the war. In this context, the somber warnings that the war would reach retirement age in 2010 and would only still be found in history books, seem premature to say the least. This is an important fact, because it shows that the war is still manifestly seen as relevant by many people, including young people. This is confirmed by the fact that various research projects and books have stirred up fierce public debate. The societal debate in the Netherlands on the nature and scope of remembrance ceremonies, carried out with great intensity, shows that the war evidently still matters. Within the limited scope of this essay I will examine some aspects of this debate and these discussions, which concern the attitude of the Dutch population with regard to the Holocaust, and which in my opinion have an educational relevance in terms of the development of civil courage.

Judgmental historians

The image of the war, and the persecution of the Jews during the war, has long been dominated by a black and white paradigm of right and wrong. Two historians in particular have helped to sustain this paradigm. Loe de Jong did so as director of the State Institute for War Documentation, which was set up only a few days after the liberation as a documentation and research institute on the Netherlands and the Second World War. Under De Jong's leadership the institute would make a significant mark on the historiography of this period. His life's work, The Kingdom of the Netherlands in the Second World War (1969-1994), consisting of 14 volumes divided into 27 sections, is regarded as the standard work on the years of occupation. What is more, De Jong reached a large audience thanks to the television series on the occupation that he presented, which was broadcast between 1960 and 1965.

'Downfall', by Jacques Presser, which sold over 100,000 copies within a year of its publication in 1965, has had a major influence on the creation of a paradigm of right and wrong, in which historiography became bound up with moral judgement. His conscious decision to carry out historical research from a personal, subjective perspective inevitably brought this in its wake. In their work both De Jong and Presser have placed a strong emphasis on the choice of individuals to take 'right' or 'wrong' actions. 'Right' actions meant resistance activities against the occupying power, and helping those who were exposed to persecution. 'Wrong' actions of course included collaboration with the enemy, but passive observation was also qualified as such. Although both historians acknowledged the circumstances that could influence the thoughts and actions of citizens during the occupation, in their eyes the choice was primarily moral in nature. For both of them, the standard for good actions was set high, and certainly when help to Jewish fellow countrymen was concerned they also arrived at harrowing conclusions. According to Presser in particular, the Dutch people had above all looked on passively as the Jews were taken away and exterminated, or in some cases had actively participated in this.

Whereas the memory of the war in the years immediately after the liberation was still defined by the former resistance movement and the role that resistance had played in the recovery of freedom and national sovereignty, with the works of De Jong and Presser the persecution of the Jews became an increasingly central theme. The right-wrong paradigm that was employed by them led to a growing awareness that the Dutch people had seriously failed in their duty to help the Jews.

The spell broken
The paradigm of right and wrong has long dominated the historiography of the war and, through that historiography, the self-image of the Dutch people. It was only in the 1980s that a paradigm shift emerged, when a new generation of historians began to place more emphasis on an analytical and academic approach, and gradually distanced themselves from the political

and moral perspective maintained by De Jong and Presser. The year 1983 can possibly serve as the tipping point in this shift. In that year two historians, Jan Bank and Hans Blom, gave their inaugural lectures on the war. Blom's lecture in particular, with its somewhat provocative title of 'Under the spell of right and wrong? Academic historiography of the occupation period in the Netherlands', set the historiography of the war on a different track. He was later appointed director of the State Institute for War Documentation mentioned above. The fact that new times had emerged was also illustrated by the fact that in 1999 Blom changed the name of the institute to the Netherlands Institute for War Documentation.

In his work Blom emphasizes the diversity of the wartime reality. He does not allow himself to become caught up in the moral paradigm of right and wrong. Although he has expressed great admiration for the work of De Jong, he sees him chiefly as a public educator, who holds up the mirror of the war for the moral edification of his fellow citizens. Incidentally, Blom does not deny the existence of right and wrong choices in the war, but he sees them as the extremes of a broad spectrum. He points out the importance of representing that whole spectrum, in all its complexity and diversity, without yoking it to moral judgments. In the 1990s there was an increasing focus on the dilemmas facing 'ordinary people' during the occupation. These dilemmas took the place of the stark black and white image of a society in which a few people had the courage and the moral strength to resist, while the rest had lent active or passive collaboration to the occupier. The growing interest in the individual memories of wartime eyewitnesses seems to have facilitated the fragmentation and disintegration of the image of the war.

The grey war
More recently, new historians and publicists have emerged who have followed the line initiated by Blom still further. They are not only interested in the actions of the great, grey majority, but even go so far as to qualify the concepts of right and wrong themselves. One exponent of this approach is Chris van der Heijden, who in 2001, with his book 'Grey Past', sounded the clarion call for a debate that is still raging with full intensity. Instead of heroes and villains, he primarily sees ordinary people with all their weaknesses, doubts and futilities. Perpetrators are portrayed as rather pathetic figures, who have ended up on the wrong side of history through a combination of

an unfortunate confluence of circumstances and weakness of character. This same weakness of character surfaces in his description of both victims and members of the resistance.

Their victimhood and their moral choices are depicted by Van der Heijden in the context of their vulgarities, improper motives and opportunistic actions. Members of the resistance were no longer the steadfast heroes of old, but adventurers and womanizers who occasionally carried out 'small acts of resistance'. Victims were not only helpless and innocent, but were also quite prepared to take advantage of others if this served their own interests. Helpers were not only altruistic, but also interested in the money they could make. The choice between right and wrong is no more than coincidental, it would appear. In Van der Heijden's view of humanity, the dividing lines between perpetrators, victims, helpers and bystanders dissolve in a sea of shades of grey.

Wir haben es nicht gewusst
More recently, the publication of the book 'We Know Nothing Of Their Fate' by historian Bart van der Boom of Leiden University provoked the inevitable commotion. The title, derived from the diary of the Jewish girl Etty Hillesum, who was killed in Auschwitz in 1943, refers to the question of whether Dutch citizens – Jews and non-Jews – knew of the fate that awaited the Jews. The subtitle refers to 'ordinary Dutch people'. In fact, Van der Boom poses the 'Was haben wir gewusst?' question, but this time to the Dutch people. In Van der Boom's view, this question is relevant to the understanding and appraisal of the attitude of Dutch citizens towards the persecution of the Jews. On the basis of a study of 164 wartime diaries, Van der Boom concludes that the vast majority of Dutch people at the time of the occupation had no knowledge of the Holocaust. He extends this notion to the victims themselves, who also did not know what awaited them. The majority of them acquiesced in their own arrest and deportation in the hope that, although they would suffer, they would still survive. And if the victims offered no resistance, what could then be expected of their non-Jewish countrymen? For the critic Robin te Slaa of the *Volkskrant* newspaper, the conclusion was clear: Van der Boom's study meant the definitive end of the myth of 'guilty bystanders'.

The return of the heroes

As could be expected, a reaction has now commenced against the 'greying' of the image of the war. And once again this has originated from the Netherlands Institute for War Documentation, and its director Marjan Schwegman. 'Where are the heroes?' she wondered when she took up her post as director of the institute in 2007. Schwegman regrets that, because of the overriding emphasis on nuances, heroism is being written out of history. Where Van der Heijden condescendingly speaks of adventurers and womanizers, Schwegman sees an exceptional and unconventional character as a key source of an attitude of resistance. Heroes cross boundaries, they tolerate no infringement of their inner freedom, they overcome obstacles, and they show us that everyone has the choice to do good. Two other female historians from the institute, Jolande Withuis and Evelien Gans, concur with Schwegman in her opposition to the 'grey paradigm,' although each of them does so in a different way and on a different terrain. Gans in particular repudiates both Van der Heijden and Van der Boom, who in her view seriously obfuscate and ultimately extenuate the image of the Holocaust and the attitude of the non-Jewish Dutch people to it.

Too many shades of grey?

On his retirement in 2007, Blom observed that the abandonment of the right-wrong paradigm he had argued for in 1983 had indeed taken root in historical science, but not yet in public opinion, which in his view was still under the spell of right and wrong. How Blom arrived at this opinion is somewhat unclear. The strictly professorial eye may very well have played a role, because for years public debate has been dominated by the apologists of 'greyness' and the reactions to them. For that matter, this debate does not appear to concern the necessity of focusing on the great difference between right and wrong so much as the question of whether we have gone too far in putting right and wrong into perspective, and in that sense obscuring our image of the Netherlands during the occupation rather than clarifying it.

Otto Frank had his own opinions on the attitude of the Dutch people towards the Jews during the war. When, in 1979, an interviewer from the *Basler Magazin* remarked that the Dutch people had behaved in an exemplary way towards the Jews, Frank replied: 'Yes, the Hollanders helped us tremendously. Where and when in history have you ever seen such a thing?'

131

The National Remembrance Ceremony and the Holocaust
The image of our country at the time of the occupation, and particularly of the attitudes of the Dutch population, has also had its repercussions on remembrance ceremonies. The intention and the scope of the most important ceremony, the National Remembrance Ceremony on May 4 in Amsterdam, has been the subject of discussion for years. A commemorative text, the so-called Memorandum, lies at the heart of the National Remembrance Ceremony. It reads: "During the national commemoration of Remembrance Day we remember all those – civilians and soldiers – who have been killed or murdered in the Kingdom of the Netherlands or anywhere else in the world in war situations or during peace-keeping operations since the outbreak of the Second World War."

On its website, the National Committee for May 4 and 5 explains that this concerns Dutch victims, and therefore not perpetrators or victims of other nationalities.

The most frequently heard criticism of this intention concerns the fact that no special place is set aside for the Jewish victims of persecution. They are commemorated of course, but only grouped together with civilians and soldiers in war situations and peace-keeping operations. In view of the magnitude of the Holocaust and its impact on Dutch society, there are many people, both Jews and non-Jews, who do not understand this. The above-mentioned historian Jolande Withuis has referred to it as a 'hotchpotch commemoration', which has lost significance by lumping everything and everyone together. The addition of other wars and peace-keeping missions in particular has led to a universalization that is seen as problematic. The criticism of this general character of the National Remembrance Ceremony cannot be seen completely separately from the criticism of the passive or even collaborationist attitude of Dutch citizens towards the persecution of the Jews. Among the circles of Holocaust victims and their surviving relatives in particular, the current intention of the commemoration is felt as a lack of recognition of the events of those times, and of the circumstances under which the persecution could occur.

Controversy
In 2012 a great controversy arose surrounding the National Remembrance Ceremony because of the original decision to have a fifteen year old boy read

out a poem about his great-uncle, who had voluntarily joined the Waffen SS during the war and had died while fighting on the Eastern Front. That seemed suspiciously similar to the commemoration of perpetrators, partly because the poem ended with an appeal not to forget the great-uncle, after whom the schoolboy was named. The committee emphasized that this concerned the educational meaning of the poem, which showed what the consequences of making a wrong choice can be. Nevertheless, it was ultimately decided, partly in the context of the ongoing debate on the intention of the remembrance ceremony, to omit the reading from the ceremony. Whether no perpetrators are in fact remembered on 4 May is questionable. What is certain is that Waffen SS volunteers later fought as volunteers for the Netherlands armed forces in the Dutch East Indies and in Korea.

Brüder, reicht die Hand zum Bunde!
The step towards the commemoration of perpetrators on 4 May has in fact currently been taken on a local level. The best-known example is from the village of Vorden in the eastern Netherlands, where ten German military personnel who died when their aircraft was shot down in March 1945 are buried in the local churchyard. In 2012, the plan was to stand at these German graves after the conclusion of the official remembrance ceremony for an austere commemoration, accompanied by the Vorden Male Voice Choir singing the hymn *Brüder, reicht die Hand zum Bunde!* The court put a stop to this, however, with a noteworthy judgement. The court prohibited the ceremony, because the commemoration of German military personnel would be disrespectful to other surviving relatives. This judgement was overturned on appeal, however. There are therefore no legal impediments to the commemoration of deceased members of the German occupying forces during the National Remembrance Ceremony on 4 May.

The planned commemoration of Germans on 4 May drew a great deal of national publicity. There were sharp protests, particularly from Jewish circles and circles surrounding the former resistance. Set against these protests were declarations of support for the initiative in Vorden, which were based on a variety of considerations. Some stressed the importance of reconciliation, so many years after the war. Others felt that these fallen warriors should also be regarded as victims. After all, in many cases they were just boys, who had not been capable to make their own decisions.

The controversy surrounding the commemoration in 2012 did not take place in a vacuum. Commemorations are the prism through which a country views its own past. They incorporate the outcomes of academic research and public debate, even though this is usually delayed. In the discussions regarding commemorations we can recognize elements of the historiography of the war over recent decades. The clear black and white perspective of right and wrong has been replaced by a nebulous image with many shades of grey. That can make commemoration a sometimes uncomfortable affair.

Educational tasks
The question is how the developments in the historiography of the Second World War, the remembrance of that period and its commemoration affect education, which has traditionally been linked to remembrance and commemoration. Can the remembrance of the war still play a role in the moral education of young people if all we have to offer is a muddy palette filled with shades of grey? Can we mold them into unconventional free spirits who, when push comes to shove, will combine their 'small acts of resistance' with heroic deeds? Are we, with all our weaknesses and futilities, still able to develop civil courage when we need it or, rather, when others ask that of us because they are in peril? Will we be able to make it clear to young people that you do not need to know what 'their fate' is in order to take action when, right in front of you, your neighbors are first treated unjustly and then taken away? These questions are relevant, but also difficult to answer.

Education is not like physics, where in many cases effects are predictable. Nevertheless, in a general sense we can indeed make a statement about the moral education of young people, the usefulness and necessity of which few would dispute. A major purpose of this education is to create awareness of certain patterns in how people think and act. In extreme situations such as the Second World War these patterns become highly visible, and can become associated with specific roles: perpetrator, helper, victim and bystander.

Against this background, I would like to discuss two aspects that, in my opinion, are of vital importance for a meaningful educational approach in the context of academic research on the one hand and commemoration and remembrance on the other.

The value of right and wrong

Firstly, the moral distinction between right and wrong continues to be essential in the development of values and standards. The history of the Second World War and the Holocaust can play a major role in learning about that distinction. The fact that the historical reality has been infinitely more complex, or 'greyer,' in no way detracts from this. The education of young people is not so much concerned with that historical reality itself as with shedding light on particular patterns within that reality that can serve as positive, or indeed negative, examples. This means that education based on the Second World War and the Holocaust must by definition maintain a certain distance from, in the words of the German historian Leopold von Ranke, 'wie es eigentlich gewesen'.

Education is more concerned with a well-founded schematization of that reality in models that offer starting points for the achievement of particular educational objectives. Of course new insights arising from academic research can be incorporated in this schematization, but it primarily remains a model constructed for educational purposes. Influencing the behavior of young people does not proceed via specific historical events or individuals, but by revealing patterns of behavior from the past and their possible consequences. Education is concerned with the categorization and raising of awareness of actions, within which lie choices. By placing the emphasis on patterns of thought and action, it is also possible to examine the relevance of the past to the present in a more general sense or, in more popular terms, to find out what we can learn from history. Such an approach avoids crude comparisons between historical developments or events, which commonly lead to fruitless discussions of similarities and differences.

Different functions

Secondly, it is important to keep a clear sight of the different functions of commemoration and remembrance on the one hand and education on the other. The tendency to give an increasingly educational content to commemoration and remembrance as the distance in time from the Second World War becomes ever greater can easily lead to misfortune. For as long as a personal element is still present in the remembrance of fellow human beings, a certain restraint is appropriate when it comes to connecting that remembrance to an educational mission. Of course commemorations inspires reflection, and this does not confine itself to the past. That is also the way it should remain, and this can also be taken into account in the formulation of the ceremonies. But contrived attempts to seize upon remembrance ceremonies for ill-considered and somewhat sentimental reconciliatory gestures, or for messages about making the world a better place, are deleterious to both the importance of remembrance and the aim of education. That same restraint is also appropriate where the connection between places of remembrance and education is concerned. Visitors to the Anne Frank House will not be terribly receptive to debates on right and wrong or human rights when they are standing in Anne's room. That little room is a place of remembrance and reflection, not of education.

Back to Miep Gies and Mohamed Taha El Idrissi. Anyone carrying out research into these two heroes would undoubtedly encounter people of flesh and blood, with both good and less good character traits. But they are also Righteous Among The Nations and Amsterdammer of the Year. We learn exactly what that means when we have to go into hiding from persecution, or when we fall into an Amsterdam canal. Because one day our lives too may depend upon the right and wrong choices of others.

Stockholm: Antisemitism, ambivalence and action

> *"We didn't have a question about race in our forms, but we did ask about religion. It is of some interest to us, when it comes to the planning of relief efforts and to be at service to all the different rescue organizations. At that time, before the world war, when we started to get so-called racial refugees, it was of utmost concern to get this information. [..] If they [converted Jews] came as refugees, they were kept in the books as M. The purpose was evidently to get a grip of the actual refugee problem."*

> Carl Christian Schmidt, former head of the Foreigner's Bureau,
> in interrogations after the war (1945)[1]

Karin Kvist Geverts

Carl Christian Schmidt, the former head of the Foreigner's Bureau, was maybe lying to the Sandler commission in the interrogations after the war.[2] Or maybe he was just telling the truth the way he saw it. To him, marking converted Jewish refugees with a "m" for mosaic confession, though they clearly did not belong to the mosaic religion, made sense. How else would the officials in Sweden be able to "get a grip of the actual refugee problem," to quote his own words? Even though Schmidt made an effort not to admit that the marking would have had anything to do with "race" or antisemitism, there is no other way we can interpret the actions today. To Schmidt, though, this was only matter-of-fact information needed to handle the applications for permits more smoothly. There is a saying in Sweden, "It's only words," however, in this case it is inaccurate. Words are important. Words matter. We use words to define and interpret everything we see and experience around us in society. If antisemitism doesn't exist, we cannot understand it and in the end cannot do anything about it. This is as true today as it was back then. Sweden and its action during World War II and the Holocaust have often

been described in heroic words as "the good Sweden," a country which rescued thousands of Jewish refugees via Count Folke Bernadotte's expedition
with the White Buses, and via Raoul Wallenberg's brave efforts in Hungary.[3]
But in order to grasp the whole picture, one needs to step back in time before
the end of the war and see how Sweden treated Jewish refugees before and
during the war. In this essay, I will explore the Swedish reactions to the Holocaust by examining the reactions of the authorities in charge of the refugee
policy, as well as the actions by single individuals and organizations in civil
society who, in the name of democracy and freedom, tried to help persecuted
Jews find a refuge in Sweden.

*"Sweden would in practice be a door through which [...] 'non-aryans' would seek
to flee"*
So, let's go back to "then," or more precisely to the fall of 1938 when more
Jewish refugees fleeing Nazi Germany also began to arrive to Sweden. Already after the German annexation of Austria, the pressure towards the
Swedish borders increased. During the summer of 1938, the now infamous
conference in the French city of Evian was held, where country after country expressed their deep regrets over the fate of the Jewish refugees, but explained, at the same time, that they were unable to do anything since they
were no country of immigration and, more importantly, since they had no
wish to "import a Jewish question." This was also the opinion held by the
Swedish officials present at the conference.[4]

The Swedish press in the 1930s was a myriad of voices but far too many
sang the same xenophobic hymn about an invasion of Jewish refugees arriving in Sweden.[5] No hard facts of course, only rumors and suspicions. It is
well known that when the shit hits the fan something that might not even
exist suddenly becomes a problem, simply because it is given a name "the
Jewish question." What where they afraid of? Maybe the same things we are
afraid of today: not the reality itself but the description of the reality. And in
1938, reality was described as if Sweden risked an invasion of Jewish refugees.

We proceed to early 1939 and despite the fact that antisemitism doesn't
exist in Sweden and despite the fact that Sweden yet lacks "a Jewish question," Swedish officials are concerned by the reports in the media. The headlines shouts "Jewish invasion in Sweden!" and troubled men in suits turn
their faces toward east. The real threat is not the well assimilated German

and Austrian Jews, but the consequences of "the open door policy," a policy if pursued would leave Sweden as the only country categorizing Jewish refugees as political such, and thus eligible for asylum.[6] In other words, the bureaucrats were afraid of the horde of eastern European Jews from Poland, Romania or Russia. Or put another way, they were afraid of the thought of what would happen if Sweden "opened the door" and gave permits to these refugees. Because no one knew exactly how many would actually try to flee to Sweden, only that it was a likely scenario that many would try. At this point in time, the officials don't even know how many Jewish refugees Sweden already hosts. So the bureaucrats intend to find out.

Already since 1932, Swedish authorities had been using a system of marking Jewish foreigners in minutes and files with "m." From the beginning, the "m" was an abbreviation of "mosaic confession," a legal expression. But despite the practice with the marking, no statistics over the amount of Jewish refugees exists. Therefore, The Foreigner's Bureau requests permission from the government to pursue a Foreigner's Census. The request was granted and between February 10 and 17 1939 every foreigner residing more than two days in Sweden had to participate in the census and fill out a form. The form asked legitimate questions about name, nationality and purpose of the stay, but question number 13 asked: "Whether either or both of the parents are Jews?" The instruction also clarified that this was regardless of whether they believed in the mosaic confession or not, i.e. regardless of religion but due to "race" in accordance with the Nuremberg Laws. In a press release where the census was presented, the Foreign Office emphasized that this shouldn't be seen as "an expression of antisemitic tendencies" Swedish newspapers didn't comment on the census but the *Daily Herald* wrote an outraged note stating that "Sweden, one of the world's most democratic nations, has apparently been forced at last by the Nazis into bowing the knee to their anti-Semitic theories," and they were surprised since they would expect "the very possibility of any discrimination between foreigners or citizens on the grounds of race or religion" to be "ludicrous to Swedes."[7]

"The stones cry out"

The war began in September 1939 and Sweden, along with the other Nordic countries, declared itself neutral. The neutrality lasted throughout the war but has been much debated, especially since the 1990s, when new research claimed Sweden paid a high price.[8] Even too high? Maybe. But was there an alternative? From the occupation of Norway and Denmark in April 1940 and after Finland in June 1941 for the second time was in war with the Soviet Union, Sweden was surrounded and also demilitarized since World War I. From a military point of view there wasn't much Sweden could have done. What would have been possible though, if Sweden would have wanted to make a difference, was to accept larger amounts of refugees early on and especially before the outbreak of war.[9] But the policy of the open door was not pursued, and the reason why was fear. Fear that "antisemitism would rise." Fear that Sweden would get "a Jewish question."[10] The pale cast of thought.

The newspapers which recently cried the hymn of xenophobia were now seemingly quieter about how Nazi Germany treated its Jewish population. Sure, there were reports in the press, but the Swedish state used censorship and confiscated papers with critical articles. The most important cog in the machinery was not the censorship though, but the self-censorship undertaken by the newspapers themselves. The pressure against the papers was hard during the winter of 1942 and in March, a large confiscation was made toward 17 papers which had reported about concentration camps.[11]

The machinery of bureaucracy kept going. More applications from Jewish refugees were rejected but some were still given a permit. There was never a complete stop – the "door" was ajar. "Race" (*"folkras"*) is an established terminology which, since 1938, together with marking with "m" separates Jewish refugees from other refugees in accordance with the "racial" definition of the Nuremberg Laws. Not according to the Swedish Law, of course, but in practice. The same practice also operated with the phrase "the usual addendum" as an explanatory statement of why applications from Jewish refugees were rejected. This phrase meant that the rejection was motivated by the ban on Jewish refugees from October 1941 leaving Germany and occupied countries. And because of the ban, their permits were rejected.[12]

The officials at the Foreigner's Bureau looked westwards to the order in Quisling's Norway. They cast worried looks eastwards toward "the Russian threat" and ponder whether Finland would make it. At the same time, Norwegian and Finnish refugees were crossing the borders. The Finns were accepted. So were the Norwegians, as long as they were not "emigrants," i.e. Jewish, and as long as they didn't try to cross at the "wrong" border control managed by the "wrong" official (*"landsfiskal"*). If so, they were told to return. If they refused, they were escorted by Swedish soldiers who returned them to the German border patrol on the Norwegian side. If they agreed to return freely, they had the opportunity to walk alongside the border and find another border control with a less strenuous official, and, if lucky, get accepted.[13]

But then something happened in Norway. There had been measures toward the Norwegian Jews already earlier. Their possessions had been registered and confiscated. But suddenly everything happened so fast. On November 26th, 1942, the first group of Norwegian Jews was forced to board the SS Donau for deportation. They arrived by train to Auschwitz-Birkenau on December 1st. The men were selected for slave labor while the women, children and elderly were immediately gassed to death in Bunker 2. The Nazis and their Norwegian collaborators worked tirelessly to make Norway "*judenrein*" and in 1944, 770 Norwegian Jews had been deported to Auschwitz. Of these, only 24 survived.[14]

Something was also happening in Sweden. The self-censorship in the press stopped and during the spring and summer of 1942 reports of the persecution and mass murders in occupied Europe were published in anti-Nazi newspapers such as *Göteborgs Handels- och Sjöfartstidning* and *Trots Allt!*.[15] Other papers also published reports, and September seems to be a turning point when *Dagens Nyheter* published the headline "The pogroms against Jews have to be stopped" and in its editorial concluded that "the persecution of the Jews" had "become harder and harsher. The end goal seems to be physical annihilation."[16] In October 1942 historian Hugo Valentin published his know famous article "The War of Extermination toward the Jews."[17]

So, when the deportations began in Norway on November 26, Swedish newspapers decided to speak out and the self-censorship that previously had been practiced was long gone. The Swedish radio reported in a telegram that "The Jewish Question in Norway seems to have found its final solution" with the deportation of the Norwegian Jews on a ship to an unknown destination.[18] The coming days, Swedish papers published several articles about the events and Swedes arranged meetings to protest the deportation, for instance held by the organization Fighting for Democracy (*Förbundet Kämpande Demokrati)* and by many women's organizations.[19] Even the churches decided to break the silence and criticize the deportations in their advent prayers. The dean *(domprost)* in Gothenburg, Olle Nystedt, turned his preaching into an outraged appeal and quoted the gospel of Luke: "if these were silent, the stones would cry out."[20] On the last day of the year, *Dagens Nyheter* published an opinion poll which showed that an overwhelming majority of the Swedes considered the deportation of the Norwegian Jews the event causing the most outrage during 1942. More than reports about the turn of the war, about Stalingrad and El Alamein.[21] How come? Because at the eve of the New Year, everyone who read the newspapers most likely knew about the persecution and the murders. Because the Jews were Norwegians, a fellow people (*broderfolk*), because they were just like us.[22]

The machinery of bureaucracy halts and slowly begins to move again; only this time in reverse. The very same officials at the embassies in Oslo and Berlin who previously argued they couldn't do anything for the refugees, because they were Jewish, now engage in the faith of the refugees simply *because* they are Jews. Norwegian Jews. This bureaucratic resistance started with the fellow people but soon embraced Jews of other nationalities as well.[23]

"A foreign element within the nation"
The shift in policy in 1942 inarguably moved Sweden from a bystander to a rescuer, but did it also lead to a shift in attitudes? Did antisemitism become visible? The answer is no, the attitudes prevailed, and part of the problem was that antisemitic attitudes weren't considered as such, but as strictly professional and unbiased matter-of-fact statements by the officials, as shown above with the statement by Carl Christian Schmidt.[24]

Since the Foreigner's Census in 1939 official statistics over foreigners and refugees separated Jews from other refugees.[25] From August 1941 this separation was also applied to the Norwegian and Danish Jews.[26] However, the separation of Norwegian refugees into "Jewish" and "non-Jewish" refugees was not seen as legitimate by the Swedish public. On September 7 1943, political economist Karin Kock formulated a harsh critique against the Foreigner's Bureau in an article in the paper *Socialdemokraten*, questioning the separation and asked about the grounds.[27] The head of the Foreigner's Bureau, Carl Christian Schmidt, replied that the separation was made before the war when the Bureau separated between refugees fleeing for political reasons and "racial refugees" and added that there was no difference in the treatment of these two groups.[28]

But Kock wasn't pleased with the answer and published yet another article in the same paper where she asked why the Bureau "separates Jews from other refugees" and accused the authorities of having "accepted the unscientific imported terminology 'race' from the south and used it as a category in Swedish statistics." She also asked if there were any reasons to keep the separation since it didn't seem to be used anyway. Finally, she connected the use of "race" with antisemitism: "Separating the Jews into special groups within each nationality gives, in its statistical objectivity, gives support to antisemitic ideas, which build upon perceptions of the Jew as a foreign element within the nation."[29] Schmidt replied that he found "no reason to – out of consideration to the antisemitic efforts, which by chance could exist in this country – suppress the objective information, which the statistic is supposed to give."[30]

When the Danish Jews fled to Sweden in October 1943, Kock again criticized the Bureau and the Foreign Office for their use of "race" (*folkras*) and asked what the officials themselves would answer if questioned about their own "race": "I don't think they know, but they do know what answer they want from the rest of us: Jew or non-Jew, or translated to another language aryan or non-aryan" and demanded that the authorities remove the question from the forms immediately.[31]

Officially, Karin Kock's protests seemingly had an effect and the Bureau no longer published statistics where Jews were separated in their own group.[32] But unofficially the separation continued, both in forms filled out by the Danish Jews rescued in October 1943, and in confidential memorandums written by the authorities.[33]

The Janus face of Swedish refugee policy

> I personally have a quite extensive experience of the difficulties for Jewish refugees to find a refuge in Sweden. I have walked the steps up to the Foreigner's Bureau, but in most cases when I have tried to get a permit for someone, my request has been rejected. So there is no doubt the right to asylum has been narrow. If we would have pursued a more liberal policy earlier than the fall of 1941 and accepted Jewish refugees, many lives could have been saved. It is very likely these refugees are now dead. *Erik Brandt in a speech in the Swedish Parliament, 1943*[34]

After the war, a commission was appointed with the task to investigate, among other things, the handling of the refugees and the official refugee policy during the war. In interrogations made by the commission with former Bureau officials, they asked whether the marking with "m" implied "race" or not. The officials denied the link as they were well aware that such a notion was illegitimate. A former head of the Bureau, Ernst Bexelius, answered: "it must have been because they belonged to the mosaic confession – we couldn't really investigate whether they were whole-, half- or a partly Jewish."

When the commission pointed out that "race" wasn't a category in Swedish official statistics, only the religious terminology "of the mosaic confession" existed. Bexelius answered that the Bureau didn't have any reason not to use the official statistical terminology.[35] When asked if he knew when the question of "race" was first used in forms he replied: "I believe it must have been in connection with the rescue efforts of these people, i.e. that it would have been positive for their chances to get here, if we knew, whether they were of the mosaic confession or not. Any other position would not have been plausible for a Swedish authority."[36] Bexelius argument made perfect sense – since antisemitism didn't exist Swedish authorities' couldn't have applied an antisemitic or "racial" vocabulary either.

The Swedish reactions to the Holocaust shifted throughout the war. The reaction of the government and its authorities was restrictive and xenophobic in the beginning and turned into a large scale reception and rescue at the end. But the prejudiced attitudes toward the Jewish refugees remained as the mentality, influenced by antisemitic perceptions which from the beginning could be uttered but not recognized as such, while at the end denied since they were no longer perceived legitimate. The Swedish refugee policy can be characterized as a Janus face – dual in its ambivalence and struck by the antisemitic background noise.

The reactions of civil society were also ambivalent, although there were always individuals, organizations and newspapers that saw the antisemitic expressions for what they were and criticized them. There were strong anti-Nazi voices throughout the period, but they fought the headwind (*motvind*) in the beginning.

Therefore, Sweden's actions during World War II and the Holocaust cannot be characterized as one and the same. In Sweden there were many who acted, and reacted. "Were the Swedish actions toward the persecuted Jews impressive or pitiful? asks historian Mattias Tydén and concludes: "Maybe it is precisely the ambivalence that should be highlighted."[37]

Notes

1   Riksarkivet (RA), Parlamentariska undersökningskommissionen (PUK), YK 984, Stenographic report of conversation with head of the Bureau Schmidt, 18.5.1945, p. 46-47.
2   The two authorities in charge of the refugee policy was the Foreigner's Bureau and the Foreign Office.
3   For a critical review, see Mikael Byström & Karin Kvist Geverts, "Från en aktivism till en

annan. Hur ska Sveriges agerande i flyktingfrågan under andra världskriget förklaras?", *Sverige och Nazityskland. Skuldfrågor och moraldebatt*, Dialogos: Stockholm 2007.

4   Hans Lindberg, *Svensk flyktingpolitik under internationellt tryck 1936-1941*, Allmänna förlaget: Stockholm 1973, p. 111.

5   Karin Kvist Geverts, *Ett främmande element i nationen. Svensk flyktingpolitik och de judiska flyktingarna 1938-1944*, Studia Historica Upsaliensia 233 & UUHGS Publications 2, dissertation, Uppsala 2008, p. 80; Svanberg, Ingvar & Mattias Tydén, Sverige och Förintelsen. Debatt och dokument om Europas judar 1933-1945, Dialogos: Stockholm 2005, p. 160.

6   Karin Kvist, "A Study of Antisemitic Attitudes within Sweden's Wartime *Utlänningsbyrån*", in 'Bystanders' to the Holocaust. A Re-evaluation, David Cesarani & Paul A. Levine (eds.), Frank Cass: London 2002, p. 203.

7   For all the quotes in this paragraph, see Kvist Geverts 2008, p. 82-84.

8   For one of the first critiques of the war years in Sweden, see Maria-Pia Boëthus, *Heder och samvete. Sverige och andra världskriget*, Norstedt: Stockholm 1991.

9   Klas Åmark, *Att bo granne med ondskan. Sveriges förhållande till nazismen, Nazityskland och Förintelsen*, Albert Bonniers Förlag: Stockholm 2011, chap. 18, and most importantly p. 657-658.

10   Kvist Geverts 2008, chap. 4.

11   Svanberg & Tydén 2005, p. 228.

12   Kvist Geverts 2008 , p. 169 & 179-180.

13   Ola Larsmo, *Djävulssonaten. Ur det svenska hatets historia*, Albert Bonniers förslag: Stockholm 2007, p. 149-150.

14   Stéphane Bruchfeld & Paul A. Levine, *...om detta må ni berätta... En bok om Förintelsen i Europa 1933-1945*, Regeringskansliet Levande historia: Stockholm 1998, p. 43.

15   Svanberg & Tydén 2005, p. 237-241.

16   "Judepogromer måste stoppas", *Dagens Nyheter*, 12.9.1942 and editorial, *Dagens Nyheter*, 13.9.1942, quoted in Svanberg & Tydén 2005, p. 241-242.

17   Hugo Valentin, "Utrotningskriget mot judarna", *Göteborgs Handels- och Sjöfartstidning*, 13.10.1942, quoted in Svanberg & Tydén 2005, p. 260-246.

18   Svanberg & Tydén 2005, p. 249.

19   Svanberg & Tydén 2005, p. 250-257.

20   Svanberg & Tydén 2005, p. 258-259.

21   "Norge främst under 1942", in *Dagens Nyheter*, 31.12.1942, quoted in Svanberg & Tydén 2005, p. 260-261.

22   Paul A Levine, *From Indifference to Activism. Swedish Diplomacy and the Holocaust; 1938-1944*, Uppsala 1998; Mikael Byström, *En broder, gäst och parasit. Uppfattningar och föreställningar om utlänningar, flyktingar och flyktingpolitik i svensk offentlig debatt 1942-1947*, Stockholm 2006.

23   Levine 1998, p. X.

24   Kvist Geverts 2008, p. 289.

25   Kvist Geverts 2008, p. 214.

26   Kvist Geverts 2008, p. 217.

27   Karin Kock, "Öppen fråga till Kungl. Socialstyrelsen", *Socialdemokraten*, 7.9.1943.

28   Carl Christian Schmidt, "Socialstyrelsen svarar docent Kock", *Socialdemokraten*, 8.9.1943.

29   Karin Kock, "Socialstyrelsen och statistiken över flyktingarna", *Socialdemokraten*, 9.9.1943.

30   Carl Christian Schmidt, "Socialstyrelsen och flyktingarna", *Socialdemokraten*, 11.9.1943.

31   Karin Kock, "Folkras? Race? Rasse? Race?", *Socialdemokraten*, 9.10.1943.

32   Se exempelvis "Utlänningar i Sverige vid årsskiftet 1943/1944", Sociala Meddelanden, 1944:2, s. 152.

33   RA, Utrikesdepartementet (UD), 1920 års dossiersystem, P:1331, PM angående antalet flyktingar i Sverige, Gösta Engzell, 15.2.1944.

34 Erik Brandt (social democrat), speech in the Swedish Parliament, Riksdagstrycket 1943, första kammarens protokoll nr. 18, p. 6-27.
35 This is a truth with a modification. Jews were categorized as belonging to "the mosaic confession", but this information was used to signal "race" since they were placed in the column "foreign races", and not, which would make more sense, "foreign religions", see Rogers, John & Marie Clark Nelson, "'Lapps, Finns, Gypsies, Jews, and Idiots'. Modernity and the use of statistical categories in Sweden, in *Annales de démographie historique*, 2003:1, s. 71–72.
36 RA, PUK, F 3:1, Stenographic report of the commissions conversation with the head of the Bureau Bexelius, 11.5.1945, p. 86.
37 Mattias Tydén, "Att inte lägga sig i. Till frågan om Sveriges moraliska skuld till Förintelsen", in *Sverige och Nazityskland. Skuldfrågor och* moraldebatt, Lars M Andersson & Mattias Tydén (eds.), Dialogos: Stockholm 2007, p. 127.

References:

Boëthus, Maria-Pia, Heder och samvete. Sverige och andra världskriget, Norstedt: Stockholm 1991.

Bruchfeld, Stéphane & Paul A. Levine, ...*om detta må ni berätta... En bok om Förintelsen i Europa 1933-1945*, Regeringskansliet Levande historia: Stockholm 1998.

Byström, Mikael, "En talande tystnad? Ett antisemitiskt bakgrundsbrus i riksdagsdebatterna 1942-1947", in Lars M Andersson & Karin Kvist Geverts (eds.), *En problematisk relation? Flyktingpolitik och de judiska flyktingarna i Sverige 1920-1950*, Opuscula Historica Upsaliensia 36, Uppsala 2008, p. 119-137.

Bystrom, Mikael & Karin Kvist Geverts, "Från en aktivism till en annan. Hur ska Sveriges agerande i flyktingfrågan under andra världskriget förklaras?", *Sverige och Nazityskland. Skuldfrågor och moraldebatt*, Dialogos: Stockholm 2007, p. 148-167.

Byström, Mikael, *En broder, gäst och parasit. Uppfattningar och föreställningar om utlänningar, flyktingar och flyktingpolitik i svensk offentlig debatt 1942-1947*, Stockholm 2006.

Folkmängden inom administrativa områden den 31 december 1939, Statistiska Centralbyrån, Sveriges Officiella Statistik (SOS), P.A. Norstedt & Söner: Stockholm 1940.

Kock, Karin, "Öppen fråga till Kungl. Socialstyrelsen", *Socialdemokraten*, 7.9.1943.

Kock, Karin, "Socialstyrelsen och statistiken över flyktingarna", *Socialdemokraten*, 9.9.1943.

Kock, Karin, "Folkras? Race? Rasse? Race?", *Socialdemokraten*, 9.10.1943.

Kvist, Karin, "A Study of Antisemitic Attitudes within Sweden's Wartime *Utlänningsbyrån*", in 'Bystanders' to the Holocaust. A Re-evaluation, David Cesarani & Paul A. Levine (eds.), Frank Cass: London 2002, p. 199-211.

Kvist Geverts, Karin, Ett främmande element i nationen. Svensk flyktingpolitik och de judiska flyktingarna 1938-1944, Studia Historica Upsaliensia 233 & UUHGS Publications 2, dissertation, Uppsala 2008.

Larsmo, Ola, *Djävulssonaten. Ur det svenska hatets historia*, Albert Bonniers förslag: Stockholm 2007.

Lindberg, Hans, *Svensk flyktingpolitik under internationellt tryck 1936-1941*, Allmänna förlaget: Stockholm 1973.

Levine, Paul A, *From Indifference to Activism. Swedish Diplomacy and the Holocaust; 1938-1944*, Uppsala 1998.

Parlamentariska undersökningskommissionen (PUK), YK 984, Stenographic report of conversation with head of the Bureau Schmidt, 18.5.1945.

PUK, F 3:1, Stenographic report of the commissions conversation with the head of the Bureau Bexelius, 11.5.1945.

Riksdagstrycket 1943, första kammarens protokoll nr. 18.

Riksdagstrycket 1939, andra kammarens protokoll nr. 12.

Rogers, John & Marie Clark Nelson, "'Lapps, Finns, Gypsies, Jews, and Idiots'. Modernity and the use of statistical categories in Sweden, in *Annales de démographie historique*, 2003:1.

Schmidt, Carl Christian, "Socialstyrelsen svarar docent Kock", *Socialdemokraten*, 8.9.1943.

Schmidt, Carl Christian, "Socialstyrelsen och flyktingarna", *Socialdemokraten*, 11.9.1943.

Sociala Meddelanden, 1939:4.

Svanberg, Ingvar & Mattias Tydén, *Sverige och Förintelsen. Debatt och dokument om Europas judar 1933-1945*, Dialogos: Stockholm 2005.

Tydén, Mattias, "Att inte lägga sig i. Till frågan om Sveriges moraliska skuld till Förintelsen", in *Sverige och Nazityskland. Skuldfrågor och moraldebatt*, Lars M Andersson & Mattias Tydén (eds.), Dialogos: Stockholm 2007.

Utrikesdepartementet (UD), 1920 års dossiersystem, P:1331, PM angående antalet flyktingar i Sverige, Gösta Engzell, 15.2.1944.

Åmark, Klas, *Att bo granne med ondskan. Sveriges förhållande till nazismen, Nazityskland och Förintelsen*, Albert Bonniers Förlag: Stockholm 2011.

Helsinki: On the brink – Finland and the Holocaust Era

"The SS leadership did not forget the Jews in Finland, but there were strong arguments for Finland not emulating German Jewish policy, at least until a decisive German victory would have been secured..."

Oula Silvennoinen

The villa by the Wannsee, near Berlin, received a number of distinguished guests in January 20, 1942. The theme to be discussed with the leadership of Reinhard Heydrich, chief of the consolidated SS security apparatus, the *Reichssicherheitshauptamt*, was a solution to the so-called Jewish question. The solution would be final. By the time of the conference, the German administrators had become frustrated by the ineffectiveness of other solutions, like emigration and resettlement, and a decision to simply kill the Jews had already been taken. To assess the size of the task at hand, estimates of the Jewish population in all the European countries were circulated. For Finland, German intelligence had arrived at a remarkably accurate figure of 2300 persons.[1]

It was clear to the participants that the destruction of European Jewry in this scale would be an immense undertaking, and so it soon came to a discussion of priorities and marching order. An undersecretary at the German Foreign Ministry, Martin Luther, rose to speak. He underscored his belief that a blunt attempt to put the envisioned operation through in the Nordic countries would lead to "difficulties." A local postponement of the Final Solution would be in order, especially as the Nordic Jewish communities tended to be very small. Luther's suggestion was accepted and duly entered into the minutes of the conference.[2]

Finland's Jews were among those Nordic communities who had thus been granted a stay of execution. But how long would it last? By the time of the Wannsee conference, the discrimination, isolation, persecution, incarceration and murder of Europe's Jews had been going on for almost ten years. Also the Finnish public had had ample time to be informed, form an opinion and react. Until now, however, the persecution of Jews had been something happening far from Finland's shores. Soon it might become a domestic policy matter. For the Norwegian Jews, destruction came already the next summer. The Danish Jews were spared from active measures until late 1943. Jews in Sweden and Finland were, for the time being, outside the grasp of Nazi authorities. Nevertheless, Sweden was surrounded by Axis-held territory and Finland was a German ally, dependent on Germany for much of its supply needs and – should the war end victoriously for Germany – obviously susceptible to further political pressure regarding the Jewish question. Finland lived, during its alliance with Germany in 1941-1944, on the brink of the Holocaust.

After Hitler's coming to power in Germany in 1933, the Nazi persecution of Jews had been restricted to Germany itself. With Germany's successful annexations, and finally war, the area of active measures against the Jews kept both widening and getting more murderous in purpose. Ultimately, the most intensive killing came to be concentrated on Eastern Europe, on former Polish, Baltic and Soviet territory the historian Timothy Snyder has labeled the Bloodlands. Outside this core theatre of the Holocaust, however, was a peripheral zone, consisting of countries like Finland. Characteristic to this periphery of the Holocaust was that everywhere within this zone the Final Solution was either postponed or limited according to local circumstances and other needs considered more pressing by the Nazi leadership. From the Nordic countries to Bulgaria, these were all countries, one way or another, on the brink.

Finland and its Jews
The Jewish community in Finland had its origins in the 19th century. Finland had been part of the Swedish Empire since the Middle Ages, until conquered in 1809 by Russia, under which it continued as an autonomous Grand Duchy. It still kept its Swedish laws, however, by which Jews were forbidden to settle or practice their religion in the realm, barring a few designated places in Sweden proper. The first openly Jewish immigrants to Finland were former members of the Russian military, allowed to settle, but living without civil rights. With the collapse of the Russian Empire, Finland among other borderlands of the Empire declared independence in 1917. This act of state

was soon followed by civil war between the insurgent, radical wing of the Social Democratic Party, and the government forces, representing the wide non-Socialist sections of society.

From the civil war and revolution both at home and in Russia, a newly created Eastern Europe emerged. The peace of Dorpat (Tarto) of 1920, a formal peace treaty with Soviet Russia, ended for Finland the period of internal upheaval, civil war and *Freikorps*-style expeditionary warfare which characterized the birth of the successors of empire in Eastern Europe. Finland settled down as a republic under parliamentary rule, seasoned with a presidency with wide powers. Politically, the country remained rather unstable, with short-lived minority governments following each other in often bewildering succession. Despite their crushing defeat in the Civil War, the Communists quickly returned to the political scene under a number of cover organizations much to the chagrin of the political Right, who saw in the republic everyday a travesty of everything they had fought for in the Civil War. Yet it was the wide political middle ground, from the moderate Right to the Center and the moderate Social Democrats, which proved to be an enduring backbone to the new state, shaken neither by the continuous schemes of the Communists to whip up societal crisis in preparation for an armed insurrection, nor the *coup d'état*-plots by numerous and sometimes influential radical Rightist cabals.

Anti-Semitism in Finland had a history quite comparable to the Scandinavian countries. Its oldest layer was Christian anti-Semitism. The Swedish Crown had seen the Jews, like other religious minorities, as a source of discord and disunity, and barred them from settling into the realm except to a few strictly defined locations in Sweden proper. After Finland's administrative ties to Sweden were severed, 19th-century developments in European anti-Semitism arrived in Finland through cultural contacts and links to both Russia and Germany. The question of civil rights for Jews, although occasionally raised, remained unresolved through opposition by the Imperial government in St. Petersburg. It was only after independence, that Finland in 1918 finally extended citizenship rights, not automatically, but upon application, to its Jewish inhabitants. Only Romania was even slower to do this among European states.

The 1917 Bolshevik coup in Russia had given Western anti-Semitism a new shot of vigor. The idea of disproportional Jewish activity in the Socialist movement was of course nothing new. The political myths of the conservative and radical Right coalesced around the central core of the incontestable but incomprehensible evil of Bolshevism, crystallizing into a thoroughly conspiratorial theory of the world and society. Western anti-Semitism became tightly intertwined with anti-Communism. At its heart was a paranoid belief of everything that happened in the world being traceable to the evil forces of world Jewry, Bolshevism and Freemasonry, seeking to undermine all that was pure and noble. The language of threatening decay, social and moral, gave particular impetus to this world-view.

Also in Finland the shrillest forms of anti-Semitism were the reserve of the ideologically enlightened members of radical nationalist, Fascist and "patriotic" circles. Nevertheless, the majority of Finns either had encountered, or shared in, the common anti-Semitic prejudices of the era, typically visible as name-calling, derogatory remarks, jokes and cartoons. The belief that the Jews were somehow behind the Bolshevik revolution and Soviet system was ubiquitous. Yet it was anti-Communism, not anti-Semitism which could move the masses in interwar and wartime Finland. As the German ambassador to Finland, Wipert von Blücher, was to remark in a report to the German Foreign Ministry in December 1942, the Finns were generally far less interested in German propaganda against the "Jews and plutocrats," than that against the Soviets. The diminutive number of Jews in Finland, as well as their almost exclusive concentration in the three largest urban centers of the country, and thus away from the experience world of the majority of Finns, did not encourage the growth of anti-Semitism into a major political topic. A "Jewish Question" failed to manifest itself as a prominent theme in Finnish politics and public discussion.[3]

Foreigners and Refugees
Hitler's coming to power and the subsequent National Socialist dictatorship in Germany did not rouse great enthusiasm in Finland. The Nazi regime with its brutal repressive measures against political opponents was widely condemned, from the Social Democratic press to the liberal and moderate Right. Exceptions to this were the numerous but diminutive organs of the Finnish radical nationalist Right and the single major political party Finnish radical nationalism was able to produce: the Patriotic Movement (*Isänmaallinen Kansanliike*), which consciously emulated the trappings of Italian Fascism by adopting party uniforms and the rudiments of a leader cult. Its organ, *Ajan Suunta*, became a mouthpiece also for Finnish self-avowed Fascist

and national socialist groups, and the newspaper remained on a steadfastly pro-German and anti-Semitic course right until its abolishment at the end of the war.[4]

The true problem from the perspective of most Finns, however, wasn't Hitler's new Germany, but the Soviet Union. The Worker's and Peasant's State remained a constant security political problem for Finland throughout the interwar period. Finnish foreign policy was aimed at restraining the Soviet regime through cooperation with other states sharing a border with the Soviet Union, as well as through the international community and the League of Nations. But no good solutions ever presented themselves. What was left was the wish, apparently increasingly realistic as the 1930's progressed, that the vocally anti-Communist National Socialist Germany would provide the necessary counterweight to growing Soviet assertiveness and power.

Nazi discrimination and terror against Germany's Jews naturally was a popular theme also in the Finnish press. It was also noted by Finland's representatives abroad, who throughout the 1930s reported to Helsinki the excesses of the regime. Towards the end of the 1930s, however, a wish to not antagonize Germany began to have an effect on the way Germany's domestic policies were treated in the Finnish press and publicly. When a Czech citizen, the Sudeten German Andre Riebling in 1936 published in the Finnish Social Democratic press an exposé of the policy of repression against the perceived enemies of the Nazi state, the Finnish Security Police drove through his deportation from Finland. Finally, the beginning of the world war caused the press in Finland to be subjected to censorship. Increasingly after 1940, Germany and its policies could not be openly criticized for fear of alienating this potential supporter. This task was left to the Swedish press, widely read and noticed in Finland as well. Criticism of Germany on the treatment of Jews was a part of public speech that was "inappropriate for a small country," as the chief of censorship in 1941-1943, Kustaa Vilkuna characterized it.[5]

Germany's Jewish policy in the 1930s had other consequences which demanded some kind of a reaction from other states. The chief manifestation was a growing number of Jews seeking emigration from Germany and German-controlled area. Throughout the interwar period, Finland had pursued a restrictive immigration policy. At its heart was a belief that the country simply could not afford to take in unproductive immigrants, even less potential troublemakers and security hazards. Finland nevertheless in the 1920s allowed into the country some 35 000 Finnic and non-Bolshevik refugees from Soviet Russia. The number was considered remarkably high in comparison to the perceived capacity of the Finnish economy and capabilities of the state. The care of the refugees was entrusted to the state-run Refugee Aid Centre (*Valtion Pakolaisavustuskeskus*).[6]

The Jewish refugee problem came to a head after the German occupation of Austria in March 1938. Among others, also the Finnish consulate in Vienna was flooded with Austrian Jewish applicants seeking visas abroad. It took some time for Germany to revoke the existing travel documents issued by the now-defunct state of Austria and replace them with German passports. The Finnish policy was to keep considering Austrian passports as valid, but refuse entry from those passengers without a right of return to Germany. In October 1938, the passports of German and Austrian Jews began to be stamped with a capital red J, signifying that the passport holder was Jewish and without a right to return to Germany. This dramatically worsened the chances of holders of such passports to be accepted anywhere.[7]

Finland's consulate in Vienna had been rather liberal in granting visas to Austrian Jews, with which a few hundred were able to enter the country. Even this small number roused the fears. In August 1938, a number of unions representing handicrafts and retail trade, fearing competition on the part of the refugee Jewish tradesmen entering Finland, appealed to the government to deport those already admitted, and prevent the entry of further Jewish refugees into Finland. The matter came to a head with the turning back in late August of a group of 53 Austrian Jewish refugees on board the steamer Ariadne, seeking entry into Finland. They were forced to remain on board and return in due course to Germany. The liberal and social-democrat press in Finland erupted in appeals for the relaxation of immigration policy, and the Swedish press soon joined in criticism of the Finnish government. But the adopted line was not eased.[8]

Apart from the state-run Refugee Aid Centre, which anyway concentrated its efforts solely on the refugees from Soviet Russia, the Finnish state had no organs or means to aid the refugees in Finland. They were thus on their own, and had to secure help through their personal contacts and the still-feeble structures of the Finnish civic society. Jewish refugees in Finland were helped by the Finnish Jewish community, certain Christian organizations and the Social Democratic Party. The National Socialist takeover in Germany had already in 1933 created pressure for European sister parties to help those Social Democrats fleeing Germany, and the Spanish Civil War further increased the need for organized aid efforts. In Finland, the Social Democratic refugee aid grew from the concept of succor to the "victims of Fascism," into whom the Jewish refugees could in time also be included.[9]

As the 1930s drew to a close, Western Europe drifted apart from Eastern Europe. European countries were more or less forced to choose between the two great dictatorships, Germany and the Soviet Union. For Western Europe the traditional enemy, the Bolsheviks and the Soviet Union, was rapidly replaced by a much more acute threat, that of a resurgent and rearming Germany. In Eastern Europe, the choice tended to be equally simple. The Soviet Union was a major security policy problem throughout the region, and its growing assertiveness led its neighbors, Poland excepted, to seek support and protection from Hitler's Germany. Finland was no exception. Finland's official policy of neutrality was dictated by the glaring lack of serious security political options and credible allies. If it came to a choice between Hitler and Stalin, few in Finland were ready to seriously consider the choice: Germany, even under the Nazi regime, was almost a foregone conclusion. As the former prime minister, future president of the republic and a towering figure of the Finnish political Right, J. K. Paasikivi, summed it up in a letter in April 1939: "should this policy of neutrality fail, we will end up under either the Bolsheviks or the Germans. And the latter option is better, even if not pleasant."[10]

In the Shadow of the War

The August 1939 non-aggression agreement between Germany and the Soviet Union carved up Eastern Europe and placed Finland within the Soviet sphere of interests. Germany accordingly did not react when the Soviet Union cancelled the Finnish-Soviet non-aggression treaty and attacked Finland in November 30. Throughout the conflict Germany maintained an official pro-Soviet policy and obstructed international efforts to deliver aid to Finland. This was in marked contrast to the wave of international sympathy, which expressed itself in efforts to help Finland both materially, and by a stream of volunteers from several countries. As a sign of inter-Nordic sympathy, the largest contingents of volunteers came from Sweden, Denmark and Norway. At the end of January 1940 the Finnish military leadership extended the call also to the foreigners residing in Finland, while at the same time exposing the most enduring ethnic prejudices even a situation of dire crisis could not erase, deciding to accept everyone "whether they have military training or not, émigrés of Russian origin and Jewish refugees from Central Europe nevertheless excluded."[11]

No amount of sympathy or volunteers could decide the war. Finland was forced to sue for peace in March 1940, had to cede considerable tracts of its eastern regions, and hastily resettle the roughly 400 000 thousand internal refugees fleeing from the area to be ceded. The fear of renewed Soviet aggression led the government to eagerly embrace any help it could get from Germany, and the first German troops entered Finnish territory in September 1940. Ostensibly, it was a question of transit traffic between Germany and German-occupied northern Norway. In Finland the agreement was widely interpreted to mean a tacit guarantee against further Soviet designs on Finland. The side consequence, however, was that Finland became irresistibly entangled in and drawn to the German plans for war against the Soviet Union. On the eve of operation Barbarossa, Germany had already almost 100 000 soldiers on Finnish territory. Even more crucial, the entire northern half of the country had been agreed to constitute a German-controlled theatre of war. This had further consequences, as the German military was to be accompanied also by the German Security Police, tasked with waging the ideological and racial war against the Soviet Union.

The German combat troops entering Soviet territory upon commencement of hostilities on June 22, 1941 were followed by special task forces of the German Security Police and the *Sicherheitsdienst* (SD). These were divided into four *Einsatzgruppen*, roughly thousand-strong each, which divided into smaller *Einsatzkommandos*. Their intended use was to pacify the occupied territory, and prepare it for the future German 'overlordship' by liquidating those strata of society deemed capable of resistance and leadership: Soviet functionaries, Red Army political officers, active Communists – and any and all Jews. Almost as an afterthought, the SS leadership in June 1941 set in motion measures to set up a Security Police and SD *Einsatzkommando* also for the German-controlled part of the Finnish-Soviet front, Finnish Lapland. The unit was hastily put together, its designated leader, *SS-Sturmbannführer* Gustav vom Felde, arriving in Helsinki in the last days of June, when the assault into the Soviet Union was already in full swing further south.[12]

In Helsinki, vom Felde contacted the leadership of the Finnish Security Police, and the guidelines for joint action in the coming campaign were laid out. The competence of the German security police and the *Einsatzkom-mando* did not extend to Finnish citizens, but both sides accepted the need to hasten the destruction of the Soviet Union, and ease the future governance of former Soviet territory, by destroying the perceived mainstays of the Soviet system. The Finnish Security Police therefore detached several of its officials to work under vom Felde's command, and he departed for Lapland.[13]

With Finland's joining the war against the Soviet Union, and the advance of Finnish troops ultimately into Soviet Karelia, tens of thousands of prisoners-of-war were taken, far more than the prisoner-of-war administration was equipped to handle. After this, there were three different groups of Jews in war-time Finland. The Finnish Jews, those either holding Finnish citizenship or being equal to citizens on the basis of an already lengthy residence, were in the most secure position. For the civilian Jewish refugees, things seemed already much dimmer. The only way to leave Finland after June 1941 was via Sweden, the only alternative being to remain in Finland, in the worst case without permission, documents, or livelihood. Non-citizens were subject to deportation should they attract the negative attention of the Security Police, and a deportation to German-controlled areas most likely ended in death. In 1941-1942, the Security Police deported a total of 12 Jewish refugees into the hands of German authorities.

The third group of Jews consisted of Soviet Jewish prisoners-of-war. Their total number in Finnish custody was recorded to be 405, but it is likely to have been higher due to the fact that many Jewish prisoners undoubtedly sought to hide their ethnic identity. The Finnish military authorities adopted the German practice of separating the prisoners suspected of political activity, commissars and *politruks* into a separate camp, from which they funneled the most troublesome into the hands of the *Einsatzkommando Finnland* in the north. A total of 521 Soviet prisoners-of-war are known to have been handed over this way, among them 49 prisoners registered as Jews. Successful war operations provided the rationale and the cover under which it was possible for the Finnish authorities to participate in the ideological and racial war of the mighty German ally.[14]

The high-water mark of Finnish-German cooperation was reached in 1941-1942. The ebb began with the waning German fortunes of war. In November 1942 the Finnish Security Police could still arrange a deportation of eight Jewish refugees from Finland into German hands, but the ensuing press clamor was already a symptom of the weakening grip of censorship, and doubts about Finland's future in the war. The German attempt to deport the Danish Jews in late 1943 caused even such highly visible friends of Germany as the philosopher Eino Kaila to publicly denounce Nazi Jewish policy in the major daily of the Finnish political Right. Finland was looking for a way out of the war, and there was less and less reason to remain politely silent about such matters.[15]

The window of opportunity when Germany could have presented Finland with an official request to deport either all, or the foreign Jews in Finland, had by 1943 closed. While all the Jews in Finland had been earmarked for destruction in due time, Finland was never put to the ultimate test. As was fitting for a small country, throughout the war Finland had sought to maintain relations to the Western Allies. Even the British declaration of war in 1941 did not frustrate this policy of insuring oneself for all eventualities. After Stalingrad, United States' support came to be seen as increasingly essential for a successful exit from the war and Finland's continued existence as an independent state. It was also important that Sweden remained a relatively free enclave, where the politicians, press and public both followed, and were keen to comment on, Finnish affairs. The SS leadership did not forget the Jews in Finland, but there were strong arguments for Finland not emulating German Jewish policy, at least until a decisive German victory would have been secured.

The Demise of Exceptionalism

Carl Gustaf Emil Mannerheim, Marshal of Finland and President of the Republic, paid a visit to the Helsinki synagogue on Finland's Independence Day, December 6th, 1944. The war on the European continent was still going on in full force, and the destruction of its Jewish population continued in the extermination camps. The old marshal was a shrewd politician who throughout his career successfully avoided compromising himself directly, even while he at times entertained the conspiratorial schemes of the radical Right. The visit to the synagogue was another clever move, with which Mannerheim sought to secure the potentially valuable loyalty of the Jewish community. That he felt it advisable to do so is an indication of the growing need to distance oneself from the still in-progress Holocaust in order to maintain political credibility.[16]

At the time of Mannerheim's visit, the battle for Finland's future course was already in full swing and the Holocaust a potential weapon in it. There were two ways to try to avoid accusations of culpability to Nazi atrocities and the accompanying political discredit: by resigning from responsibility, or by speaking out. Mannerheim, and virtually the whole Finnish political elite, chose the first course by acting as if they had nothing to explain. The reasons for their choice are to be found in the post-war position of Finland, which came to be very different from the rest of the defeated and occupied Eastern Europe. The choice was crucial in determining the shape of post-war Finnish discussion regarding the Holocaust.

Finland was never occupied, and while the Communists immediately re-turned to the political scene after the Finnish-Soviet armistice in September 1944, they failed to gain control of the key state institutions. The majority of the parliament, the civil service, courts and the military remained in the hands of non-Communists. *Status quo ante bellum* prevailed, and most mem-bers of the pre-war political elite and civil service were able to continue their business as usual also after the war. In 1941 Finland had been taken to war by a broad based coalition government including the Social Democrats, and had been governed during the war in an atmosphere of *Burgfrieden*. After the war, the Social Democrats emerged as perhaps the most active anti-Com-munists in the battle to limit the growth of the Far Left influence. While the Communists and their allies sought to change the *status quo* also through ac-cusations of Fascism and war crimes, their efforts were eventually frustrated by the fact that the vast majority of Finnish politicians had little interest in burrowing into the embarrassing details of the very recent past.[17]

Immediate post-war political necessities have continued to shape the discourse on Holocaust in Finland, to this day. Suggestions of connections between war-time Finland and the Holocaust still tend to bring forward defensive reactions, consisting of comments seeking to relativize or belittle Finnish responsibility. A typical rhetorical tactic is to divert attention to Sta-lin's crimes, which supposedly makes it superfluous to even speak about those of Hitler. The number of Jews victimized through direct acts of Finnish au-thorities is quickly declared so low as not to warrant any further discussion. Or, it is said to be preposterous to pay so much attention to the victims, when there were so many Jews who on the contrary found refuge in Finland, and whom Finland can be said to have protected. To any of these tropes a hardly veiled allegation of Far Left political sympathies can be added, intended to demolish the credibility of anyone seeking to connect Finland's history with the history of the Holocaust. They simply have nothing to do with each other, runs the creed of Finnish exceptionalism.

Defensiveness is a symptom of underlying guilt, sustained by decades of circling around but never really engaging the real issue. Finnish exceptionalism has rested on the convenient myth of the separate war, which has allowed the Finns also not confront the memory of the Holocaust. Within the exceptionalist framework, Finland is not really perceived as part of a larger whole, of Europe, or Nordic countries. Within this narrative framework, Finland fought alone against the Soviets in 1939-1940, then again simultaneously with, but independent of, Germany in 1941-1944, had virtually nothing to do with the Holocaust, instead protecting both its own Jewish minority and a not inconsiderable number of Jewish refugees, and generally being a country where "anti-Semitism simply did not exist," to borrow the promotional sleeve text of one early study. In the same narrative vein, Finland finally emerges into the post-war period with a peculiar, but actually a shrewd and very independent-minded arrangement with the Soviet Union only the unenlightened could disparage as *Finnlandisierung*.[18]

The national memory culture and historiography have both displayed a strong tendency towards isolationism. Subjects of historical study difficult or impossible to understand without an inter- or transnational background – such as cooperation with the Nazi regime, or the Holocaust – are either dismissed as being outside the Finnish experience, or are given an exclusively national, exceptionalist interpretation – like describing Finnish participation in the *Waffen-SS* as a national project aimed at securing Germany's diplomatic support without further meaningful connotations.

The fall of the Soviet Union and Finland's entry into the process of European unification seems finally to have begun to change the rules and demands to memory policy. Finnish exceptionalism regarding the Holocaust and the whole German alliance period was born out of the post-war political necessities, produced by the uncomfortably close distance to the Soviet Union. During the 2000s, research has brought forth new knowledge regarding Finland's history with the Holocaust. The public awareness is slowly digesting the fact that Finland in 1939-1945 participated in a general European conflict where it simply could not pick and choose which of its dimensions it got involved with. There were forces and people in Finland quite ready to cooperate with the Nazi regime in realizing even its most extreme ideological and racial projects, and it is time to face these unwelcome facts.

159

Bibliography

Hans-Jürgen Döscher, Das Auswärtige Amt im Dritten Reich, Berlin: Siedler 1987.

Michael Jonas, Kolmannen valtakunnan lähettiläs, Wipert von Blücher ja Suomi, Helsinki: Ajatus 2010.

Matti Lackman, Esko Riekki, Jääkärivärväri, Etsivän Keskuspoliisin päällikkö, Suomalaisen SS-pataljoonan luoja, Helsinki: SKS 2007.

Hannu Rautkallio, Finland and the Holocaust, The Rescue of Finland's Jews, New York: Holocaust Library 1987.

Esko Salminen: Aselevosta kaappaushankkeeseen, Sensuuri ja itsesensuuri Suomen lehdistössä 1944-1948, Helsinki: Otava 1979.

Oula Silvennoinen, Geheime Waffenbrüderschaft, Die sicherheitspolizeiliche Zusammenarbeit zwischen Finnland und Deutschland 1933-1944, Darmstadt: Wissenschaftliche Buchgesellschaft 2010.

Oula Silvennoinen, Paperisydän, Gösta Serlachiuksen elämä, Helsinki: Siltala 2012.

Jukka Tarkka: Karhun kainalossa, Helsinki: Otava, 2012.

Taimi Torvinen, Pakolaiset Suomessa Hitlerin valtakaudella, Helsinki: Otava 1984.

Taimi Torvinen, Kadimah, Suomen juutalaisten historia, Helsinki: Otava 1989.

Vesa Vares: Hakaristin kuva. Kansallissosialistinen Saksa Suomen johtavassa puoluelehdistössä sisä- ja ulkopoliittisena tekijänä 1933-1939, Turku: Turun yliopisto 1986.

Bernd Wegner, Oliver von Wrochem and Daniel Schümmer (eds.), Finnland und Deutschland, Studien zur Geschichte im 19. und 20. Jahrhundert, Hamburg: Verlag Dr. Kovač 2009.

Lars Westerlund (ed.), Prisoners of War Deaths and People Handed Over to Germany and the Soviet Union in 1939-55, Helsinki: National Archives 2008.

Notes

1 Hans-Jürgen Döscher, Das Auswärtige Amt im Dritten Reich, Berlin: Siedler 1987, p. 227-236.
2 Döscher, Das Auswärtige Amt, p. 227-236.
3 Michael Jonas, Kolmannen valtakunnan lähettiläs, Wipert von Blücher ja Suomi, Helsinki: Ajatus 2010, p. 270-271.
4 Vesa Vares: Hakaristin kuva. Kansallissosialistinen Saksa Suomen johtavassa puoluelehdis-tössä sisä- ja ulkopoliittisena tekijänä 1933-1939, Turku: Turun yliopisto 1986, p. 14-21; Matti Lackman, Esko Riekki, Jääkärivärväri, Etsivän Keskuspoliisin päällikkö, Suomalai-sen SS-pataljoonan luoja, Helsinki: SKS 2007, p. 323.
5 Lackman, Esko Riekki, p. 332; Taimi Torvinen, Pakolaiset Suomessa Hitlerin valtakaudel-la, Helsinki: Otava 1984, p. 110-111; Esko Salminen: Aselevosta kaappaushankkeeseen, Sensuuri ja itsesensuuri Suomen lehdistössä 1944-1948, Helsinki: Otava 1979, p. 18-22.
6 Torvinen, Pakolaiset Suomessa, p. 126-127.
7 Torvinen, Pakolaiset Suomessa, p. 91.
8 Torvinen, Pakolaiset Suomessa, p. 95-96.
9 Torvinen, Pakolaiset Suomessa, p. 127-133.
10 Oula Silvennoinen, Geheime Waffenbrüderschaft, Die sicherheitspolizeiliche Zusam-menarbeit zwischen Finnland und Deutschland 1933-1944, Darmstadt: Wissenschaftliche Buchgesellschaft 2010, p. 33.
11 Oula Silvennoinen, Paperisydän, Gösta Serlachiuksen elämä, Helsinki: Siltala 2012, p. 469.
12 Silvennoinen, Geheime Waffenbrüderschaft, p. 164-168.
13 Silvennoinen, Geheime Waffenbrüderschaft, p. 168-171.
14 Ida Suolahti: 'Prisoner of War Transfers During the Continuation War', in: Lars Wester-lund (ed.), Prisoners of War Deaths and People Handed Over to Germany and the Soviet Union in 1939-55, Helsinki: National Archives 2008, p. 154, 157, footnote 292.
15 Malte Gasche and Johan Strang, 'Der Kriegseinsatz des finnischen Philosophen Eino Kai-la', in: Bernd Wegner, Oliver von Wrochem and Daniel Schümmer (eds.), Finnland und Deutschland, Studien zur Geschichte im 19. und 20. Jahrhundert, Hamburg: Verlag Dr. Kovač 2009, p. 92-93.
16 Taimi Torvinen, Kadimah, Suomen juutalaisten historia, Helsinki: Otava 1989, p. 161-162.
17 Salminen: Aselevosta kaappaushankkeeseen, p. 52; Jukka Tarkka: Karhun kainalossa, Hel-sinki: Otava 2012, p. 26.
18 Hannu Rautkallio, Finland and the Holocaust, The Rescue of Finland's Jews, New York: Holocaust Library 1987.

Oslo: The escape from Norway

*"Regardless of how the various escapes proceeded, whether they were organ-
ised on an ad hoc basis by family and networks of friends, or were organised
beforehand, we are dealing with individuals who displayed a significant
spirit of civilian engagement and a huge amount of bravery."*

Irene Levin

Around 60 per cent of Norwegian Jews managed to escape to Sweden during the Second World War. This means a total of around 1100 people. About
35 per cent (772 people) were deported to Auschwitz, of which only 34 returned home again. An unknown number survived by remaining in Norway
and hiding in hospitals or other places. Some changed their identity and kept
this new profile after liberation. Not one woman or child survived the first
round of selections at Auschwitz (Bruland, 2008).

However, this chapter looks at the people who helped Jews to escape.
As is well known, giving assistance to Jews during the war meant the death
penalty. How then did Jews manage to escape from Norway? How were they
rescued? By whom? Were organized groups involved, or did individual Jews
organize their own escape?

In comparison with Denmark, the major *Aktion* against the Jews in Norway happened much earlier in the war. On the 26th of October 1942, all
male Jews over the age of 15 were arrested. At the same time, all Jewish
women were ordered to report to the nearest police station on a daily basis,
and Jewish financial assets and property were confiscated. Exactly a month
later, on the 26th of November, the general arrest order was expanded to
include all Jewish women and children. The subsequent deportations were
carried out using four transport ships, of which the *Donau* shipment on the
26th of November 1942 was the largest, with 532 people on board. The final deportation occurred on the 25th of February 1943 with MS *Gutenland*,

which carried 158 Jews. In addition to this, MS *Monte Rosa* carried male Jews bound for Auschwitz on two occasions (Mendelsohn, 1986).

This book deals with the flight from Norway and the role of civil society. My first question is whether Norway actually had a functioning civil society with people willing to help during the war years?

Civil society or civilian engagement?

What do we mean by the phrase "civil society"? According to Håkon Lorentzen (2007, p. 9), finding a satisfactory definition for the term "civil society" is no easy task. Sometimes, we might use a narrow definition like "non-profit" (that is to say outside of the commercial market), or "non-governmental" (outside, of the state) in order to indicate an absence of state involvement (Lorentzen, 2007). Overall, the concept of civil society has a broader and more positive tone and suggests the idea of actions and activities carried out for the general public good. In this context, civil society is posed as being in contrast to the state body. Thus, civil society exists in the nexus between the state, commercial markets and the family unit. Civil society is often described as being more caring and has warmer connotations than the state – something that has a heart, as opposed to the state body, which is often portrayed as being cold and impersonal.

Lorentzen's definition of civil society refers to that situation in peacetime. But what about wartime? In Norway, the state was taken over and administered by the Nazis, and the government was in exile in London. Clearly, the Nazified Norwegian regime had a different attitude to civilian alliances than the Norwegian government in exile. In fact, the Nazi regime carried out an extensive analysis of popular and voluntary organizations.

A key element within the concept of civil society refers to civilian engagement; that is – when civilians engage with some body or group that is larger and exterior to themselves (Lorentzen, 2007, p 9). In this context, one might ask whether the more organized resistance struggle throughout the Second World War can be seen as an example of activity engendered by civil society? This is difficult to answer where Norway is concerned, because we soon get into the question of the voluntary nature of the resistance movement. For example, was membership in the resistance organization, Milorg, voluntary? Of course, it is true that there was a voluntary element at play. But at the same time, members were obliged to submit to a military command structure running along hierarchical lines (Kragelund, 2013). Were individuals free to cancel their membership just as in any normal civilian association? Presumably, this would have been frowned upon given that those involved were in possession of very sensitive information that could not be shared outside the group. If a member were to pull out, this would possibly raise suspicions about loyalty and betrayal. Some people solved this dilemma by getting over the border to Sweden, but even as a refugee in Sweden one was expected to support the overall goal: Norway's liberation (Kragelund, 2013).

The central motivation, therefore, for any kind of "peoples movement" is civilian engagement. In other words, when separate individuals, based on an "inner conviction that an important issue is at stake are moved to form an alliance, civilian engagement has been established" (Lorentzen, 2007, p 10).

During the war, many citizens were involved in various forms of civilian engagement. The fact that civilian engagement was present does not rule out the possibility that this involvement was politically motivated. However, the motives could have arisen from religious convictions via Norway's state church congregations, for example. Even though the church is part of the state structure, genuine civilian engagement cannot be ruled out. And it is precisely in this concept of a public spirited *civilian engagement*, it seems to me, that we find the motivation for the help given to fugitives and refugees, rather than from civil society as a whole. The term civilian engagement also has the advantage that we are not obliged to link the various activities to one particular sector of society. Civilian engagement transcends the civil society framework and can thus be located in a wide variety of social scenarios. In what follows, we will examine the way civilian engagement proved to be a decisive factor in the escape of Jewish people from Norway as their situation worsened.

Different forms of escape

The deportation of Norwegian Jews took place between October and November 1942. The war had not yet turned against the Nazis at this point. In this period, the Jewish community in Norway was just at the beginnings of an integration process (Banik and Levin 2010). There had been Jews in Norway since 1851, but at the beginning only very few Jews settled in Norway (25 per year).[1] Jewish immigration did not become numerically significant until 1880-1890, and the largest number came in around the year 1905. By the time the Second World War broke out, the integration process was well under way. There can be no doubt that Jews welcomed this process. The ability to speak fluent Norwegian was highly valued amongst Jews resident in Norway. In fact, those speaking with a marked *gebrokken* pronunciation were even ridiculed by their own kinsmen. Norwegian Jews followed the cultural customs and practices observed by most Norwegians – they adopted Norwegian values like a love of the great outdoors, rambling, hiking and similar pastimes. They also changed their surnames so that Norwegians would find it easier to pronounce them (Banik and Levin, 2010). However, despite these attempts at integration, Jews did not have a high profile in wider Norwegian society. They were too few in numbers and had not established sufficiently deep roots in society for that to happen.[2]

When the situation became much more fraught in the late autumn of 1942, Jews resorted to four main types of escape. These escape routes were not always sharply delineated and civilian engagement manifested itself in slightly different ways depending on the form of escape chosen, which can be summarized as:

1. Unaided escape
2. Escape organized on an *ad hoc* basis by family units and extended family networks
3: Escape routes organized beforehand by, for example, the "Carl Fredriksen Transport"
4: Escape routes organized to save particular groups – for example, children from the Jewish Nursery School.

Unaided escapes

Most Jews in Norway got across to Sweden via one or more helpers. But a number of them made their own way there – either because they did not have the necessary resources, or because they lacked the right contacts (Tangestuen 2004, Levin, 2007). In these instances, it was the Jews themselves who possessed the requisite civilian engagement and courage.

In order to be part of an organized escape, one had to pay. There is precious little record of what Jews actually paid for escape operations. Presumably these sums were calculated on the basis of ability to pay. There is an example of a well to do family that paid NOK 6000 for each person included in the rescue operation. In all, this involved seven persons who in total paid NOK 42,000. Whilst others had to hand over between NOK 600 and 1000 per person, all according to how their financial situation was assessed. In

Skien, there was a ship's captain who demanded 15,000 Swedish kroner to ship a mother and her three children across to Sweden. As the family involved could not pay this kind of money, the Norwegian helper resorted to threatening the captain with his gun so as to get the family across to safety. Mats Tangestuen (2012) has described how the rescue operation called the "Carl Fredriksen Transport Operation" required NOK 150 from each participant, but that nobody was refused because of an inability to pay (see below for more on the Carl Fredriksen operation). Thus, no Jew was refused participation in the Carl Fredriksen operation because of a lack of funds. However, Jews were not aware of this fact. Moreover, the Carl Fredriksen plan was not put into effect until after the MS *Donau* had departed from Oslo quay on November 26, 1942 and many Jews had already managed to get over to Sweden by that point.

Escape organized on an ad hoc basis by family and extended family networks
This form of escape developed spontaneously when individual citizens came to recognize how dangerous the situation had become for Jews. The link person involved was often a friend or neighbor. He or she would then contact someone else who, in turn, would contact an appropriate person. Thus a contact chain, inspired by civilian engagement and courage, was established by a set of individuals. The exact nature of each chain depended on the individual situation. The person whom the neighbor or friend contacted on behalf of the escaping Jews would often be another immediate family member or relative who they could trust implicitly. For our purposes, we can talk of family and extended family networks.

Whilst seeking a hiding place, the helpers would invariably end up coming into contact with the resistance network. It is estimated that in order for one or two people to be rescued, a chain of 9 to 25 helpers would have been needed. All links in the chain were equally important in achieving a successful result. But, of course, the chain was completely dependent on someone starting it in the first place.

After the arrest order for all Jewish men was issued on October 26, 1942, Fanny Raskow was to be found pacing backwards and forwards across the floor of her little apartment in Oslo and crying. She was pregnant and her husband Herman had gone into hiding a couple of miles away. Then there was a knock at the door. It was Fanny's neighbor Einar Follestad who asked: Do you know where Herman is?

"That's the problem," Fanny replied. "He could turn up here any minute and there's nowhere for him to hide in this place. This apartment's not safe." Einar's wife Agnes had contacted her parents the day before and expressed her concern about the fate of their Jewish neighbors. "Bring them here if things take a turn for the worse," her parents had told her. In this way, Agnes Follestad had begun to prepare for what was to come next.

When Fanny and Herman arrived at the home of Agnes's parents the next day, her father immediately telephoned Professor Kristine Bonnevie who was related to Agnes sister, Alfhild Bonnevie. "We have two bags of turnips for you" were the code words used. When the Jewish couple got to Kristine Bonnevie, she rang her nephew Harald Bryn who, accompanied by his wife Nanti, left a dinner party to join them immediately. After an hour of questioning (they could have been spies) Harald Bryn slammed his hand down onto the table and said: "They arrested my good friend Professor Goldsmidt at the border. I'm going to help you." Harald Bryn contacted his close friend and art critic Finn Nielsen who was himself an artist. The Raskows were then hidden in the ceiling of Finn Nielsen's studio. After a week passed, Nielsen returned to say that he too was being sought but that he had found a hideaway for them at a place belonging to some friends across the street.

In this new place of concealment, Fanny and Herman had neither food supplies nor fuel to warm the apartment. Nor had the contact who was supposed to knock on the door three times ever shown up. In the end, Fanny telephoned a doctor with a made up story that her husband was on the verge of suicide. The doctor understood right away what was really going on and placed Herman into a psychiatric hospital.

One day, when Fanny went to visit her husband, the head doctor warned her that she should make plans to escape because "they did not know how much longer they would be in control of the hospital." The warning from the doctor seemed to present Fanny with an impossible task as she did not have the kind of contacts that were required. But as soon as she got back to her mother's apartment, where she was staying at the time, she received a telephone call: "I know you are in difficulties. Bring 1000 kroner per person and your ration cards with you tomorrow and stand outside the entrance to the psychiatric clinic at 6pm." It was clear that the doctor had arranged this contact with these helpers. The next day, Herman was discharged and they stood waiting for a taxi at the agreed time of 6pm. No taxi came. Nor was there a taxi at 7, 8 or 9 pm. They understood that something had gone wrong. But what about Herman who had now been discharged from the hospital? The Nazis rang the hospital every day to get the names of those who had

*been admitted or discharged. Showing huge courage, the doctor allowed Herman to
sleep overnight in his office and the taxi finally arrived the following day.*

*At this point, Harald Bryn re-enters the story. For the taxi driver was Bryn's
friend and Harald Bryn had chosen their escape route. However, they got no
further than a kilometer – to Kirkeveien – before they were stopped at a mobile
checkpoint that formed part of a general raid in the area. The street was full of
State Police and Gestapo officers. A Norwegian police officer asked the driver for
his «Schein» (license), but the driver did not actually possess a driver's license. Suddenly the driver said:*

"Is Thoresen on duty tonight?"

*"No Thoresen is not on tonight, but drive – and I mean quick," the Norwegian
policeman replied.*

*It transpired that this police officer and the driver just happened to be in the same
resistance network. "Thoresen" was one of their codewords. It is true that this was
pure luck, but it was also dependent on the fact that a number of Norwegians had
decided to actively support the resistance movement and had shown great bravery,
even when their own lives were at risk.*

In the above story, the rescue chain was created by an *ad hoc* group of citizens, who all gave a large amount of support and showed no little bravery.
All the links in the chain were equally important. What also becomes clear
is that the helpers knew each other, either via family or extended family connections. In certain specific instances, there was also a connection between
close friends. Harald Bryn was a member of the civilian resistance movement (Sivorg) and had responsibility for the escape routes in the "Østland"
(South East) area of Norway (Ulstein, 1975). These were used for any Jew or
Gentile who needed get out of the country. Even though the above type of
escape operation was ad hoc in nature, it eventually linked into a more or less
well established resistance network. The Raskow couple arrived at Sweden's
"Kjäseter" internment camp on the 15th of November 1942. At that point,
they had been on the run just under three weeks.

Organized escape routes: the "Carl Fredriksen Transport Operation"
Another escape option was to avail of escape routes that had been set up
from the very beginning. The Carl Fredriksen Transport Operation is one
example of this. The "Carl Fredriksen" route was a cover name that played on

the name of the Norwegian King Haakon VII, whose actual title was "Prince Carl". Haakon was the son of King Fredrik VIII of Denmark – hence "Carl Fredriksen". Understandably given their codename, those involved used the motto: We drive for the King! The Carl Fredriksen Transport Operation represented Norway's biggest single transportation of refugees and fugitives during the Second World War. In all, 1000 persons were saved, of which around 400 were Jews. The whole operation took place within six weeks – from the end of November 1942 to the middle of January 1943 (Tangestuen, 2012).

Alf Pettersen was from an area close to the Swedish border and had previously helped several persons to get across to Sweden before the situation became highly dangerous for Jews towards the end of 1942. Pettersen had already received a warning from the police because he had refused to obey the new rules and laws that had come into force such as giving a Nazi salute when in the presence of German officers. Once the deportation of Jewish men, woman and children had taken place on November 26, 1942, Pettersen was contacted by a gardener, Rolf Syversen, who proposed an expansion of escape route operations to Sweden (Tangestuen, 2012). Two days after this, on November 28, Pettersen was again contacted – this time by Reidar Larsen who carried a message from a somewhat peripheral Milorg leader, Ole Berg. The message was that they would soon have to start moving fugitives/ refugees across the border. This applied both to Jews and also other Norwegians who needed to get out as quickly as possible (Ulstein, 1970, 1975).

Deciding to get involved in such a dangerous venture was not easy. Alf Pettersen's wife was pregnant with their first child. And from his wife Gerd's point of view, it was perhaps more a case of not being able to say no. However, Gerd Pettersen was herself to become centrally involved in such operations, keeping a record of who was being moved across and minding the account books. In fact, she came to be known as the brains behind everything. Alf Pettersen made certain demands upon those who had approached him before he agreed to lead the transport operation. First of all, he himself would decide who was to be involved in the operations and nobody would be allowed to use a cover name because he wanted to know at all times whom exactly he was dealing with. The escape party should be armed but not be a part of Milorg (Tangestuen, 2012). The Jews that Pettersen and Syversen were meant to get across the border were those who had gone into hiding during the general "Aktion" against the Jews on the 26th of November 1942.

The transportation operation was very carefully planned and recruits for the job also included police officers. Pettersen was especially keen to get serving police officers involved as they offered a better chance of ensuring the success of the rescue operation. Amongst other things, they were able to get fuel for the vehicles at a time when this was not readily available. Policemen also had much easier access to weaponry and ammunition where this proved necessary. Syversen was entrusted with the responsibility of organizing the collection point at his market garden premises. Reidar Larsen meanwhile knew a lot of drivers and was able to procure a fleet of lorries. Pettersen was very precise in his planning of times and distances (Tangestuen, 2012, p 6). He then set up an effective modus operandi with scouts along the route. Thus, the operation was to start at 9:00 pm precisely. Pettersen had set up a whole system of signals involving branches, twigs and the like. These were to be placed along the route and would signal either danger or a free passage.

All the Jews to be transported were then brought to Syversen's market garden premises at Økern, east of Oslo. They were shipped in lorries in groups of 20 per trip. They lay hidden under tarpaulins and each journey was fraught with risk. On several occasions, they were stopped by German border patrols, but miraculously managed to get through. On another occasion, Pettersen drove so close to a mobile German troop column that guards at a checkpoint believed his lorry was part of the column and so let him through unchallenged. Not even the Jews themselves knew which transport column they belonged to.

The main players in the Carl Fredriksen Transport were Alf Tollef Pettersen, Gerd Julie Bergljot Pettersen, Rolf A. Syversen and Reidar Larsen. In addition, a range of other people also played their part in ensuring that the rescue plan would be a success. Gerd and Alf Pettersen themselves were forced to flee to Sweden after their escape operations were compromised by two infiltrators during one of the missions in January 1943. Rolf Syversen was taken to Trandum Forest and executed in November 1944. There can be no doubt that the Carl Fredriksen group is an example of significant civilian engagement and courage and that its actions managed to save the lives of a large number of persons in the Second World War.

Escape routes in order to save particular groups – for example children from the Jewish Nursery Home
Once the *Anschluss* had taken place in 1938, approaches were made to the Jewish congregation in Oslo requesting that Jewish children from Vienna and elsewhere be allowed to spend their summer holidays at a Jewish chil-

dren's holiday home at Bærum (Nøkleby and Hjeltnes, 2000) and then subsequently at a Jewish nursery home in Oslo. The proposal was for 21 Jewish children to stay in Norway for three months at a time during the summer. Norway had strict rules with regard to immigration (Johansen, 1984, 2005) and Under Secretary Platou at the Department of Justice advised that these Jewish children should not be given temporary residence permits – or at least, not those children who were without parents, because these children might subsequently become a burden on the Norwegian state (Waal 1991). Once Norway was occupied by the Nazis on April 9, 1940, all the children's parents were contacted to establish whether they wished their children to remain in Norway or be sent back home. Six sets of parents requested that their children be sent back. All these children were murdered. Another two children who were loosely connected to the nursery, and happened to be with their parents/foster parents when *Aktionen* were carried out, were also murdered (Levin, 2009). However, all 14 children from Austria and Czechoslovakia who were still based at the nursery in Oslo were rescued. This rescue mission was only possible because of clear planning and a large degree of civilian engagement, not to speak of the courage displayed by several people.

In the interwar period, the head Nina Hasvold née Hackel from St Petersburg had met with the well known female child psychiatrist Nic Waal whilst attending the "Wilhelm Reich Kinderseminar" in Berlin. A very close friendship then developed between the pair – a friendship which would not only prove significant for themselves, but also in terms of the rescue operation at the nursery. Nic Waal brought Nina to Norway and when, in 1938, the Jewish Community in Oslo found a need for a headmistress for its newly established nursery, Nina was an obvious choice for the job.

In the period immediately after the arrest order for all Jewish men on the 26th of October 1942, Nina and Nic began to work out contingency plans in the event that a similar order was issued for Jewish women and children. Nic was active in the resistance movement (Ulstein, 1975) whilst Nina had a "J" stamped in her passport and had submitted the form given to all Jews in late January 1942. The fiancé of the cook at the nursery, Gudrun Fjeld, also had connections with the resistance movement. The eldest boy attending the nursery, Siegmund Korn (12 years), was given the job of bringing in NOK 10,000, which was hidden in his boots. This money was to be passed on to Gudrun's fiancé, who lived in another part of Oslo. The money was to be used for the taxi transportation that would bring them over the border to Sweden in the event that immediate flight became necessary. Thus, a partial escape plan was already in place.

But several groups were aware of the threat that now hung over the children. The night before the general "Aktion" was begun by the Nazis, a telephone call was made to an executive officer of the Nansen Committee – Sigrid Helliesen Lund. «Yes, there's going to be another party this evening – it's the small parcels they are picking up this time» the caller said (Lund, 1981). After several moments of deliberation, Helliesen Lund realised that Jewish woman and children were now also going to be arrested (Wright, 1974). The first thought that came into her mind was the nursery. But she was also aware that Nic and Nina had the situation under control. They had already been informed of what was about to happen. This gave Sigrid Helliesen Lund the chance to use the time to warn other Jewish families to find safe houses or hideouts.

Early in the morning of November 26, the children at the nursery home were roused from their sleep and told that things had become dangerous: "More serious than the events of April 9," as Nina described it. They were told to dress quickly, putting on two items for each clothes part, instead of the usual one, and then to go out quietly via the back staircase. The procedure that then followed was not only executed with great proficiency but was also imbued with great care and love of the children in the situation where, once again, a huge element of civilian engagement was present and also a large element of courage. At no point were the children nervous. Their trust in their head Nina was total as they gravely and diligently carried out their part of the escape plan as per their leader's instructions.

With their hiking boots in their hands, they went down to Nic Waal's waiting car. As a doctor, Nic Waal had a special driving license and coupons for the purchase of petrol. In two round trips, she moved the children over to a safe house – a villa on the west side of Oslo. Gerda Tanberg lived at this address. After day or so, some of the children were moved to other addresses in Nic Waal's extended family network. Meanwhile, Sigrid Helliesen Lund kept an eye on the children and managed to get enough ration cards to ensure that the children did not go hungry whilst in hiding.

A week later, the escape route was ready. Taxi driver Martin Solvang moved the first group of children to the border south of Elverum. Border guide and farmer Ola Rauken was the man who had been tasked with taking them across. However, he was due to help with slaughtering a pig on the agreed day. Ola was wary of *arousing suspicion by putting the arrangement off, so the escape plan was tempo-rarily delayed. The children stayed overnight in a log cabin where they took turns in tending the fire throughout the night. The following day they were placed into the hands of a different border guide, Ola Breisjøberget, who then led them across the last 3 km to the border. Nina Hasvold suffered a gallstone attack during this fi-nal leg of the journey and one of the boys carried her rucksack. "As far as I remember the escape operation, it was not that dramatic; presumably because it was so well planned and because luck was with us," one of the children would subsequently recall (Levin, 2006, 2009). After a week had passed, Martin Solvang[3] moved the remaining children across via the same route. The children were housed at Alingsås outside Gothenburg for the rest of the war in a house which had been purchased by the Jewish congregation.*

Thus, this rescue mission was a complete success. Saving 14 Jewish children and getting them across to Sweden during the Nazi occupation of Norway is nothing short of a great and heroic feat and it is surprising that so little is known of this episode in Norway itself. In other words, the story has not entered the collective narrative of what happened during the occupation. By comparison, some of the stories of daring and great courage from the time of the occupation are so well known that key words from them have entered into general use in the Norwegian language. One needs only to utter just one of those words or phrases and everybody knows what is being referred to. For example, the expression "ni liv" (nine lives) serves as an immediate metaphor for the fairy tale rescue of Jan Baalsrud. This illustrates how Baalsrud's story has gone into the collective folk mythology surrounding the war. But why then has the rescue of 14 children from a Jewish nursery in Oslo not gained the same status as a valued symbol of resistance against the Nazis? No doubt there are many different reasons for this. I would suggest that the combina-tion in the story of women, children and Jews has contributed to the silence with regard to this story in post-war Norway (Levin, 2009). This may suggest that the rescue of the vulnerable, or groups that are seen as "weak" in society, is not given the same heroic luster. As far as I am aware, no resistance fighter has ever been bestowed with hero status because of his or her part in rescu-ing Jews in Norway – even though the awareness of what actually happened to Norwegian Jews during the occupation has grown in more recent times.

"The ordinariness of goodness"

Regardless of how the various escapes proceeded, whether they were organized on an *ad hoc* basis by family and friend networks, or were organized
beforehand, we are dealing with individuals who displayed a significant spirit
of civilian engagement and a huge amount of bravery. They risked their lives.
Research on helpers and rescuers in the Second World War points to precisely this kind of special phenomenon, where individual citizens put their
own lives at risk in order to save their fellow human beings. "We didn't really
think we were doing anything that special. We just got on with it." is a typical
kind of sentiment expressed by those involved. Without hesitating, without
dwelling too long on the possible repercussions, they placed their own lives
in danger. This is the highest form of civilian bravery and engagement with
other citizens. In the literature that describes the helpers and rescuers during the Nazi occupation of different countries, the question has been raised
as to whether these citizens really were heroes, or whether it was simply a
case of "the ordinariness of goodness" (Rochat and Modigliani, 1995, p. 210).
Thus, whilst Hannah Arendt discusses "the banal nature of evil," Rochat and
Modigliani assert the natural presence of a general form of human goodness
(the ordinariness of goodness). Many of those who gave assistance had some
kind of connection with the resistance network. But this simply proves that
we cannot make sweeping judgments on people. For even though the resistance movement did nothing as a movement to save Norwegian Jews, there
were individuals connected to the resistance who displayed a simple, human
"ordinariness of goodness."

References

Bruland, Bjarte, 2008. Det norske Holocaust, i Bernt Hagtvet (red) *Folke-
mordenes svarte bok*. Oslo: Universitetsforlaget.

Banik, Vibeke Kieding og Irene Levin, 2010. Jødisk liv i etterkrigstiden.
Integrering og egenart. I Anne Bonnevie Lund og Bente Bolme Moen
(red) *Nasjonale minoriteter i det flerkulturelle Norge*. Trondheim: Tapir.

Johansen, Per Ole, 1984. *Oss selv nærmest. Norge og jødene 1914-1943*. Oslo:
Gyldendal.

Johansen, Per Ole, 2005. 20 år for en jøde. *Materialisten*, 4.

Kragelund, Ivar, 2013. Personlig samtale. Hjemmefrontmuseet i Oslo.

Levin, Irene, 2001. Taushetens tale, *Nytt norsk tidsskrift*, 3.

Levin, Irene, 2006. Barn på flukt. 26. november 1942. *Barn Spesialnummer for Per Olav Tiller.* 2.

Levin, Irene, 2007. Flukten. Jødenes flukt til Sverige under annen verdenskrig. *HL-senterets serie.*

Levin, Irene, 2009. Det jødiske barnehjemmet og Nic Waal. *Tidsskrift for norsk psykologforening.* 46.

Lorentzen, Håkon, 2007. *Moraldannende kretsløp. Stat, samfunn og sivilt engasjement.* Oslo: Abstract.

Lund, Sigrid Helliesen, 1981. *Alltid underveis.* Oslo: Tiden.

Mendelsohn, Oscar, 1986. *Jødenes historie i Norge gjennom 300 år. Bind II.* Oslo: Universitetsforlaget.

Nøkleby, Berit og Guri Hjeltnes, 2000. *Barn i krig.* Oslo: Aschehoug.

Rochat, Francois og Andre Modigliani, 1995. The Ordinary Quality of Resistance: From Milgram's Laboratory to the Village of le Chambon, *Journal of Social issues,* vol 51, 3.

Tangestuen, Mats, 2004. «Også jødene kom for øvrig over grensen høsten 1942» jødiske flyktninger fra Norge til Sverige 1940-1945. Hovedoppgave i historie.

Tangestuen, Mats, 2012. *Carl Fredriksens transport – krigen største redningsbragd.* Uro/Koro hefte.

Ulstein, Ragnar, 1970. Intervju med Alf Pettersen (interview with Alf Pettersen).

Ulstein, Ragnar, 1975. *Svensketrafikken.* Oslo: Det norske samlaget.

Waal, Helge, 1991. *Nic Waal. Det urolige hjertet.* Oslo: Pax.

Wright, Myrtle, 1974. *Norwegian Diary. 1940-1945.* London: Friends Peace International Relations Committee.

Noter

1   In the Norwegian Constitution of 1814, Jews had no access to the Kingdom (section 2). This was abolished in 1851.
2   There were never more than around 2.200 Jews in Norway. The highest number was just before the Second World War.
3   Martin Solvang continued to ferry fugitives/refugees across the border until February 1943 when he was arrested and sent to Grini prison camp.

Copenhagen – Refugees and rescue: The ambivalence of Danish Holocaust history

"The very system which in the 1930s was so busy protecting itself and its own by keeping Jewish refugees out was the same system that during the Jews' flight to Sweden cared for their belongings back in Denmark."

Cecilie Felicia Stokholm Banke

In early 2000, just after the first Stockholm International Forum in January, an article in the daily *Berlingske Tidende* argued that the Danish authorities during the Second World War refused 21 Jewish refugees from Nazi Germany entry into the country, and sent them back to an unknown fate, ultimately meaning death in Auschwitz. The story generated considerable controversy, and the political response was a government-financed investigation into the official Danish policy towards German-Jewish refugees.

Considering the well-known history of the rescue of the Danish Jews in October 1943, it may in some ways seem odd that Denmark should also examine its response to the killings of European Jews during the Second World War and its national share of guilt. To quote just one author who wrote on the Jewish rescue, Nechama Tec:

"Denmark, for example, represents a very special case: the conditions for the collective rescue of Jews were favorable in virtually every regard, and the Danes took full advantage of them. First, Danish Jews numbered only 8,000, making up a mere 0.2 percent of Denmark's total population. Second, this small group was highly assimilated. Third, the Nazis defined the Danes as a superior 'Aryan' race. Partly because of this definition, they were left in charge of their own political destiny retaining the pre-war government. One effect of Denmark's local autonomy was that the Jews were left alone."[1]

Tec, who bases her description of the Danish circumstances primarily

176

on Raul Hilberg and Lucy Davidowicz, authors of two of the classics in Holocaust literature, also states that it was "precisely the minimal interference of the Nazis in the internal affairs of Denmark that made the idea of a righteous Denmark superfluous." Circumstances changed, however, in the fall of 1943, when a plan for the deportation of the Jews of Denmark was concocted in Berlin. For, as Tec writes, "the Danes refused to obey."

According to Tec, Jews in Denmark were considered Danes, and therefore the Danes refused to hand over their Jews, even when ordered to do so. Instead, a heroic rescue action took place during the first days of October, when the Danish underground in cooperation with other Danes relocated the country's Jewish population to Sweden. The Danish resistance to the Nazi authority even saved the 481 Danish Jews who were actually being deported to Thereisenstadt. Compared to the treatment of other deportees, the Danes in Thereisenstadt experienced far better conditions, and were not transferred to Auschwitz, as was the fate of many others. When explaining the reason for the Danes' protection of their Jews, Tec emphasizes a low degree of anti-Semitism and 'a strong adherence to democratic principles.'

Yet this extremely favorable image of Denmark as a kind of safe haven for Jews has gone through changes during the past decade, following new trends and tendencies within both the scholarship of a new generation of historians and a new European political culture, influencing the way national history is being interpreted. New books about a less flattering side of Denmark's history during the occupation have tainted the previously pristine image and have fuelled renewed controversy about the hitherto widely accepted 'policy of cooperation' raising questions about whether it was the wisest path a small occupied country like Denmark could follow, given the circumstances.

The current historical debate in Denmark can be seen as taking place between two main schools: the moralists and the realists. Those who maintain a practical view as to what was possible represent one side of the debate, and those who hold a more moralistic view as to what Denmark could have done and how Denmark should have behaved, the other. I think this division reflects how differently history can serve a society in the present, and how things that seem just and fair to one generation, can be considered opportunistic by another.

The Danish case, like so many others, shows to what extent the Holocaust as a scholarly field has been dramatically Europeanized during the past ten to fifteen years, raising new questions and provoking renewed debate in national historiography. I will come back to this issue later, because it can be explained by changes within European political culture following the fall of the Berlin wall, and because it can also be explained by mounting interest in the Holocaust.

The thesis of this article places me somewhere in the middle, between the realists and the moralists. The thesis argues that Denmark followed a very restrictive refugee policy towards German Jewish refugees during the 1930s, not because of widespread anti-Semitism in the Danish government or society, or simply in order to please the Germans, but rather because of simultaneous efforts made by policy makers and social-liberal politicians to establish what later became a national welfare state.

Although the term, *welfare state*, was not used at the time, important steps were taken during this period towards building a universalistic welfare state with a high degree of social planning, which aimed to improve not only the living standards of the population, but also, through social engineering, the general quality of it. This effort, which I call *prophylactic social policy*, had the goal of creating a better population through progressive social planning – it really had a qualitative dimension – and avoiding future social problems.

At the same time Hitler was creating a new refugee problem for Germany's neighbors with his anti-Jewish laws, the Scandinavian countries were in the middle of a socio-economic debate about demographics and declining birth rates. This issue had been a general European concern since the First World War, especially in countries like France, Germany, and Great Britain, but it was first put on the political agenda in Scandinavia in 1934 by the Swedish social democrats Alva and Gunnar Myrdal with their classic work '*Kris i befolkningsfraagan*' (*Crisis in the Population Question*).

When I initiated my study on refugee policy in 2000, my knowledge of the Holocaust and my expertise in anti-Semitism and Jewish history did not exceed what could be expected from an average historian trained in 20th Century European History. However, I did know something about social policy during the 1930s and the ideas developed throughout the decade about a progressive, caring, and protective national welfare state.

Before delving into Holocaust studies, I dealt with the relationship between state and society in 19th and 20th Century Europe. My dissertation from 1999, '*Social ingeniørkunst i Danmark: Familie, stat og politik fra 1900 til 1945*' (*Social Engineering in Denmark: Family, State and Politics from 1900 to 1945*) describes the ideas behind social planning that emerged in Northern Europe as a response to the First World War and were later further developed by several European governments. As part of my research, I also came across the relative influence of fascist ideas on social thinking, not only among right-wingers, but also in social democratic circles (Banke 1999).

Therefore, I proposed a study examining the development of national welfare with a view to refugees. I wanted to see how these two topics intermingled in the general discussions at that time (Banke 2001).

My initial inquiry involved how Denmark could maintain a restrictive policy towards "German-Jewish emigrants" (a misleading term used officially and publically for people who were, in fact, political refugees) allowing only approximately 2,000 to enter Denmark between 1933 and 1940, most during the first two years of Nazi rule, while policy makers and demographers were simultaneously debating the future of the total population.[2]

In my research, I read headlines like "Will Denmark become a nation of geriatrics?" referring to the declining birth rate, and articles suggesting that "Sweden will have to import Danes." If the declining population was considered a looming threat, and if the prospects of a nation getting older and older haunted the public debate, why not let German Jewish refugees in?

Of course, this was a rhetorical question, and I could easily come up with an explanation, as had scholars before me, citing the economic crisis, unemployment, and, to a certain extent, the fear of anti-Semitism. Nevertheless, I wanted to combine these two types of social questions, immigrants and welfare, because to me they are crucial to understanding the European nation-states. Who were considered members of the national community? In what way did the emerging national welfare state respond to people who did not belong? Could they become 'belongers'? What was the reaction in neighboring Denmark to the persecution of Jews in Germany? At a certain level, this question is unique to Denmark, since the relationship between Germany and Denmark was based on mutual esteem and admiration, but also on fear, anxiety, and feelings of inferiority.

You may notice that my way of framing this research made it into a general examination of how the state acted when confronted with a new group of immigrants, and how it defined itself in relation to this new group of 'others.' I was lucky to be part of a larger research team, which allowed me to do this kind of study.

My colleague Lone Rünitz completed the archival work in the Justice Department. Aided by a group of research assistants, she went through 80,000 files on foreigners coming to Denmark from 1933 to 1945. Among the 80,000, approximately 8,000 left Germany as a result of political, religious, or racial persecution. It is very uncertain if any Sinti or Romas at all came to Denmark during the period. Most of the refugees were political, either communists or social democrats, and Jews. Not surprisingly, several were both, especially during the first wave, that is from 1933 to 1935 (Rünitz 2005, p.13-15).

What my research describes, then, is not so much the exact treatment of the refugees by the Danish government, but the public debate about Jews, about refugees, and about the so-called 'Jewish question', which was discussed among writers and intellectuals in the more politically correct circles. And finally, whether anti-Semitism was an issue at all.

So, what did I find out? Was my approach a fair one within the field of Holocaust studies? This concern actually prompted serious deliberations. The more I delved into the history of the refugees, and thus, by extension, into the Holocaust, the further away I got from my original thesis, which concerned the relationship between the creation of a progressive and universalized welfare state and the treatment of German Jewish refugees.

I found out that, to a certain degree, the social thinkers and policy makers inspired by socialist ideas were not trained, or willing, to see 'the Jewish question' as more than a social and economic problem. The research I conducted into the debate among the progressive left-wingers uncovered that the 'Jewish problem' was considered superfluous, contrived by the reactionaries, and as something that would disappear the moment a classless society came into existence. When that happened, all social and economic inequalities would vanish, and so would anti-Semitism and the 'Jewish question'. Both were regarded as mere products of a capitalist society.

This reaction was, of course, very romantic, but it shows how the persecution of Germans of Jewish backgrounds was not fully understood in these circles. I believe that this is still one of the crucial questions within Holocaust studies, i.e. the repercussions of anti-Jewish policies as shown by both Raul Hilberg and Saul Friedländer.

However, it was among the same libertarian circles in the Danish public sphere that I would find opposition towards the government's restrictive refugee policy. Unsurprisingly, the resistance was driven by a strong aversion towards the social democrats and their government, whom the left-wingers, or 'libertarians,' as they would call themselves, saw as renegades and outright class traitors, working as lackeys for the Nazi government in Germany. The social-liberal government was considered a front for 'the exploitatious dictatorship of capitalist society'. In that sense, the German refugees became part of an internal discussion within the labor movement about how to achieve a socialist society – through reform and negotiations, or through revolution.

What, then, could I conclude from a broader perspective? Was my research framework suitable for the subject? And how could I solve the problem with Holocaust studies and my thesis? Could a description of how the emerging welfare state responded to a refugee crisis be combined with Holocaust studies? This was a big dilemma for me, and I am still not sure I have solved it.

One of my answers would be that since the Holocaust, in my view, has become a paradigm, it would be reasonable also to view Holocaust studies as a unique prism for understanding 20th Century European history, which is in fact what I did in my book. I used the Holocaust as a prism to discern some of the crucial facets of developing the European nation-states.

According to British historian Tony Kushner, a special field within Holocaust research has emerged during the past decades focusing on the liberal democracies' reaction to the Nazi persecution of the Jews. Most of this research concerns the refugee policies in the individual countries and how they responded at the political and administrative levels. This area of research studies the reaction of the bureaucracy to a refugee crisis, and how the solution of this crisis depended on the international situation (Kushner 1994; Morse, 1968; Wyman, 1968; Friedman, 1973; Feingold 1970; Sherman; Gilbert 1981; Moore 1986).

Important political decisions must also be seen in light of the circumstances under which these decisions are made. These circumstances not only include the international events, but also the national contexts and the attitudes of the population. Especially in a liberal democracy, an understanding of the popular reactions can contribute to a more complete picture of the reality in which politicians acted. In trying to explain the reaction of the liberal democracies to the Nazi persecution of Jews, including the individual refugee policies and what affected them, analysis of the political and administrative level must be complemented by a study of public attitudes. What did people actually think about the Jewish refugees? What did the politicians need to consider in their political and administrative choices?

However, in contrast to the United States and Great Britain, where opinion polls were carried out and could be used as indicators of public attitudes, no such system existed for the Danish population. Gallup polling had not yet been established in Scandinavia, so in order to conceptualize the *Zeitgeist*, so to speak, I used what Timothy Garton Ash has labeled "history of the present," namely writings from journalists and others describing what was going on at the time (Garton Ash 2000). I went through vast amounts of newspaper material, journals and books and combined these readings with research in the archive.

Very early on, from when the Nazis came into power in Germany, the Danish press was placed under restrictions by foreign minister Peter Munch, who encouraged Denmark's newspaper and magazine editors to handle the 'emigrant question' with the utmost caution. This caution served to constrain the emergence of a genuine debate about refugee policy, just as it hampered the actual flow of news from Germany.

As a result, the refugee question could not become the kind of topic which engages the public today. One could be shocked over the Nazis' persecution of the Jews, but there was little coverage of Danish government policy toward the refugees. As I explained earlier, the refugees were labelled as emigrants, both by the German regime and the Danish authorities and aid committees, and this is also what they were called in the public sphere. This distinction only served to underscore the lack of recognition of the refugee problem, which Germany imposed on other countries at the time. The term 'emigrant' was in fact directly misleading, inasmuch as the term 'emigration' connotes a voluntary departure from a country. Whether they were social democrats, communists, or Jews, all had been forced to flee as a result of the political conditions in Germany. They were all political refugees, not emigrants.

In the same way as the refugees were euphemistically referred to as 'emigrants', Danish refugee policy was not discussed in the public sphere. The Danish government maintained a very low profile, and this was reflected in the reduced coverage of the refugee question in the media of that time. Under these circumstances, opposition to the existing policy could not be anything but sporadic. Such opposition was limited to the 'libertarian' circles, as mentioned. These were the public *dissenters*, opposing both the Nazi regime and the restrictive refugee policy. But it existed, and made its views felt in the discussion of the 'Jewish question' and of the Nazis' persecution of the Jews.

As mentioned earlier, Denmark has been hailed within the field of Holocaust research as one of the few countries that managed to rescue its Jewish population. The Danish rescue in October 1943 stands as an exemplary model for how a democracy, despite everything, took action under Nazi occupation. Around seven thousand Danish Jews were saved from deportation to the concentration camps.

But how did liberal, democratic Denmark react *before the war* toward the very un-liberal phenomenon in neighboring Germany, the persecution of the Jews? And how should we understand the connection between Denmark's restrictive refugee policy in the 1930s and the rescue of the Danish Jews today? Is there any connection at all?

I believe there is, and it has to do with the emerging welfare state and the well-defined national community. The very system which in the 1930s was so busy protecting itself and its own by keeping Jewish refugees out was the same system that during the Jews' flight to Sweden cared for their belongings back in Denmark (Bak 2007). If one looks for an explanation, in a comparative perspective, for unique rescue operation of Jews in Denmark, it relates to the following: Danish Jews were considered members of the national community. It was the same sense of belonging that made the rescue operation possible. While the Danish state was reluctant to take in Jewish refugees during the 1930s, the same state would take action when helping Jews in Denmark fleeing persecution during the fall of 1943. This paradox is what I have described as the ambivalence of Danish Holocaust history. How could Danes be restrictive against German Jewish refugees on the one hand while on the other perform a remarkable act of civil courage helping Jews escape to Sweden?

The answer lies within the historical context. The German Jewish refugees of the 1930s came to Denmark as immigrants, especially in the beginning, and they were considered a threat to Danish labor and to the social stability of Danish society. If the Danish state took in too many immigrants with Jewish background, there was a risk that Denmark, like Germany, it was believed, would get a 'Jewish problem'. The general assumption within the Danish administration was thus that too many immigrants with Jewish background would create a 'Jewish problem' and with that also widespread anti-Semitism. And anti-Semitism would lead to social instability. The restrictive refugee policy was in that sense both a way to protect the Danish labor market from immigrant labor and to avoid anti-Semitism and social instability.

As Tony Kushner writes, the Nazi persecution of the Jews was an attack on one of the most fundamental features of liberalism, namely the freedom of the individual. An essential aspect of the liberal credo, especially in British and American liberalism, was the idea of tolerance (Kushner 1994).

Nevertheless, the reaction of the liberal democracies toward the persecution of the Jews was full of contradictions and very complex. It was precisely the strong belief in liberal tolerance which prevented democracies such as the United States and Great Britain from conducting a more refugee-friendly policy.

The belief in the infallibility of liberalism and in the system itself, i.e. the state bureaucracy, led to complacency and passivity regarding the issue of the Jewish refugees. The liberal system could not err, and, in this case, acted ostensibly as it had in all other cases, both rationally and justly. The problem, however, was that the persecution of Jews was both irrational and unjust, so that aiding them required a completely different mindset in terms of liberal tolerance.

In this sense, the refugee issue clashed with what sociologist Max Weber has described as one of the most characteristic features of the modern state, the bureaucracy, where the system's rules and regulations have a higher priority than humanitarian considerations. This characteristic feature of modern bureaucracy is prevalent in many of the cases described by Lone Rünitz and her research team (Rünitz 2001).

Reason triumphed over emotions, *realpolitik* over humanitarian considerations and charity. Some people were surprised by the Nazis' actions and attempted to explain the 'Jewish problem' in Germany by the country's complex nature as a nation. Others ultimately came to assign Jews a part of the blame – had the Jews been better at integrating themselves into the nation-states, there would presumably have been no 'Jewish problem' in the first place. In other words, some thought that there was some truth to the accusations that "the Jews" controlled all the money and ran the world.

In this sense, liberal tolerance had its own limitations. The liberal democracies viewed the Jewish minority in terms of how good they were at assimilating bourgeois national values. In Denmark as well, the discussion about 'the Jewish question' reflected the extent to which Jews were viewed as a part of the national community.

For Denmark, the 1930s was the decade during which a new social contract was finally established. Denmark became a national community consolidated around the state as the all-embracing instrument of social security. The 1930s saw the groundwork laid for the post-war welfare state, even though two decades would pass before the 'welfare state' concept first appeared in the public debate. The rudiments of a social security system, based upon universalism and preventive measures, were already present in the 1930s. And it was this system that confronted the German-Jewish refugees escaping Nazi persecution.

The welfare state can be interpreted as a way of managing modernization and the break-up of the village community and its replacement by life in the big city. The welfare state is a modern form of social patronage, where the state, in the same manner as the feudal lord, takes care of its populace. According to this new social contract, the state offers social security in exchange for individual contributions thrown into the common pool, administered by the state bureaucracy.

The progressive economists and politicians of the interwar period used much of their energy to develop and disseminate precisely this idea and thus could not immediately grasp the repercussions of the refugee problem that the Nazis had created with their policies.

They could condemn it, they could distance themselves from it, but they could not bring refugees into the new social patronage model. Refugees lay outside their field of vision.

Yet, if one examines an economic analysis of the 'Jewish problem' at the time, it becomes clear how much immigrating Jews were placed outside the economic community in the nation-state. We can see how Jews were considered a problem, and we can see how many people really wanted Jews, especially the East European Jews, out of Europe in order to avoid a social problem.

The idea of justice that was pursued in the crisis-ridden Denmark of the 1930s was a form of social justice. It was aimed at the population as a national collective. That was as far as rights-based thinking had developed in Denmark. It was limited to ensuring social rights for its citizens, and this necessarily led to limitations for those who were not viewed as members of the national community. The idea that non-members of the community, i.e. non-citizens, also had rights – what we today call human rights – had not yet penetrated into the Danish social justice discourse.

The period between the First and Second World Wars reveals efforts made by several states to integrate the citizens into a social whole and make them a part of a community where all are economically and socially equal; these efforts are especially prominent in Northern and Western Europe. It was a norm meant to ensure stability and welfare and consolidate the community around the common foundation, around the state. However, the welfare states which evolved after the Second World War were based on homogenous national states which had already constituted themselves as cultural nations. These states were based on what nationalism researcher Anthony D. Smith calls 'ethnic nations' (Smith 2003; Smith 2000; Gellner 1994; Hettne, Sörlin & Østergård 1998).

The welfare state takes as its point of departure the principle that it can only be effectuated on an exclusionary basis. We can therefore examine how this exclusionary principle began to operate, whether it was immediately before the war or after the war, or even earlier.

The important point here is that the social economic thinking of the 1930s about an all-embracing, equality-based state – whose primary task was to prevent social discontent – led to a system which viewed refugees in a rigid, restrictive manner, based, as it was, on the principle of protecting the country's own citizens and its national labor market.

Hence Denmark had to be protected against immigrant labor, even if these immigrants were, in fact, refugees from a totalitarian system, fleeing discrimination, persecution, and eventually deportation as well. In this sense, the national community that had been the foundation for the welfare state turned out to be a very closed community, unable to meet the challenges of ethnic and religious persecution in a neighboring state.

The interesting point here is that the exclusion of Jewish refugees to Denmark was not based on Danish racism, it was based on a Danish welfare ideology. Danes sought to be both humanistic and exclusionary at the same time, which is one of the many paradoxes in the history of the Holocaust.

The Danish state's administration of immigrants and refugees during the 1930s says something decisive about the fundamental nature of a national community. It reveals something about who were viewed as members, and how central liberal values such as tolerance and individual freedom were interpreted.

The encounter with the German Jews as 'the Other' became the litmus test of how far this liberal credo extended. That there were limitations to liberalism in the 1930s only emphasizes the degree to which liberal democracy was actually in crisis also in Denmark during this period.

References:

Timothy Garton Ash, *History of the Present: Essays, Sketches and Despatches from Europe 1990s*, 2000.

Cecilie Felicia Stokholm Banke, *Demokratiets skyggeside*, 2005.

Cecilie Felicia Stokholm Banke, 'Flygtninge i velfærdsstaten', in: Banke (Ed.) *Folk og fællesskab*, Arbejdsrapporter fra DCHF, 2001.

Cecilie Felicia Stokholm Banke, *Den sociale ingeniørkunst i Danmark. Familie, stat og politik 1900-1945*, 1999.

Sofie Lene Bak, 'Indtil de vender hjem', in: Peter Henningsen & Rasmus Mariager red. *Strenge tider*, 2006.

Lucy Davidowicz, *The War Against The Jews, 1933-1945*, 1975.

Henry Feingold, *The Politics of Rescue: The Roosevelt Administration and the Holocaust 1938-1945*, 1970.

Saul P. Friedman, *No Haven for the Oppressed: United States Policy Toward Jewish Refugees, 1938-1945*, 1973.

Saul Friedländer, *Nazi Germany and the Jews*, Vol. I+II, 1997 and 2007.

Ernest Gellner, *Conditions of Liberty*, 1994.

Martin Gilbert, *Auschwitz and the Allies*, 1981.

Björn Hettne, Sverker Sörlin and Uffe Østergård, *Den globala nationalism*, 1998.

Raul Hilberg, *The Destruction of the European Jews*, 2003 (1961).

Tony Kushner, *The Liberal Imagination*, 1994.

Bob Moore, *Refugees from Nazi Germany in the Netherlands 1933-1940*, 1986.

Arthur Morse, *While Six Million Died*, 1968.

Lone Rünitz, *'Af hensyn til konsekvenserne...'*, 2005.

Lone Rünitz, 'Familien Baum. En flygtningefamilies møde med det danske statsapparat', in: Banke (ed.), *Folk og fællesskab*, 2001.

A. J. Sherman, *Island Refuge: Britain and Refugees from the Third Reich, 1933-1939*, 1973.

Anthony D. Smith, *Nationalisme*, 2003.

Anthony D. Smith, *The Nation in History: Historiographical Debates about Ethnicity and Nationalism*, 2000.

Nechama Tec, *When Light Pierced the Darkness: Christian Rescue of Jews in Nazi-Occupied Poland*, 1986.

David Wyman, *Paper Walls: America and the Refugee Crisis 1938-1941*, 1968.

Notes

1　Tec, 1986, p. 5-10.
2　In April 1940 there were 2.198 refugees in Denmark. 302 were German social democrats and intellectuals. 142 communists. 1.680 were Jewish refugees, divided into three main groups: 377 Hechaluzs with a temporary permission to stay to learn agriculture and prepare for Palestine, 265 were Alijah-children aged 13-16 years, and 1.000 Jewish refugees coming to Denmark on individual basis. See Kirchhoff & Rünitz 2007, p. 35-37 & p. 419-431.

Contributors

SOFIE LENE BAK – Ph.D, Associate Professor in History at the Saxo Institute, Copenhagen University and author of a series of books and articles on the Holocaust in Denmark and on Anti-Semitism before and during the Second World War, including "Dansk Antisemitisme 1930-45" [Danish Anti-Semitism 1930-1945] (2004), "Nothing to speak of: Wartime Experiences of Danish Jews, 1943–1945" (2011) and "Da krigen var forbi. De danske jøders hjemkomst efter besættelsen" [When the war was over. The return of the Danish Jews after the German Occupation] (2012).

CECILIE FELICIA STOKHOLM BANKE – Ph.D and MA, is Senior Researcher at the Danish Institute for International Studies where she works with Danish and European foreign policy, specializing in how societies come to terms with their atrocity past. From 2009-2013 she was in charge of Holocaust and genocide studies at the DIIS, and has been a member of the Danish Delegation to International Holocaust Remembrance Alliance since 2005. She has published on the Danish refugee policy during Nazism, Holocaust memory in postwar Europe, and the politics of memory in Europe since 1989.

RICHARD BREITMAN – Distinguished Professor, American University, is the author or co-author of ten books and many articles in German history, the history of the Holocaust, and American history. His most recent book, co-authored with Allan J. Lichtman, *FDR and the Jews*, was published by Harvard University Press in 2013. He is editor of the scholarly journal *Holocaust and Genocide Studies*. He took part in a U.S. government effort to declassify documents related to the Holocaust and war crimes and war criminals, which resulted in the opening of more than 8 million pages of documents in the U.S. National Archives.

KONSTANTY GEBERT – International reporter and columnist at *Gazeta Wyborcza*, Poland's largest daily newspaper, and associate fellow at the European Council on Foreign Relations. He was an underground journalist in the 1980s under martial law, and later founded the Polish Jewish intellectual monthly *Midrasz*. He has written ten books on a variety of topics including the Polish democratic transformation, the European 20th century, the Yugoslav wars, the wars of Israel, Torah commentary and post-WWII Polish Jewry. His articles have appeared in newspapers in Poland and around the world.

ANTHONY GEORGIEFF – A writer and journalist who has worked for the BBC/World Service in London; Radio Free Europe/Radio Liberty in Munich and in Prague; and for a variety of Danish and Bulgarian media. His books include a novel, *Vienna* (2001), as well as non-fiction works *Hidden Treasures of Bulgaria* (2005), *East of Constantinople/Travels in Unknown Turkey* (2008), *Jewish Bulgaria* (2011), *A Guide to Ottoman Bulgaria* (2011), and *The Turks of Bulgaria* (2012).

KARIN KVIST GEVERTS – Ph.D, is a teacher and researcher in the Department of History and the Hugo Valentin Centre at Uppsala University, Sweden. Her dissertation, *Ett främmande element i nationen. Svensk flyktingpolitik och de judiska flyktingarna* 1938-1944 (A Foreign Element Within the Nation. Swedish Refugee Policy and the Jewish Refugees, 1938-1944; 2008) dealt with Sweden and the Holocaust, more specifically with the attitudes and actions of the Swedish Immigration Authorities towards Jewish refugees during the Second World War. She has written articles on antisemitism as well as the bystander issue, and she is the co-editor of a forthcoming anthology on antisemitism in Sweden, *Tankar i "judefrågan. Nedslag i den svenska antisemitismen.*

ULRICH HERBERT – Prof. Dr., holds the Chair for Modern History at the Freiburg University. From 2007 until 2013, he was Director of the Freiburg Institute for Advanced Studies, School of History. His books include: Best. Biographische Studien über Radikalismus, Weltanschauung und Vernunft, 1903-1989, Bonn 1996, 52008; National-Socialist Extermination Policy. Contemporary German Perspectives and Controversies, New York und Oxford 1999 (ed.); Hitler's Foreign Workers. Enforced Foreign Labor

in Germany under the Third Reich, Cambridge 1997; Die nationalsozial-
istischen Konzentrationslager 1933 bis 1945. Entwicklung und Struktur, 2
Bände, Göttingen 1998 (ed.) Editor of „Europäische Geschichte im 20. Jahrhundert", 10 vol.; Co-editor of the source book Die Verfolgung und Ermor-
dung der europäischen Juden durch das nationalsozialistische Deutschland,
1933-1945, 16 vol. , München 2007 ff.

ANDERS JERICHOW – Senior Correspondent and columnist, *Politiken*,
Copenhagen. Chairman of Humanity in Action (Denmark) and Danish
PEN. He has authored a number of books on human rights and international development, questions of freedom of speech, Middle Eastern affairs.
Jerichow has also published a major source collection *Oktober '43* on the fate
of Danish Jews in 1943 (2013). Finally, he has contributed to a number of
publications on genocide and human rights questions.

RONALD LEOPOLD – Born in 1960. From 1978 to 1985, Leopold
studied history and literature at the University of Groningen. He wrote his
doctoral thesis in Budapest, where he lived for two years. Since 1985, he
has lived with his wife and daughter in Amsterdam. Following his studies,
Leopold held a number of positions at the General Pension Fund for Public
Employees. In 1990 he moved to the Pension and Benefit Board, a public
agency responsible for the implementation of legislation offering financial
support to victims of the Second World War. Ronald Leopold has been the
executive director of the Anne Frank House since January 2011.

BOB MOORE – Born 1954, Moore is Professor of Twentieth Century European History at the University of Sheffield. He has published extensively
on the history of Western Europe in the mid twentieth century, including
*Victims and Survivors: the Nazi Persecution of the Jews in the Netherlands,
1940-1945* (1997); *Refugees from Nazi Germany and the Liberal European
States* (with Frank Caestecker, 2009) and his latest monograph, *Survivors:
Jewish Self-Help and Rescue in Nazi-Occupied Western Europe* was published
by Oxford in 2010.

OULA SILVENNOINEN – Ph.D, is a Finnish historian working in Helsinki. He earned his doctorate in 2008 with a work dealing with Finnish-German security police co-operation between 1933-1944 (translated into German as *Geheime Waffenbrüderschaft: Die sicherheitspolizeiliche Zusammenarbeit zwischen Finnland und Deutschland 1933-1944*, Darmstadt: Wissenschaftliche Buchgesellschaft, 2010). His current research interests include the history of the Holocaust and its legacy both in Finland and abroad, the history of European Fascist and radical nationalist movements, as well as the history of policing and police institutions. His most recent international publications appear in Kinnunen, T. and Kivimäki, V. (eds.): Finland in World War II, Leiden: Brill 2012 and in Muir, S.
and Worthen, H. (eds.): Finland's Holocaust, Basigstoke: Palgrave Macmillan 2013.

ANETTE WIEVIORKA – Historian and Senior Fellow at the French National Center for Scientific Research, Paris. Annette Wieviorka has worked on the history of the Jews in the 20th Century, the memory of the Holocaust and the history of Communism. She is notably the author of *Déportation et génocide: Entre la mémoire et l'oubli* (1992); *L'ère du témoin* (1998); *Maurice et Jeannette: Biographie du couple Thorez* (2010); *A l'intérieur du camp de Drancy* (with Michel Laffitte). Her intellectual work has been the object of a book of interviews with Séverine Nikel, *L'heure d'exactitude. Histoire, mémoire, témoignage* (2011).

Acknowledgements

This anthology is published as part of a series of events in Copenhagen commemorating the 70th anniversary of the flight and deportation of Danish Jews in October 1943. In Denmark the events and books are sponsored by the Oak Foundation, Sportgoods Foundation, Jyllands-Posten Foundation, Politiken Foundation, Johannes Fogs Foundation, Marcus Choleva, Frimodt-Heinike Foundation, Letterstedtska Förening, Foundation for Danish-Swedish Cooperation, Knud Højgaard Foundation, IK Consultancy, Aage og Johanne Louis-Hansen Foundation, Oticon Foundation and supported by the Federal Republic of Germany, Federal Foreign Office.

The English edition and commemorative events in the United States have been sponsored by generous contributions from Richard D. Bernstein, Stuart A. Bernstein, the Keith and Carol Brown Family Foundation, the Elizabeth and Richard Dubin Foundation, Douglas Durst, Irwin P. Edlavitch, Melvyn J. Estrin, Laurie S. Fulton, the Annette M. and Theodore N. Lerner Family Foundation, the John L. Loeb, Jr. Foundation, Mauree Jane Perry and the Charles E. Smith Family Foundation.